It's me.

The "Hello God...it's me" devotions and prayer prompts are intended to be conversation starters between you and God. Our hope is for you to be so well known by God that you can talk to Him about anything. Any time. Any where.

Journaling lines are included so you can write prayers, record His answers, share dreams, respond to the devotions, or ask questions. An "amen" may be the only dialogue you need on some days, and others you may use every line. This is a safe place for you and God to get to know one another better. So dig in. Read. Write. Pray. Be inspired.

You're a Wonder

Praise the LORD, my soul; all my inmost being, praise his holy name. Praise the LORD, my soul,
and forget not all his benefits—who forgives all your sins and heals all your diseases,
who redeems your life from the pit and crowns you with love and compassion,
who satisfies your desires with good things so that your youth is renewed like the eagle's.
PSALM 103:1–5 NIV

They are called the seven natural wonders of the world: Aurora Borealis, Grand Canyon, Paricutin, Victoria Falls, Mount Everest, Great Barrier Reef, Harbor of Rio de Janeiro. When you see them they evoke a response of wonder and awe. They're one of a kind.

Go ahead and add yourself to that list. You are a wonder. You're one of a kind. God made just one of you—only one person with your exact looks, your exact set of abilities and interests and background and experiences.

And while those seven wonders of the world are there for us to simply look at and enjoy, you are created for a reason. You have a job to do on this planet in this particular span of years that only you can accomplish.

The new year dawns—a new year of hopes and possibilities. They're all yours for the taking. They're all yours for the doing.

Are you ready?

Hello God...it's me. This year renew a fresh wonder in me for all things "You."

A Divine Hunger

What is more, I consider everything a loss because of the surpassing worth of knowing Christ Jesus my Lord,
for whose sake I have lost all things. I consider them garbage, that I may gain Christ.
PHILIPPIANS 3:8 NIV

It is almost impossible to fathom how a world so full of information can be lacking in understanding. And yet it is true. We are challenged to pursue advanced degrees, prompted to keep up with the newest trends, urged to stay competent in the latest technology. But have such endeavors filled our lives with meaning and hope? No. One problem is that these endeavors—as worthy as they are—aren't big enough to capture our hearts.

A believer has a more exalted, more compelling goal: to know God. Not just to know about God or gather facts concerning God or memorize a creed regarding God, but to have a *relationship* with the living God. The difference is as vast as knowing the recipe for your favorite pie—or actually sinking your teeth into a fresh-out-of-the-oven slice. Formulas cannot do justice to the experience.

Once we know God, once we experience Him, we will only hunger for more of Him. Pursue Him with all your passion.

Hello God...it's me. This year, I desire to know You more. Please develop that desire into a passionate hunger.

It Doesn't Make Sense

And you, being dead in your trespasses and the uncircumcision of your flesh, He has made alive together with Him, having forgiven you all trespasses, having wiped out the handwriting of requirements that was against us, which was contrary to us. And He has taken it out of the way, having nailed it to the cross. Having disarmed principalities and powers, He made a public spectacle of them, triumphing over them in it.

COLOSSIANS 2 :13–15 NKJV

Christianity is full of paradoxes: One must die to live, give to have, mourn to be happy, be poor to be rich, surrender to be victorious. But no greater paradox exists than Jesus's cross: love birthed in hate, beauty arising from ugliness, a good man dying so bad men could be saved. The cross was the Roman Empire's torturous instrument of death. The victim hung suspended between heaven and earth. The crossbeams stood in paradox— the vertical beam jutting upward toward heaven, like a champion thrusting his fist into the air, satisfying the demands of God's holiness; the horizontal beam reaching outward toward the earth like a father's arms, signifying the embrace of God's love.

It doesn't make sense, does it? Paradoxes don't. But that doesn't make it any less true. Delight in the cross.

Hello God...it's me. Thank You for the wonders of Your goodness that go beyond my understanding.

A Paradigm Shift

Now may the God of peace...equip you with everything good for doing his will, and may he work in us what is pleasing to him, through Jesus Christ, to whom be glory for ever and ever. Amen.
HEBREWS 13:20–21 NIV

What do you hurry to do each day? Sometimes we rush through the activities of our day to get to what we think is the best part: quitting time, mealtimes, bedtime. We don't have to be forced to do the tasks we *really* want to do: play a sport we love, spend time with our family, read a good book. We give to the tasks we love our best energy and purpose.

Does the performance of "every good work" stir the same energy and readiness of mind? If we're honest, we'll probably say, "Not always." Sometimes we approach our service to the Lord with reluctance, knowing the limitations of our strength or desire. But it's time to make a paradigm shift. We can readily "perform every good work" when we know that the God of peace equips us. Relying on His limitless strength instead of our flagging energy or desire enables us to rejoice in the tasks to which He has called us.

Ready to rejoice? Rely on God.

Hello God...it's me. This year, I would like a passion and deep desire to accomplish every good work You have planned for me.

Closest of Friends

*When he heard this, Jesus said, "This sickness will not end in death.
No, it is for God's glory so that God's Son may be glorified through it."*

JOHN 11:4 NIV

Gayle King. Lem Billings. Guy Pelley. These aren't household names. But the names of their best friends are. As close friends to people like Oprah Winfrey, Princes William and Harry, and John F. Kennedy, these individuals have a different perspective when it comes to the faces the rest of us only recognize. To them, Winfrey, Kennedy, and the princes aren't just famous people; they are friends who have cared for them.

Jesus had a close personal friend named Lazarus. Jesus often visited Lazarus and his sisters in their small hometown of Bethany. On one occasion, however, it appeared that Jesus wasn't there for His friend. Having received word that Lazarus was deathly sick, Jesus didn't show up until days after Lazarus had died. But when Jesus did arrive, it was clear that He cared deeply for His friend. After weeping, Jesus raised Lazarus from the dead. What appeared at first to be indifference was in fact Jesus demonstrating a radical love and exhibition of His glory. And this is what God does in our lives. Though He may seem to be uninvolved, He has a plan and is going to work all things together for His glory *and* your good. This is what Jesus does for His friends.

Hello God...it's me. Help me to look for You daily, like I would seek out a friend.

What Does God Want?

He has told you, O man, what is good; and what does the Lord require of you but to do justice, and to love kindness, and to walk humbly with your God?

MICAH 6:8 ESV

Most families, schools, places of employment, and neighborhoods have rules or expectations of behavior. The wise person learns what is required of him or her inorder to be a successful participant. When a group's rules are unspoken, however, frustration can quickly set in as those new to the group try to meet expectations they can only guess at.

Have you ever asked yourself what God wants from us? Some believers fear that God has unspoken requirements they can't meet. They consult self-help books or the advice of other believers, all the while fearing God's anger if they get His requirements "wrong."

But God doesn't leave us to wonder what His expectations are; He tells us clearly in His Word. So what does God require? Sincere gratitude and worship. You can never go wrong when you praise God with a thankful heart. You don't need special skills to tell God thanks. Just be willing to spend time with the Father who loves you!

Hello God...it's me. Thank You for clearly revealing Your desires for us through Your Word.

Love That Lifts

*I learned God-worship when my pride was shattered. Heart-shattered lives
ready for love don't for a moment escape God's notice.*

PSALM 51:17 MSG

In 2012, a documentary about three under-privileged student-athletes transcending inner-city Memphis shocked Hollywood and won an Oscar. The stars of *Undefeated* were underdogs in every way. America is an underdog culture. Her people cheer the loudest for the war veteran skiing on prosthetic legs, the small-town soprano with an unpolished voice and a dream, the lowly beagle vying for Best of Show.

Underdog status is hard-won, usually signaled by broken hearts, little pride, and even less hope. Perhaps that is why God is so ready to love and use those who are overlooked.

Consider the shepherd boy who would be king, wielding only a slingshot and five smooth stones. Or the outcast prostitute who helped bring down a city. Or the unwed pregnant teenager who bore a Savior. God roots for the shattered because they need His compassionate love in difficult circumstances against very poor odds. They're more willing to ask for it, receive it, and humbly praise Him for it, recognizing that real strength comes from God, and that human limitations and inadequacies provide opportunities for His power to shine. The glory is all His.

Hello God...it's me. When I'm feeling down and overlooked, will You remind me to seek Your outstretched arms?

Praying God's Heart

Let us go right into the presence of God with sincere hearts fully trusting him.... Let us hold tightly without wavering to the hope we affirm, for God can be trusted to keep his promise.

HEBREWS 10:22–23 NLT

Have you ever noticed an elderly couple who bears a uncanny resemblance to each other? They may mirror each other's expressions and mannerisms. It is said that the more time two people spend together, the more they look alike.

The same is true with God. The more time we spend in His Word, the more His words echo from our tongues. The more we invest in prayer, the more His thoughts reverberate within our hearts. If we want to look like Him, we will hang out with Him.

We know that God can be trusted to keep His promises, so we enter boldly into His presence in prayer. We present our requests, not like slaves or servants trembling before a harsh ruler but as dearly loved children approaching a gracious Father. We trust that God knows what we need. We believe that when our hearts seek His will, He will answer. We know that He is good and faithful to guide our prayers until they become His very promises breathed out through us.

Hello God...it's me. Thank You that You don't want us always second-guessing our worthiness to approach You but desire that we boldly approach.

Adjusting Our View of Self

Through the grace given to me I say to everyone among you not to think more highly of himself than he ought to think; but to think so as to have sound judgment, as God has allotted to each a measure of faith.

ROMANS 12:3 NASB

How many times each day do you hear messages in advertisements and media that tell us that we are important, that our needs and desires are paramount, and that we should not let others stand in the way of our goals and happiness? We are inundated with these messages daily.

Yet that is not the radical approach to life that Christ modeled for us. His thinking goes against our modern times, but it also went against the messages conveyed throughout all of human history.

If we truly want to walk closer to Christ and follow His plan for our lives, we must be willing to humble ourselves and submit to Him—and to others. This attitude of selflessness is certainly difficult and not of this world, but it's necessary.

Scripture reminds us not to think too highly of ourselves and commands us to treat our neighbors as we want to be treated. This radical, biblical challenge is filled with wonderful possibilities.

Hello, God...it's me. Thank You for giving me an abundance of both humility and self-confidence.

The God of Contentment

I can do all this through him who gives me strength.
PHILIPPIANS 4:13 NIV

The world had rarely watched an athlete as closely as they did the quarterback for the University of Florida. At least, that's what the Internet seemed to indicate on Saturday nights. Every Saturday for his games, Tim Tebow would don a black strip with a Bible verse reference written in white underneath his eyes. Whichever Scripture reference Tebow wore would be the most heavily searched on Internet engines over the next twenty-four hours. A Bible verse that Tebow wore frequently was Philippians 4:13.

While many fans interpreted this verse to be about winning a game, it was, of course, composed in the middle of a much more serious circumstance. These words were written by the apostle Paul while he was in prison for his faith. Hungry and isolated, Paul declared that he was content. He had learned the secret of relying on Christ, who filled him with the supernatural power to remain strong.

The strength that God provides is a beautiful testimony to His love. Whether our bank account is full or pitifully sparse, whether we dine on filet mignon or macaroni, His grace makes contentment and peace possible.

Hello God...it's me. This year, will You train my heart to look to only You for contentment?

Boldness for the Timid

For this reason I remind you to fan into flame the gift of God, which is in you through the laying on of my hands, for God gave us a spirit not of fear but of power and love and self-control.

2 TIMOTHY 1:6–7 ESV

Psychologists tell us that there are four basic personality types: choleric (excitable), sanguine (confident), phlegmatic (calm), and melancholy (persistent). Depending on your temperament the thought of being a bold witness for Christ might ignite a fire in your soul or it might fill you with dread. As Christians we need to remember that being a witness for Christ doesn't depend upon our personality but on the Spirit of God working in our lives.

Each of us has spiritual gifts bestowed upon us by our Creator. God created our personalities, and He calls us to be bold witnesses for Him whether we are assertive or timid by nature. Our hope in Christ doesn't spring from our temperament but from our salvation.

Scripture urges us to always be willing to share the hope that is within us, in the ways God has prepared for us.

Hello God...it's me. Today, I will anticipate Your goodness and know You will give me what I need for everything that comes my way.

Cry Out to God

Call on me in the day of trouble; I will deliver you, and you will honor me.
PSALM 50:15 NIV

Are you experiencing difficulty today? Perhaps you are struggling through a painful situation or bearing the burden for another who is suffering.

The apostle Paul knew hardships firsthand. He was persecuted, beaten, shipwrecked, and imprisoned. He also suffered from a burden so painful that he described it as a "thorn in his flesh." Paul was honest with God, asking Him to take the thorn away. But God reminded him that His grace was all Paul needed (2 Corinthians 12:7–10). His faithfulness is tried and proven.

Whatever difficulty you face today, cry out to God. Pour out your heart to Him in prayer and lay all of your pain at God's feet. His power is perfected in our weakness, and His grace is just as sufficient for us today as it was for the apostle Paul.

Hello God...it's me. Thank You for the beauty of Your perfected power in my weakness.

Stooping to Help Us

The blessing of the Lord makes rich, and he adds no sorrow with it.
PROVERBS 10:22 ESV

A shepherd wandering in darkness and danger to find and rescue one little lamb. A father setting aside his dignity and running to welcome home the son who rejected him and squandered his money. The Son of God reaching out to touch the hand of a leper. Jesus noticing and praising the generosity of a poverty-stricken widow.

So many of the images we have of God, in the parables and in the human face of His Son, show God stooping down to our level.

Christ was willing to humble Himself so that He could help those who were in need. And He continues to reach down to us so we might receive His strength when temptation hits. He is eager to help us. Every time we reach the end of our strength and can't find our way out of difficult circumstances, we need to stop and ask Him for help. He is never too proud to stoop to our level to give us the help we need—dare we be too proud to ask?

Hello God...it's me. Please take away any pride that keeps me from running to You.

January 14

Bootstraps

For I will not trust in my bow, nor shall my sword save me. But You have saved us from our enemies, and have put to shame those who hated us. In God we boast all day long, and praise Your name forever. Selah.

Psalm 44:6–8 NKJV

Americans love the idea of self-sufficiency. From the first day at kindergarten to the last overpriced therapy session, we are told over and over that we are "good enough" and that we can do anything if we just "believe in ourselves." Publishers sell millions of self-help books, all of which encourage us to "pick ourselves up by our bootstraps."

But no matter how good these platitudes may sound, they don't reflect reality. Why?

Because self-sufficiency is impossible. As much as we hate to admit it, no one can get through life on his or her own strength. At some point, we all need help, and self-help can't cut it.

God knows we can't get by alone. That's why He didn't leave us to pick ourselves up by our bootstraps; He reaches down to help us up.

Hello God...it's me. I want You to know how much I love You for not subscribing to the bootstraps mentality.

Bruised Christians

Lord God of Israel, no other god in heaven or on earth is like you! You never forget the agreement you made with your people, and you are loyal to anyone who faithfully obeys your teachings.
1 Kings 8:23 CEV

Like a toddler just learning to walk, we followers of Jesus sometimes stumble as we make our way along the narrow path. Some days we get by without a scratch; still other days we barely limp through, bruised and bleeding.

The amazing reality about our spiritual journey is that we don't take it alone. We have other believers before us, behind us, and beside us to pick us up when we fall. Better still, we have our Savior who wipes away the tears, cleans our wounds, and applies the healing salve of forgiveness.

When we stumble, we learn from our mistakes. Having come through the rough times, we have the wisdom to help others in similar situations. God knows we don't like to stumble, but He makes sure that everything works together for good—our good and the good of His kingdom.

Step forward boldly, knowing He walks with you.

Hello God...it's me. Will You help me not to miss one opportunity to lift someone up?

Consider His Mercy

All bitterness, anger and wrath, shouting and slander must be removed from you, along with all malice. And be kind and compassionate to one another, forgiving one another, just as God also forgave you in Christ.
EPHESIANS 4:31–32 HCSB

The honey locust thorn tree is a great provider of shade. Yet it has one drawback: long, sharp thorns. Botanists have determined that the thorn is the tree's means of self-defense. A prick from the thorn can cause a very painful wound that can lead to swelling and infection.

Sometimes we use prickly words as our self-defense against hurt. Yet a careless word is like the thorn of the honey locust thorn tree—it can cause a deep wound that can lead to the "infection" of bitterness setting in and causing even more problems. Believers should stop and consider the love and mercy of God before allowing thorny words to hurt others.

This is especially true when it comes to our interactions with other believers. When we consider how much God has forgiven us, we should be eager to forgive. As our hearts are filled with God's love, we should honor Him by choosing words that express mercy and kindness. Our words can be honeyed, rather than barbed. The choice is always ours.

Hello God...it's me. By Your power, I will reveal Your love and kindness with my words.

Questions and Answers

Let the words of my mouth and the meditation of my heart be acceptable in Your sight,
O Lord, my rock and my Redeemer.
Psalm 19:14 NASB

The best way to help people who are encountering huge problems is just to be present. There are no quick fixes for the agony of losing a loved one or the shock of being diagnosed with a serious illness. Still, grieving people need to be able to talk to someone, to voice their frustrations, to ask their questions. They need to feel heard.

A real friend will be that listening ear.

For each of us, the situations life throws at us produce any number of questions that we will need to direct to God—questions He already knows are coming. And He intends to resolve every one. Perhaps not in our timing or in the manner we would desire, but He *will* resolve them.

Hello God...it's me. Thank You for Your guidance even in the questions.

Seeing Things Clearly

Then I saw that wisdom excelleth folly, as far as light excelleth darkness. The wise man's eyes are in his head; but the fool walketh in darkness: and I myself perceived also that one event happeneth to them all.

ECCLESIASTES 2:13–14 KJV

Colors didn't seem as bright to Reginald. Street signs were getting harder to read. For a long time he didn't notice, and then he shrugged it off as a normal consequence of getting older. But the doctor told him cataracts were causing his problems. If he had them removed, he could again have clear eyesight. Now that he has had the surgery he can see again, even without glasses. Proper focus has helped Reginald enjoy his daily walks again—and to drive more safely too.

How about you? Do you need a vision check? Is Jesus out of focus on the edges of your life? Spend some time with the Eye Doctor of your soul, and ask Him to remove any obstructions so you can see clearly again. Doing so is a way to honor Jesus and put your faith in the proper perspective.

Hello God...it's me. Will You remove any attitudes or other obstructions that are keeping me from seeing Your loving control of my life today?

Changed by Tragedy

Yet you brought me out of the womb; you made me trust in you, even at my mother's breast.
From birth I was cast on you; from my mother's womb you have been my God.
Do not be far from me, for trouble is near and there is no one to help.
PSALM 22:9–11 NIV

The Thursday before Easter in 2007, a tragic car accident took the life of a high school senior, Chris. A girl who barely knew him was shaken. A young Christ-follower, she'd distanced herself from God. As her shock from Chris's death changed into fear and tears, she returned, weeping, to God's arms. She took comfort in His Word, explored it more, and clung to its truth. She rested in God's strength, found peace in knowing that He was in control, and drew closer to Him than she ever had been before. The direction of her life changed. Without Chris's death, she might have remained distant from God for much longer. Her love for God and others would have grown more stagnant. The tragedy served as a reminder to her of what was really important.

Although most of us want a life filled only with joy and blessings, God knows that sometimes we must endure difficult circumstances and tragedies in order for Him to build the strength of character He wants in us. Unexpected tragedies reveal what is most important in our lives—and they often lead us to the arms of the One who is the Source of life.

Hello God...it's me. Increase my faith in Your goodness, no matter what my day looks like.

Unlimited Knowledge

O Lord, you have examined my heart and know everything about me. You know when I sit down or stand up. You know my thoughts even when I'm far away. You see me when I travel and when I rest at home. You know everything I do. You know what I am going to say even before I say it, Lord.

Psalm 139:1–4 NLT

God is the only being to possess limitless knowledge. He knows all that ever occurred in the past. He knows everything that is happening at this moment. He knows what will happen in the future. He is prepared to meet our needs even before we know we are in need.

Because God knows the future, nothing can surprise Him. He not only knows the circumstances we are facing, but He knows the way through them.

Why do we so often think we know better than God? So often we second-guess His plans for us. Sometimes we even go so far as to think He doesn't understand what we are going through. At times, we even think that God has forgotten about us.

But God loves us and wants to guide us into the future that only He knows. Let us sit at His feet, soaking up all He has to teach us.

Hello God...it's me. Will You show me what it is like to sit at Your feet even during my full schedule today?

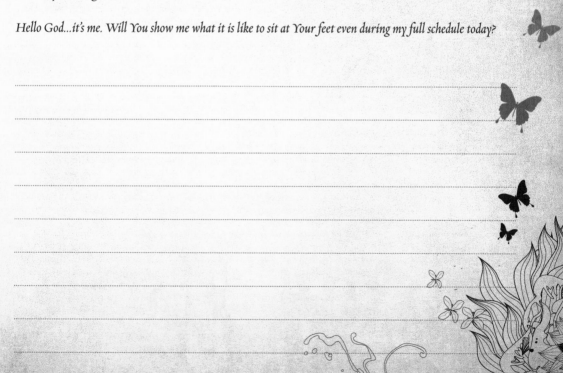

The Dirtier Face

Why do you look at the speck in your brother's eye, but do not consider the plank in your own eye?
Or how can you say to your brother, "Let me remove the speck from your eye";
and look, a plank is in your own eye? Hypocrite! First remove the plank from your own eye,
and then you will see clearly to remove the speck from your brother's eye.
MATTHEW 7:3–5 NKJV

Catherine diligently worked on her chalk drawing for the entire hour of art class. She had blended colors, swirled sponges to darken or fade hues, and used a heavy piece of soft black coal to outline a border. Looking over at her friend Anna's smudged attempt to make a chalk drawing of a face, Catherine laughed. "That's one of the messiest faces I've ever seen," she said critically. Anna first looked offended, then amused. She reached into her purse, extracted a compact, and held the mirror in front of Catherine. "Not as messy as this face," Anna countered. To her surprise, Catherine saw her reflection, her sweaty cheeks smeared with chalk colors.

Too often we criticize the flaws of others without realizing our own flaws. It's easy to point out the failings of others instead of examining ourselves to discover our sin. Yet acceptance and love do far more to help others than insults and ridicule. Instead of pointing out others' sins, let's confess our own sins to God. Then, cleansed by His forgiveness, we can reach out to others with kindness and love.

Hello God...it's me. Thank You for Your love that gently shows me a true reflection so You can begin to transform.

Cause and Effect

All of you angels in heaven, honor the glory and power of the Lord!
Honor the wonderful name of the Lord, and worship the Lord most holy and glorious.
PSALM 29:1–2 CEV

Cause and effect is simple. Every junior-high science student understands that adding some substances to others creates a reaction—sometimes positive, sometimes negative. You might get a compound of beautiful color and scent; you might get an explosion.

How we worship is based on *why* we worship—cause and effect. Are we worshiping because it's the thing to do, because our friends do it, because it's a habit? If so, our worship will be stale, flat, without emotion. In fact, it might not be true worship at all.

However, if we are worshiping because of our love for this God who saves us, transforms us, and promises us eternity with Him, then our worship will reach to heaven and bring us close to Him. In order to worship God as He should be worshiped, we need to focus completely on who He is and what He has done. Cause and effect.

Hello God...it's me. I often feel so scattered. Will You show me how to completely focus on You to give You the worship You deserve?

Unlocked Potential

Now you are the body of Christ, and members individually. And God has appointed these in the church: first apostles, second prophets, third teachers, after that miracles, then gifts of healings, helps, administrations, varieties of tongues. Are all apostles? Are all prophets? Are all teachers? Are all workers of miracles? Do all have gifts of healings? Do all speak with tongues? Do all interpret? But earnestly desire the best gifts.

1 CORINTHIANS 12:27–31 NKJV

Go into any local bookstore and you'll find shelves lined with self-help books that tout the authors' ability to unlock the potential of a person. And in sold-out conference centers and arenas, motivational speakers assure us that if we would just follow these seven steps or buy this product, then we will notice a difference in our lives in a matter of days.

Yet God alone is the ultimate locksmith of our hearts. He can unlock potential no one even dreamed of, because He designed it and put it there. He has given each of us specific gifts and abilities and dreams. He knows the full measure of our potential. Best of all, He doesn't assign an "expiration date" or an age limit for the realization of that potential. You can be all that God calls you to be whenever God wills.

Lay your heart before the One who knows it better than even you do. Let Him unlock your potential.

Hello God...it's me. Will You help me to partner with You to unlock the potential You've placed in me?

True Light

*The true light, who gives light to everyone, was coming into the world. He was in the world,
and the world was created through Him, yet the world did not recognize Him.*
JOHN 1:9–10 HCSB

Ever worry about how to share your faith? Perhaps you worry not only about who you'll talk to but what you'll say and how you'll say it. The good news is that God does the bulk of the work in spreading the Good News. As you share your faith with others, He not only reminds you of the truth but He also shines His light through you.

The apostle John wrote of Jesus as the Light who revealed Himself to a people trapped in darkness. While some preferred the darkness, others gravitated toward the light of His truth. The more they sought the light, the more they saw how splendid it was and how desperately they needed it. After His resurrection, Jesus sent the Holy Spirit to help bear witness of His truth to them and to you.

Ask God to show you someone you can talk with about your faith. The Holy Spirit will help you be a light in a dark world.

Hello God...it's me. Show me how I can be a light to the world around me.

....

....

....

....

....

....

....

Small Acts

We should think about others and not about ourselves.
1 CORINTHIANS 10:24 CEV

We can certainly express our love for someone by doing big things for our beloved, but faithfulness in doing the small things quickly adds up. The loyal husband of many years who still leaves love notes on his wife's pillow and comes home every evening to help her with the kids and household chores is as valued and appreciated as the one who dazzles his bride with expensive jewelry and presents.

This is especially true in our interactions with God. Not every Christian can do something stupendous for the Lord. There are very few people like Billy Graham or Mother Teresa, recognized for their huge contributions to the faith. But plenty of us live for Jesus every day doing our little, unnoticed pieces of obedience. We can honor Jesus in what we do, no matter how insignificant it may seem, by doing it with all of our heart.

God regards not the greatness of the work, but the love for Him with which we do even the smallest act.

Hello God...it's me. Thank You, Lord, for seeing my heart.

Big Shoes to Fill

*When he had finished washing their feet, he put on his clothes and returned to his place.
"Do you understand what I have done for you?" he asked them. "You call me 'Teacher' and 'Lord,'
and rightly so, for that is what I am. Now that I, your Lord and Teacher, have washed your feet,
you also should wash one another's feet. I have set you an example that you should do
as I have done for you.... Now that you know these things, you will be blessed if you do them.*
JOHN 13:12–15, 17 NIV

When you were little, did you ever try to walk in your dad's shoes? Your small feet felt dwarfed in your father's shoes. The size of the shoes affected your ability to walk. But when your dad slipped his feet into those shoes and balanced your feet on top, you could walk just fine.

Following Jesus's perfect example can seem like slipping on a pair of shoes that are too big for us to handle—or so we think. But through the Holy Spirit, Jesus's feet are still in the shoes. His feet are underneath ours, guiding our steps and equipping us to do what He has called us to do. We can follow His example gladly, because He goes with us. And as we walk with Christ, others may be inspired to follow along behind us.

Feeling like you have big shoes to fill? Relax. His feet are under yours, guiding you each step of the way.

Hello God...it's me. Will You help me to walk in Your footsteps today?

In Plain Sight

For what can be known about God is plain to them, because God has shown it to them.
For his invisible attributes, namely, his eternal power and divine nature, have been clearly perceived,
ever since the creation of the world, in the things that have been made. So they are without excuse.
ROMANS 1:19–20 ESV

In 1987 a children's book titled *Where's Wally?* was published in England (later published in North America as *Where's Waldo?*). The book featured double-page illustrations of people doing a variety of things at a given location. The goal for the reader was to locate Wally. Since he wore a red-and-white-striped shirt and hat, along with big black-rimmed glasses, you would think Wally would be easy to locate. But the illustrator included several decoys within the already jumbled pages, making it a challenge to find him.

Thankfully, God has not set up the world in a way that makes Him hard to find. As a matter of fact, all one has to do to see God's character is to look out the window. Though He is invisible, God has not hidden Himself.

Look around your world today. Let your eyes rest on the things not made by human hands—the very pages of God's artistry. As you stare at these things, try and imagine the One who made them. As you do, you will find your heart being filled with a renewed sense of wonder.

Hello God...it's me. Thank You that I can see You in the beauty that surrounds me.

God in Our Weakness

He said to me, "My grace is sufficient for you, for my power is made perfect in weakness."
Therefore I will boast all the more gladly about my weaknesses, so that Christ's power may rest on me.
That is why, for Christ's sake, I delight in weaknesses, in insults, in hardships, in persecutions,
in difficulties. For when I am weak, then I am strong.
2 Corinthians 12:9–10 NIV

Sometimes it feels like we're not strong in Christ at all. We falter. We trip. We try and fail. We serve to the point of exhaustion. How can we possibly be of any value to God and His kingdom?

Oddly enough, it is in our weaknesses that God works in us the most. His strength gives us power even when we don't realize it. The weaker we feel, the more of God we bring to the situation. This is when we make the strongest impressions on others. We fade into the background as God's presence and glory are revealed through our weaknesses. We become the strongest of examples for Him when we least know it.

In those weak moments, we sow seeds of faith. Under God's watchful eyes, those little seeds, sown in the dust of our daily lives, will blossom into immortal flowers of eternal life.

Keep planting. God will tend the garden and produce the growth.

Hello God...it's me. Thank You for Your strength that goes out to those of us who are humbly aware of our need for You.

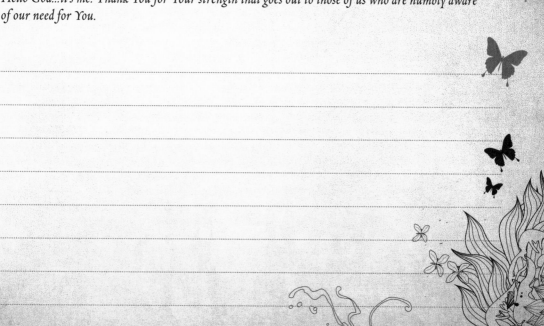

Welcoming God's Trials

No discipline seems pleasant at the time, but painful. Later on, however,
it produces a harvest of righteousness and peace for those who have been trained by it.
HEBREWS 12:11 NIV

When we are sick, the doctor often prescribes medication to treat the illness that can taste terrible and have negative side effects. Even without adverse effects, our daily dose of medicine is a daily reminder we are sick. This is sort of like trials from God. Who wants them? But trials are necessary to strengthen our faith and improve our spiritual health.

Trials don't usually appear to be helpful, but cruel, unfair, and unloving. Why would a good God send trials into our lives? But sometimes the Great Physician sends trials into our lives as a form of spiritual medicine. God's discipline isn't much fun at the time, Hebrews 12:11 tells us, but it bears the fruit of righteousness and peace. The Lord loves those He tests. God's discipline shows that we are truly His sons and daughters.

So the next time we want to complain about the pain, or worse yet, consider abandoning our faith, ask the Lord for strength to endure the trials—realizing that, like medicine, they are for our good, as much as we might not want to take it.

Hello God...it's me. I want You to know that, with Your strength, I am choosing to trust You.

But God…

When we were utterly helpless, Christ came at just the right time and died for us sinners.
Now, most people would not be willing to die for an upright person….
But God showed his great love for us by sending Christ to die for us while we were still sinners.
ROMANS 5:7–8 NLT

God is sometimes incorrectly labeled as unreasonable or cruel. Unbelievers think that like a callous judge, God thunders from heaven with anger, malice, or punishment for the slightest infraction. Some people argue that God is a celestial killjoy, taking away our pleasure with a list of "Thou shalts" and "Thou shalt nots."

Praise God that He is not like that! Instead of delighting in our downfall, the Bible tells us that God, in His goodness, is a God of second chances. He comes to the rescue of His children, even when their difficulties are of their own making. The Bible lists many instances of trials that changed to blessings simply because God intervened. *But God…* "is a mediator," "had mercy," "disciplines us for our good," "promised a legacy," "raised Jesus," "remembered the needy," "answered," "listened," "preserved," "testifies," "gave protection and warning."

Perhaps the loveliest "but God" in the pages of Scripture is found in Romans 5:8: "*But God* demonstrates his own love for us in this: While we were still sinners, Christ died for us" (NIV).

Hello God…it's me. Help me to bring out the "but God" side when I hear people talk bad about You.

A Joyride with God

Jesus said to him, "I am the way, and the truth, and the life; no one comes to the Father but through Me."
JOHN 14:6 NASB

God's attributes draw us to Him. This unique list of what can make a heart swell with love for God gives us the opportunity to look at our loving Father in new and exciting ways.

He is the Center, the point around which everything else in life revolves. No spinning out of control when God is your Center. He is the Peacemaker, bringing peace to your worried heart, to broken families, to a dying world. He is the Passport to adventure.

When you become a citizen of heaven, that passport grants you entry to places unknown, places of adventure God has prepared for you. He is a Joyride, taking you through life with your hands in the air and the wind in your hair. Above all, He is the Answer to any and all longings, whatever yours may be.

With God, your life is an adventure—a veritable joyride!

Where is God taking you today?

Hello God...it's me. Help me to look intently to You, expecting joy.

February 1

Ignore the Mess

The LORD sits enthroned over the flood; the LORD is enthroned as King forever.
The LORD gives strength to his people; the LORD blesses his people with peace.
PSALM 29:10–11 NIV

Ever wish you could find a restart button to push when life gets messy? That frustrating job. That complicated friendship. That circumstance that seems to get more and more untidy the more you try to fix it. Sometimes our difficult situations can feel like a skein of yarn that keeps getting more and more tangled as we work through the knots.

In the midst of the mess, it's easy to forget that God promises to bless His people with victory and peace. He invites us to take our messes to His cross and leave them there, instead of making them our focus. The cross is a restart button. Even when our difficult situation wildly beckons us and ignites our worry, we can choose to believe that God is still in control and He can bless our messes.

Choose to take Him at His word. Give Him your doubts and your fears. Accept His hope.

Hello God...it's me. Help me to remember that there is nothing complicated about Your love for me.

A State of Genuine Joy

Let the field be joyful, and all that is therein: then shall all the trees of the wood
rejoice before the Lord: for he cometh, for he cometh to judge the earth:
he shall judge the world with righteousness, and the people with his truth.
PSALM 96:12–13 KJV

Katelyn struggled with the mistakes of her past. Over and over, she mentally replayed the memories of the nights she'd snuck out of the house, the secrets she'd kept from her parents, the lies she'd told. Guilt dominated her life, filled her thoughts, controlled her actions, and contorted her expressions. Plagued by the thoughts and emotions of her past sins, she was never truly happy.

After accepting Christ in her life, Katelyn confessed her sins to God and repented. She told her parents about her deceptions, and her parents forgave her. Still, for Katelyn, the feelings of guilt remained. God and her parents had forgiven her, but she couldn't accept their forgiveness. Unable to comprehend the depth of their love, Katelyn couldn't fathom the idea of total forgiveness for all the wrongs she'd done.

The gospel—that God sent His Son to save us from sin, that God forgives us completely—is the greatest reason for us to be joyful. Let's show our faith through our words, our thoughts, our actions, and our smiles. We are forgiven.

Hello God...it's me. Help me to roll my daily burden of guilt onto You.

He Kept Going

I do not have time to tell about Gideon, Barak, Samson and Jephthah, about David and Samuel and the prophets, who through faith conquered kingdoms, administered justice, and gained what was promised; who shut the mouths of lions, quenched the fury of the flames, and escaped the edge of the sword; whose weakness was turned to strength; and who became powerful in battle and routed foreign armies.... These were all commended for their faith.

HEBREWS 11:32–34, 39 NIV

Chris Gardner had a stack of parking tickets he couldn't pay. After a short stay in jail for failure to pay the tickets, he landed an internship by his character, not his clothes.

Gardner had no job, no car, and no place to live, only a thousand-dollar-a-month stipend from his internship and a young son to take care of. He worked at his internship like a madman, arriving early and leaving late. He did what he could to keep his son safe and their homelessness private, even sleeping in the locked bathroom of a transit station.

In time Gardner's perseverance paid off: he became a full-time stockbroker. Had he given up at any point, *The Pursuit of Happyness*, the movie from his memoir of the same title, would never have been made.

Are you far from your own happily ever after today? Take courage in this: God knows the end of your story. Look to Him as you persevere day after day.

Hello God...it's me. I want You to know I'm trusting You for my happy ending.

A Mighty Power

Now I am going to him who sent me. None of you asks me, 'Where are you going?' Rather,
you are filled with grief because I have said these things. But very truly I tell you, it is for your good that
I am going away. Unless I go away, the Advocate will not come to you; but if I go, I will send him to you.
JOHN 16:5–7 NIV

Imagine what it would have been like to be a follower of Jesus while He was on earth. He might have come to you and said, "Stop what you are doing; come, follow Me. I am going to make you a fisher of men." You would have been there when He gave sight to the blind, strength to the lame, and food to more than five thousand people from just five small loaves and two fish. You would have watched in awe as evil spirits and raging waters obeyed His every command.

Then you learn that He is leaving and returning to His Father in heaven. Doubts flood your mind and fear grips your heart as you ask yourself, "How can I go on? Without Jesus here with me, I can't!"

On Pentecost, the Holy Spirit, the power of God from on high, descended into that first band of timid disciples and empowered them to carry out God's mission. For every Christ-follower since, the same Holy Spirit enters our hearts and pulsates the power of God into us day by day.

Hello God...it's me. Will You help me to be more aware of Your power in me?

God Our Shelter

The world is full of so-called prayer warriors who are prayer-ignorant. They're full of formulas and programs and advice, peddling techniques for getting what you want from God. Don't fall for that nonsense. This is your Father you are dealing with, and he knows better than you what you need. With a God like this loving you, you can pray very simply.
MATTHEW 6:7–8 MSG

When you were a child, where was the first place you ran when you were scared or overwhelmed? More than likely a parent's arms offered the perfect place of safety. Your fears about the monster lurking in the closet or the bad storm outside gave way in the presence of a parent's strong and steadfast love.

When we get older, problems and temptations become like monsters in our closet that don't go away, no matter who hugs us. Victory eludes us as long as we focus on our faltering ability to fight. So where can we turn?

If you're in the midst of the fray today, become like a child again. Seek shelter in the loving arms of your heavenly Father. Jesus taught us to run to God in prayer whenever we feel afraid or overwhelmed by the struggles in this world.

Need shelter? Your heavenly Father eagerly waits with outstretched arms to comfort and protect you.

Hello God...it's me. Will You show me how to take shelter in You?

God's True Love

God is love, and the one who abides in love abides in God, and God abides in him.
1 JOHN 4:16 NASB

Divine love. How do we even begin to comprehend it? It is so far beyond what we know as love—our earthly passion for another person.

We may be willing to sacrifice some of our own desires for one we love, but our noble gestures pale in comparison to the ultimate sacrifice our loving heavenly Father made. He sent His Son to give His very life for us. And He did it while we were still sinners, while we were far from being worthy of such a great love.

In our own relationships, how often do we perform a kind deed for our beloved in the hope of receiving a reciprocal response? But God, in His divine love, does not love us in order to get something from us. He simply offers His love as a gift, freely, with no ulterior motive or hope of reciprocity.

The choice is ours.

Hello God...it's me. I ask for Your help in loving like You do.

He Carries It All

*Come to Me, all you who labor and are heavy laden, and I will give you rest.
Take My yoke upon you and learn from Me, for I am gentle and lowly in heart,
and you will find rest for your souls. For My yoke is easy and My burden is light.*

MATTHEW 11:28–30 NKJV

The famous poem "Footprints" reminds us that in life's most difficult seasons, Jesus does not abandon us; rather, at the times we are unable to go on, He picks us up and carries us.

We are amazed by the picture of a burden-bearing Savior. He took our sins upon Himself so that we might have freedom. He takes up our shame so that we are no longer hindered by it. What other burdens have never landed on our shoulders because He would not allow it? What other burdens has He taken upon Himself rather than letting them fall to us?

Whatever is loading you down today, you need carry it no longer. Jesus will scoop the weight in one arm and put His other arm around your tired shoulders. Gently He'll remind you that it is for these very things that He sacrificed His life.

Today, feel Him removing the weight of your burden and holding you near.

Hello God...it's me. I want You to know that I love You, and I do not take Your gentle and self-sacrificing character for granted.

....

....

....

....

....

....

....

Restless Hearts

So God created man in his own image, in the image of God created he him; male and female created he them. And God blessed them.... And God saw every thing that he had made, and, behold it was very good.

GENESIS 1:27–28, 31 KJV

Watch any amount of television and you will come away feeling sorry for the people who are seeking fulfillment in a job, a friend, a lover, a flawless body or a perfect performance. Nothing on this earth—no amount of fame, notoriety, or perceived perfection—can bring rest to our restless hearts. We find peace in God and God alone.

This is how God made us. Humanity is not a random accident. We were created on purpose by God Himself, who made us in His image so that we might commune with Him, love Him, and be loved by Him. He made us for Himself. And only when we find our rest in Him will our hearts stop seeking.

When we find Him, we find everything we need in this life and in the life to come.

Hello God...it's me. Thank You for Your peace that surpasses understanding.

Let Us Love Like Jesus

For God so loved the world that He gave His only begotten Son,
that whoever believes in Him should not perish but have everlasting life.
JOHN 3:16 NKJV

What is love? In a word, it's Jesus. He embraced the cross because He loved us. He died so that none of us would perish. He gave the ultimate sacrifice out of godly concern and compassion for us—a people who didn't deserve it. Christ's love looked beyond His needs to the needs of others.

Are we willing to follow His lead, loving as He did with giving, selfless, humble love?

While we can't die for someone else's sins, we can set aside our love of work so we can spend more time with our family. Or reconnect with an old friend when it would be easier not to. Or forgive someone who hurt us. Whatever the sacrifice, can we do it for Jesus, uniting our hearts with His? When we do, we are united with God. The power of love does that.

Hello God...it's me. Thank You for leading my heart to love as steadfastly as Jesus does.

Come Away

My beloved spoke and said to me, "Arise, my darling, my beautiful one, come with me."
SONG OF SONGS 2:10 NIV

Put down the phone. Push away the keyboard. Turn off the television. God asks you to stop and spend time with Him alone.

Like an excited fiancé who wants nothing but to enjoy time with his beloved, God seeks you out to simply be with Him. He doesn't need pious prayers. He doesn't ask for lofty commitments or ritualistic practices. He asks for you. You, there in the middle of work's madness. You, tired and longing for someone to notice. You, broken and distant. He wants your company and will not tire in searching you out.

Sometimes God's silence compels us to run and find Him. Other times, the glowing sun outside the kitchen window signals us to drop the ordinary and be captivated by Him...just for a moment.

Bring your open heart today and allow yourself to be drawn near to Him.

Hello God...it's me. It is hard to comprehend, but I know it's true: thank You for seeking me out, for pursuing me.

First Love

Father, I want everyone you have given me to be with me, wherever I am. Then they will see the glory that you have given me, because you loved me before the world was created.

JOHN 17:24 CEV

Parents love a child before he or she ever arrives. Announcements are mailed, rooms are redesigned with vibrant colors and cribs, siblings are prepared for the arrival, and the family begins the Herculean task of name selection. All of this takes place before the baby is delivered. The parents' love comes first; the child doesn't earn the love of its parents. The love is present before that baby boy or girl even enters the world.

The Father loved the Son before there was anything. Before the creation of light and dark and fish and birds and creeping things and trees and fruit and man and woman. God loved His Son before the world was breathed into being. And that same wondrous love is what the Son showers on us by His life, death, burial, and resurrection.

God's love is always first, before anything else. He is the initiator of love, of our communion with Him. We don't earn His love; it is unconditional and a gift of His grace. Before the world was created, the Father loved the Son. Before we knew Him, God loved us.

Hello God...it's me. I love that Jesus was so secure in Your love. Help me to be like Him.

The Reason Is Love

This is how God showed his love among us: He sent his one and only Son into the world
that we might live through him. This is love: not that we loved God,
but that he loved us and sent his Son as an atoning sacrifice for our sins.

1 JOHN 4:9–10 NIV

It's a classic story. Geppetto the wood-worker carves a boy out of wood and wishes he would become real. His wish is granted, and Pinocchio is transformed into a real boy with a mind of his own.

Pinocchio's boyish ideas land him in the wrong crowd and he runs away from home. This act of rebellion breaks his father's heart, causing Geppetto to experience the ache of separation between himself and the child he has created.

Knowing full well that mankind would make a similar decision to rebel, God created us anyway. He knew our outcome before He formed the dust we were made from, and yet, with love immeasurable, He formed us and shaped us. The human race soon rebelled, but God's love didn't waver.

His love for you doesn't waver either.

Hello God...it's me. Thank You for creating us with choices. I chose You.

I Love You

Two others—criminals—were also led away to be executed with Him. When they arrived at the place called The Skull, they crucified Him there, along with the criminals, one on the right and one on the left. [Then Jesus said, "Father, forgive them, because they do not know what they are doing."] And they divided His clothes and cast lots.

LUKE 23:32–34 HCSB

A Jew enduring torture during the Holocaust looks up at her torturer and says, "I love you." A POW in Vietnam raises his bleeding head and tells his tormentor, "I love you." A person walking through the wrong neighborhood says "I love you" to the gangster whose gun is against his head.

"I love you." These are not words usually spoken to try to change an adversary's mind. These are words of honesty and truth, used to express what is in a loving person's heart.

But these three words of immense meaning gain even more profundity when uttered in perilous situations toward one's enemies.

How is it possible to love someone who causes so much pain? How could we possibly love our enemies? Ask God, because that's the way He loves us. While we were still God's enemies, He loved us enough to send His Son to die on the cross in our place. And He continues to demonstrate His love for us yet today.

Hello God...it's me. Thank You for Your love given to us that transcends our own.

First in Your Heart

So watch yourselves, that you do not forget the covenant of the LORD your God which He made with you, and make for yourselves a graven image in the form of anything against which the LORD your God has commanded you. For the LORD your God is a consuming fire, a jealous God.

DEUTERONOMY 4:23–24 NASB

When a bride and groom stand before the altar, they promise love and devotion "till death do us part." How can they make such a promise? How can they know that they will always feel this way? It's easy in the beauty of the wedding ceremony; unfortunately, it's not easy when the pressures of life mount in the coming years.

But that's just the thing—the promise is not to feel that way forever, the promise is to live that way forever. To always live in love and devotion, to act with love and devotion, regardless of how we feel at the moment.

Every one of us longs to be loved—to be first in someone else's thoughts, to sense devotion that overwhelms us with joy. God wants us to put Him first in exactly this way. To live with love and devotion, regardless of the doubts, the problems, or the fears. He wants to be first in our lives. He deserves nothing less.

Hello God...it's me. Will You help me to put You first?

Loved Divinely

We are more than conquerors through Him who loved us. For I am persuaded that neither death nor life, nor angels nor principalities nor powers, nor things present nor things to come, nor height nor depth, nor any other created thing, shall be able to separate us from the love of God which is in Christ Jesus our Lord.
ROMANS 8:37–38 NKJV

Throughout the ages humanity has been drawn to the image of the eagle. Nobility in particular often used this bird to represent their strength.

God has been portrayed in literature as the Divine Eagle who soars above all, including kings and emperors. And yet surprisingly, this Divine Eagle, so mighty and majestic, longs to draw us to Himself. In fact, His love for us is so great that He suffered and died in order to give us an eternal home.

How shall we respond to so great a love? By offering our lifelong love in return.

Open your heart to God. Dwell each day under the wings of the One who gave His very life for you and who longs to teach you to soar with Him.

Hello God...it's me. I desire to soar with You—will You teach me?

Done!

Our Lord Jesus Christ...died for us, that whether we wake or sleep, we should live together with Him.
1 THESSALONIANS 5:10 NKJV

From the start we have been taught that we have to earn what we want. No handouts. No free lunches. If you want it, you work for it. So we labor to earn a living, to earn a position in the company, to earn status in the community.

We think such a strategy works to secure God's favor too. It sounds logical. Yet we will never be good enough in God's eyes. In fact, we can't earn His acceptance because He has already done everything for us.

Following Jesus is not about what we do to earn God's favor, but what Jesus has already done for us. Jesus satisfied God's demands. All we have to do is accept His gift.

Because of Jesus we are approved.

Hello God...it's me. Thank You for the tremendous gift of Your Son.

Hand in Hand

*The Lord makes firm the steps of the one who delights in him;
though he may stumble, he will not fall, for the Lord upholds him with his hand.*
Psalm 37:23–24 niv

As the mother and her young child prepare to cross a busy street, the mother grasps her child's hand. A young man bends his knee before the love of his life and puts a ring on her finger. A man and woman with crowns of gray and wrinkled smiles walk hand in hand as they stroll a sandy beach.

Hand in hand we touch, we hold, we love, we protect. Remember the first time you reached out to God and put your hand in His? Perhaps it was a prayer for help, or a prayer for a desperate need, or a prayer of surrender.

Your Father's hand is always there, reaching out to you, holding you, loving you, protecting you. He has not released His grasp. When your prayer of faith touched the heart of God, Jesus took your hand in His with a promise to hold it forever.

If you are in need of a gentle touch today, whisper a prayer asking Jesus to take your hand in His and hold on.

Hello God...it's me. Thank You for Your gentle touch, today and always.

I'm Listening

We are confident that he hears us whenever we ask for anything that pleases him.
1 JOHN 5:14 NLT

Listening is a mark of love. When you are sure of being heard you can share your thoughts, your hurts, your emotions, your dreams with your beloved. Listening is key to a lasting and healthy relationship.

God is good at listening. He is never too busy for us. He demonstrates His love by speaking through His Word and listening to our voice. He is a two-way communicator. He hears the hurt in our tone. He sees the need in our nuances.

God is a ruler who calms the stormy waves of our lives. God is also a presence who walks the dusty roads with us. He talks with us. And, better still, He listens to our pleas, our tirades, our doubts, and our anguish. He responds as a cherished lover.

What do you need to say to God today? He's listening.

Hello God...it's me. Thank You that I am like Your cherished lover, and You wait to hear from me.

The Inside Job

May the righteous be glad and rejoice before God; may they be happy and joyful.
PSALM 68:3 NIV

"I just want to be happy." Plenty of people say those words. People of every age, social standing, vocation, culture, and disposition. Americans have embedded "the pursuit of happiness" into the Constitution. Happiness is a right. Right?

The tragedy is that people look for happiness on the outside—by earning more money, accumulating more stuff, taking more vacations, manufacturing more changes. Once they have fulfilled all their desires, then they will be happy.

Wrong!

Happiness is an inside job. No amount of nipping or tucking, investing or traveling will make us permanently content. Happiness is a by-product of the internal filling of God. He cannot give us happiness apart from Himself. Why? Because happiness simply does not exist without Him.

Hello God...it's me. Thank You for fullness of joy in You presence.

Transcendence

"Come now, let's settle this," says the LORD. "Though your sins are like scarlet,
I will make them as white as snow. Though they are red like crimson, I will make them as white as wool."
ISAIAH 1:18 NLT

How do we transcend ourselves? Great thinkers have been trying to answer that question for centuries, often telling us to look within and rely on the resources deep inside ourselves. Indeed, as individuals who possess more than a physical body, we are endowed with inner qualities that go beyond genetics and physiology. We have something intangible about us, something spiritual and eternal that surpasses biological and chemical matter. But it's far from pure or strong; it's sinful and in need of cleansing. Only God, the Creator, can re-create us. He made us and knows our true nature. We are nothing without Him. With Him, we are capable of leaving our human failings behind.

Our true transformation is initiated and completed by God alone. We transcend ourselves not by looking within, but by looking at the cross and the only Savior who can make us all He created us to be.

Hello God...it's me. Thank You that Your presence makes me brand new.

Precious in His Sight

Whoever welcomes one of these little children in my name welcomes me.
MARK 9:37 NIV

During the American Civil War, composer George F. Root wrote a tune for the war song "Tramp, Tramp, Tramp." Later, one of Root's favorite lyricists, C. Herbert Woolston, would provide these lyrics for the wartime melody:

Jesus calls the children dear,
"Come to me and never fear,
For I love the little children of the world."

The refrain to Woolston's song has become a song unto itself, often sung by children. We know it simply as "Jesus Loves the Little Children."

Woolston was right; Jesus does indeed love all the children of the world. On more than one occasion, Jesus would bring children to His side to illustrate what He was teaching at the time. If someone tried to turn those little ones away, that person would be greeted with a firm rebuke. Why? Because Jesus loves the little children.

Here is a wonderful thought to consider: God refers to those who believe in Him as His children. With eyes of affection and tender hands of mercy, God welcomes us as His very own.

What a wonderful Father!

Hello God...it's me. I love how You stopped what You were doing to give Your attention to the children. Thank You for Your undivided attention.

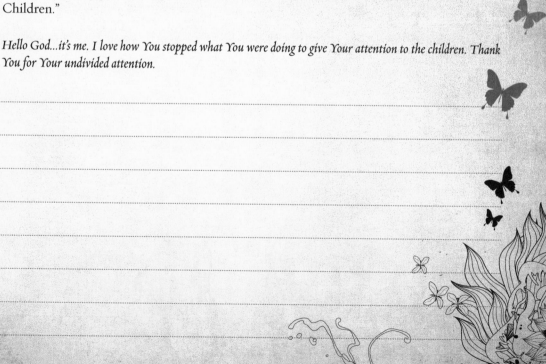

Precious Communion

Truly I tell you that if two of you on earth agree about anything they ask for, it will be done for them by my Father in heaven. For where two or three gather in my name, there am I with them.
MATTHEW 18:19–20 NIV

With Christ in us, we have communion with God and with one another. What a wonderful reminder of the oneness we have in Jesus—the answer to His prayer that we would be one, even as He and the Father are one (John 17:11).

How blessed is that communion! The moment we discover that we are fellow believers in Christ, we feel a closeness with complete strangers that we have not felt before. It may be a group gathered at church, students meeting in the local school for a prayer meeting, or even words spoken across the checkout line. The family of God enjoys immediate fellowship within its circle. And where two or three are gathered in Christ's name, He is present.

We cannot remain ignorant of His presence, for it is what draws us together in the first place. No wonder we are at home wherever we find fellow believers.

Hello God...it's me. Thank You for the home You create for Your own.

February 23

Sailing in Storms

Be strong and courageous, do not be afraid or tremble at them,
*for the L*ORD *your God is the one who goes with you. He will not fail you or forsake you.*
DEUTERONOMY 31:6 NASB

Have you ever had a day when everything fell apart at once? A day when, suddenly, all the careful plans you laid blew up spontaneously?

These days happen to all of us. Everyone who makes plans will, someday, see them fall apart. In our corrupted, imperfect world, nothing is permanent. Something will break. At times, it seems Murphy's Law is as reliable as gravity.

In sailing, often the best way to survive an awful storm is to lower the sails and ride it out. The same is true in life. Though it goes against our every instinct, in time of trouble we must lower our sails—whatever we seem to have control over—and ask God to carry us through the storm.

Take heart; God has not left you. He loves you, and He will not let you down. Remember that when He is at the helm of your life, you can ride along on His grace as He carries you through.

Hello God...it's me. Please give me peace that You are controlling the things that I can't.

Illumination

For God, who said, "Let there be light in the darkness," has made this light shine in our hearts so we could know the glory of God that is seen in the face of Jesus Christ.
2 CORINTHIANS 4:6 NLT

To the one feeling around in the darkness when thunderstorms knock out all electricity, light is not to be taken for granted. At that moment, it is seen for the miracle it is, and—for a moment, anyway—valued as a lifesaver. Light keeps the right path in sight and chases fear out of the corners.

Light is everywhere in the Bible—figuratively, as an emblem of knowledge, purity, and truth; and literally, as electromagnetic radiation created by the great Fountain of Light. In every instance, the light pours from the same source of power and divinity, beauty and holiness, integrity and certainty: the one true God.

The Father not only created first light, He actually illuminates the human heart with a light that "shines"—it does not blind; it does not burn. It is a splendid, cheerful, alluring glow...because it reflects the glory of God in the face of His Son.

Everything is made clear when held up to the light of Jesus. Even the darkness flees in His presence.

Hello God...it's me. Let me be one who reflects Your glory.

The Message Is the Mission

Pray for us, too, that God may open a door for our message,
so that we may proclaim the mystery of Christ, for which I am in chains.
COLOSSIANS 4:3 NIV

"We find that after years of struggle, we do not take a trip," said author John Steinbeck; "a trip takes us."

A trip indeed "took" the apostle Paul—hundreds of miles over many, many years. He was heartily welcomed, met with a Roman governor, and drew large crowds. He was thrown out of one city and fled another. He was stoned and left for dead. Imprisoned, he was still eager to spread the mysterious plan of Jesus. He was compelled by God's powerful and appealing message...and determined to deliver it.

Churches take missionary trips in stride now, but to the early saints in AD 44, a trip to proclaim the gospel of Christ was unimaginable. It was a new and dangerous idea. Yet despite difficult trials and horrendous persecution, God was equipping Paul and the other disciples to spread the gospel, and they gave God all the glory.

He is amazing this way. Only He can give the tools and the resources and prepare the way. Only His Spirit can keep the fires of the message alive. He is faithful and true and opening doors every day.

Hello God...it's me. Thank You for opening doors and preparing the way for me.

A Stubborn People

He said, "Go out and stand on the mount before the Lord*." And behold, the* Lord *passed by, and a great and strong wind tore the mountains and broke in pieces the rocks before the* Lord*, but the* Lord *was not in the wind. And after the wind an earthquake, but the* Lord *was not in the earthquake. And after the earthquake a fire, but the* Lord *was not in the fire. And after the fire the sound of a low whisper.*

1 Kings 19:11–12 ESV

God speaks, but how seldom do we hear Him? We enjoy our pleasures—the very pleasures that come from His hand—and forget to thank Him. He loves to bless us, and in those blessings He whispers His love to us. But then bad news comes. The doctor delivers an unexpected diagnosis. The relationship hits a rocky road. The choices that seemed right suddenly look very wrong.

Again God speaks. We search for the meaning and take a sidelong glance at Him. Finally, when the full force of adversity hits us, when the pain becomes all too real, only then does God successfully get our attention. This is beyond what we can bear. This needs extra help. This needs God.

We forget that God wants us to hear Him all the time. Times of pleasure, times of pain—what is He saying to you today?

Hello God...it's me. I want to thank You now for all the goodness You've given to me.

Ultimate Love

God demonstrates his own love for us in this: While we were still sinners, Christ died for us.
ROMANS 5:8 NIV

Oscar Wilde once said, "Every saint has a past, and every sinner has a future." Pretty simple, really. We were lost, and yet while we were wandering hopelessly, God sent His Son to atone for our sin though we did not deserve or earn His mercy. God's love was demonstrated in tandem with His unsurpassed grace, so that now we with our sinful pasts have a future.

It's a powerful show of love. We mortals can try to understand it, and offer gifts to the Father in return, but eventually we come to the truth: He loves us. He wants to share life with His created ones. He chose to demonstrate His love in an excruciatingly costly gift—His Son.

To Him be the glory for this unmatchable, indescribable act of love.

Hello God...it's me. Thank You that Your love and mercy cover my past.

Following in Our Footsteps

Imitate me, just as I also imitate Christ.
1 CORINTHIANS 11:1 NKJV

Billy Graham once told of a man who was walking to a bar one winter night during a new snowfall. His seven-year-old son called out, "Take smaller steps, Daddy. I'm walking in your tracks." The man turned around and was horrified to see that his son was following in his footprints. The man hugged his little boy, took him home, and swore off alcohol. Until that moment, he had never understood that his actions were being emulated by his son.

Which young people might be imitating your life? Perhaps children or grandchildren, nieces or nephews, or even the kids in your church or neighborhood. They all need adults who reveal the qualities of God.

You never know how your life will affect the young ones around you. What children are in your circle of influence? Pray that your life shows them a true reflection of Jesus.

Hello God…it's me. Will You show me where my reflection of You needs polishing?

Undying Light

I did not see a temple in the city, because the Lord God Almighty and the Lamb are its temple. The city does not need the sun or the moon to shine on it, for the glory of God gives it light, and the Lamb is its lamp.

REVELATION 21:22–23 NIV

Romance, mystery, and wonder surround the moon. And why not? The moon is the only natural satellite of the earth. Once a month, it completes its orbit, its angle slightly changing, which creates the illusion of a change in shape. What's more, the gravitational pull between the moon and the earth has a huge effect on our planet: it causes the oceans to ebb and flow, creating high and low tides.

What sky-gazers might find surprising is that the apostle John pointed to a glorious future and a city that will need neither sun nor moon. The risen Savior, Jesus Christ, will be the Source of energy, a Source that will never fade or dim. The glory of God will be our everlasting light; no other source will be necessary.

On the cross, Jesus—who described Himself as the Light of the world (John 8:12)—defeated the power of darkness once and for all. By the power of His Spirit, may you walk in that light today, tomorrow, and always.

Hello God...it's me. I want You to know: I can hardly wait to live in that city lit by Your glory.

God's Paradise

The Lord your God is living among you. He is a mighty savior. He will take delight in you with gladness.
With his love, he will calm all your fears. He will rejoice over you with joyful songs.
ZEPHANIAH 3:17 NLT

We think of paradise as a perfect place. A place of refuge. A mighty fortress. We find our paradise in the shadow of the Almighty.

But God? He finds paradise in a soul... the soul of a person who is fair, honorable, upright, and filled with His righteousness.

Do you wonder how that can be? Think of your heart as a cup. Take a deep, deep breath and envision God filling your cup—your soul—with Himself. Seek His righteous presence.

Imagine His delight as He pours goodness, justice, fairness into you.

Imagine His delight when you take that justice into your world!

Hello God...it's me. Please fill my soul with more of You.

Our Joy Source

By these He has granted to us His precious and magnificent promises, so that by them you may become partakers of the divine nature.... Now for this very reason also, applying all diligence, in your faith supply moral excellence, and in your moral excellence, knowledge, and in your knowledge, self-control, and in your self-control, perseverance, and in your perseverance, godliness, and in your godliness, brotherly kindness, and in your brotherly kindness, love. For if these qualities are yours and are increasing, they render you neither useless nor unfruitful in the true knowledge of our Lord Jesus Christ.

2 PETER 1:4–8 NASB

It's no secret that many people suffer from depression. While some people endure clinical depression, many of us just find ourselves under a cloud of gloom once in a while, and we wonder why. As believers we are not immune to depression, so how can we find joy?

Our joy comes from God. Second Peter 1:3 says that God "has given us everything," which tells us that God began giving in the past and continues giving right into today. God never stops giving. As our source, though, He gives what "we need for life and godliness" and not everything we want—not always what is easy, luxurious, and successful. Yet God gives His children what we need so we are more satisfied in Him, not less satisfied in Him. Our joy source is God, who can fill us so we are overjoyed on our saddest and happiest days.

Hello God...it's me. Thank You for caring about my satisfaction and joy.

_____

_____

_____

_____

_____

_____

A Protected Heart

*Therefore let us be grateful for receiving a kingdom that cannot be shaken,
and thus let us offer to God acceptable worship, with reverence and awe.*
HEBREWS 12:28 ESV

How difficult it is to be grateful in our daily lives. We are constantly making comparisons. We compare children, hoping ours are the smartest and the strongest. We compare our talents with those of others—and our possessions. But watch out: comparison is a dangerous game. Sadly, we often come up on the short end—the losing side—and it breeds resentment and gloom.

God never intended for us to compare our lives or our stuff with others. Instead, He commanded us to look to Him—the giver of life, hope, peace, love, security. Understanding His gifts causes our hearts to well up with gratitude. He gives so much; we deserve so little. Only in acknowledging the Giver, appreciating His unwarranted, incomparable, and unmerited gifts, will our hearts be safe from bitterness and depression.

Hello God...it's me. Thank You that You are not a Father who ever compares Your children.

God's Perfect Timing

*God did this according to his eternal plan. And he was able to do what
he had planned because of all that Christ Jesus our Lord had done.*
EPHESIANS 3:11 CEV

"All good things come to those who wait" is an adage with little charm if you happen to be the one in the middle of waiting. Waiting demands patience, and patience calls for being still and knowing God as all-wise, trusting His perfect timing.

Our culture today demands instant satisfaction. Instant food. Instant solving of problems. Instant relief of pain. Yet wise parents do not succumb to a child's "I want it now" tantrums. God is no different.

Whether you are waiting for the weather to change, the flowers to bloom, the toddler to learn to walk, the pain to cease, the hurt to heal, or for God to answer prayer for a loved one...be patient. Trust God's timing and wisdom. He knows the perfect time for all good things to burst forth in bloom.

Hello God...it's me. Please help me to trust Your timing.

Behind It All

Jesus has been found worthy of greater honor than Moses, just as the builder of a house has greater honor than the house itself. For every house is built by someone, but God is the builder of everything.
HEBREWS 3:3–4 NIV

Frank Lloyd Wright spent more than seventy years creating designs that revolutionized the art and architecture of the twentieth century. Many innovations we see in buildings today are products of his imagination. All in all, he designed 1,141 works—including houses, offices, churches, schools, libraries, bridges, museums, and many other types of buildings. Of that total, 532 resulted in completed works, 409 of which still stand.

But who built or created Wright? Who is behind the imaginative genius that crafted so many works of art and left a challenging legacy for future generations? The supreme Architect behind all that was and is and is to come is God, the Master Builder. This is His world, and all its majesty, both natural and man-made, can be traced back to His divine imagination and creative genius.

God is behind it all. His signature adorns everything that is beautiful, inspiring, or uplifting to the senses, soul, and spirit—whether the human artist knows it or not.

Hello God...it's me. Thank You for being the ultimate Creator, and for sharing that characteristic with Your creation.

Staying in Tune

Hear, O ye kings; give ear, O ye princes; I, even I, will sing unto the Lord;
I will sing praise to the Lord God of Israel.
JUDGES 5:3 KJV

The composer and the conductor—both are indispensable to an orchestra. As the musicians follow both the notes that have been written and how they are being directed, a beautiful piece of music results.

God is our Composer and Conductor; our faith is the orchestra. As He creates the beautiful tune of His grace in our lives, we must keep our eyes on Him. Let outside pressures fade into the background as you keep your eyes on God and what He is doing. Ignore the audience's rustling programs, hacking coughs, and cell phones that haven't been silenced. Take captive any doubt, fear, or anxieties that try to discourage you as you play. Be confident in a Conductor who knows what He's doing because He has composed the music.

And if you experience a day, or even a season, when your notes sound off-key or you can't seem to keep the beat, retune your instrument. Remember God's faithfulness in the past and pick up where you left off. There's another recital tomorrow.

Hello God...it's me. I want You to know I am trusting Your faithfulness.

A Magnificent Artist

For the word of God is living and active, sharper than any two-edged sword, piercing to the division of soul and of spirit, of joints and of marrow, and discerning the thoughts and intentions of the heart.
HEBREWS 4:12 ESV

A snow-capped mountain in the distance. Majestic. Powerful. Steep.

Come. Step closer. Magnificent details abound in this painting. Nestled in the brushstrokes are beautiful plants, trees, and rivers. Hikers, snowboarders, and skiers crisscross the mountainside. Smoke wafts out of chimneys. It's a mountain scene both majestic and alive. And the more you study it, the more you are drawn into its splendor.

You feel like you're hiking the mountain yourself. Snow sprays your jacket as skiers swoosh past you down the mountain. Steam rises off the frozen river. Your boots crunch the snow in steady rhythm as you walk.

God's Word is like that painting. Come, step closer—the museum's protective rope is down. It's a painting you can touch, feel, and experience. And the artist is giving autographs. He'll engrave His very name upon your heart.

Hello God...it's me. Please put Your signature on my heart for all to see.

Not My Will, but God's

Father, if it is Your will, take this cup away from Me; nevertheless not My will, but Yours, be done.
LUKE 22:42 NKJV

Jesus didn't mince words. When facing the horror of the cross, He asked God to take it away. But then came the words that bring us to our knees: He said, "Not My will, but Yours be done." Jesus knew His prayer wasn't about getting His way; it was about doing God's will and trusting it.

Confirming who we are to God's will is a process that takes a lifetime. The refining never ends.

Maybe you're in a situation where you're thinking, *I don't want God's will this time!* That hard conversation at home? Deductions at tax time? Choosing to give away money earmarked for a TV?

When those times come, you know it's time to get in God's presence and ask Him to realign your priorities—not your will, but His.

Hello God...it's me. Will You help me to submit my will to Yours, trusting that You will take care of me?

Living Between the Steps

*God is able to make all grace abound to you, so that always having
all sufficiency in everything, you may have an abundance for every good deed.*
2 CORINTHIANS 9:8 NASB

Common sense makes sense. We have confidence and certainty in what we know. Lest life become dull and routine, God challenges even our certainties. Every step for a believer is a step of faith, filled with grace—moving ahead in harmony with God's character.

Gracious uncertainty understands the remarkable gift of today. Mindful that every step is rich with opportunity, we take each one, reflecting God's love. Grace causes us to give more than expected, to serve beyond our time, to help when we are tired, to love when the feelings are gone. Grace upgrades and expands our lives.

Uncertainty forces us to walk by faith—knowing that God walks with us, assured that God directs our steps, confident that we make an impact by the way we love. The unknown becomes an adventure to dispense God's grace.

Step lightly. Walk boldly. Live with gracious uncertainty.

Hello God...it's me. Thank You for enabling me to peacefully trust You.

God's Unfathomable Love

*For as the heaven is high above the earth, so great is his mercy toward them that fear him.
As the east is from the west, so far hath he removed our transgressions from us.*
PSALM 103:11–12 KJV

The Neil Armstrong quote, "One small step for man, one giant leap for mankind," gave the world a sense of pride when man landed on the surface of the moon. Still, the moon seems puny in comparison to the vast expanse of space yet to be seen or explored. Like the Energizer Bunny, there are spacecraft traveling through deep space today that keep going and going with no known end point.

We measure distance in space by light-years. One lightyear is estimated at 6 trillion miles, and the farthest galaxy the Hubble space telescope has seen so far is 13 billion light-years away. Incredible. Unfathomable.

But not as immense as God's great mercy toward us.

His miraculous love sweeps away the weight of our sin through the redemption of Jesus Christ, removing it so far from us that no trace of it is left. There are no corners in heaven where our sins are stockpiled. God alone accomplishes this wonderful feat. Hallelujah!

Hello God...it's me. Have I thanked You lately for forgiving me?

Be Contemptible

Rejoice, inasmuch as ye are partakers of Christ's sufferings; that, when his glory shall be revealed, ye may be glad also with exceeding joy.... If any man suffer as a Christian, let him not be ashamed; but let him glorify God on this behalf.

1 PETER 4:13, 16 KJV

Jesus was hated by much of the world, and that hatred still exists today. Then, as now, He was "despised and rejected of men" (Isaiah 53:3 KJV).

In spite of rejection, He died for us.

Being like Him means being willing to be viewed with contempt in the eyes of the world. What does that look like today? Others may feel contempt for us when we refuse to bend God's rules, or stand up for what is right, or go against the norm. In spite of that rejection, we are called to rejoice always, to honor Christ in all we do, to never be ashamed of the gospel message, to lift Him up everywhere we go, and to extend grace to whomever crosses our path.

Being contemptible in the world's eyes means being like Jesus.

Hello God...it's me. Thank You for enduring so much rejection for me. Please enable me to do the same for You.

In the Waiting

So the Lord must wait for you to come to him so he can show you his love and compassion.
For the Lord is a faithful God. Blessed are those who wait for his help.
ISAIAH 30:18 NLT

Patience is a gift. Many say it's one they don't have. Regardless, we wait. Every day. In the store checkout line, as the boss makes a final decision, at the doctor's office, at the busy intersection. Sometimes we must wait in order to wait some more.

Even though it's unavoidable, waiting in the daily details is an unpleasant part of life. And when a mundane job remains mundane, or physical pain clings like a bad shirt, or an anticipated situation refuses to evolve as we dreamed it would, questions arise. What is God doing? Why doesn't He fix it? What's His purpose in allowing the unwanted circumstances to persist?

Your daily routine that seems to never change may last for just one more day. But it could be yours for another month, another year, or even more. What will you do in the waiting? Dear friend, take a new look at this season. Fight your frustrations, and trust that this place of preparation is of great importance.

Hello God...it's me. I want You to know that starting today, I am choosing to trust Your timing.

Surrounded

With your powerful arm you protect me from every side.
PSALM 139:5 CEV

When we are aware of people's presence, we are careful about what we say and how we act. When the boss is present, we're sure to be seen diligent and not wasting time. We may talk differently with our friends if we know our parents can overhear us. How would we live if we knew that every moment, Christ is beside us, in front of us, behind us, within us, above us, beneath us?

Would knowing that He is within earshot affect what we say? Would knowing that He is in front of us affect our attitude toward the future? Would knowing He is behind us make us less fearful? Would knowing He is above and below us make us stronger in our convictions? Would knowing He is within us make a difference in how we act?

The fact is, Christ is indeed in all of those places. What does that mean for you as you walk into today?

Hello God...it's me. Will You make me more aware of Your presence today?

Enduring Faith

Through him we have also obtained access by faith into this grace in which we stand, and we rejoice in hope of the glory of God. Not only that, we rejoice in our sufferings, knowing that suffering produces endurance.
ROMANS 5:2–3 ESV

Trying out for the varsity team as a tenth grader, young Michael was told that he just wasn't good enough. Hurt by being cut from the team, the teenager determined to make the team the following year. Practicing relentlessly in all his spare time, Michael developed the kind of skills that would not only allow him to make the squad the following year but eventually become the star of that team. Were it not for the disappointing rejection he suffered as a high school sophomore, Michael Jordan might never have discovered the inner determination and endurance needed to become one of the greatest professional athletes the world has ever seen.

Following God requires much endurance. But the endurance we need is supplied by God as a gift. In fact, the same grace that *places* us in Christ *keeps* us in Christ. And God, in His wisdom, knows the heartaches and trials that will produce a holy endurance in us.

God takes the ugly and turns it into the beautiful, and in the end we are blessed by it.

Hello God...it's me. Thank You that I don't have to muster up endurance on my own.

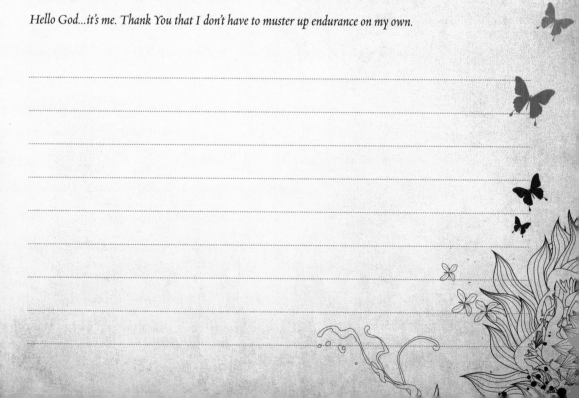

March 15

Heavenly Healer

In the same way the Spirit also helps our weakness; for we do not know how to pray as we should, but the Spirit Himself intercedes for us with groanings too deep for words; and He who searches the hearts knows what the mind of the Spirit is, because He intercedes for the saints according to the will of God.

ROMANS 8:26–27 NASB

A man with pain in his lower right jaw went to the dentist assuming further drilling on his recent root canal was necessary. Once he'd been examined, he was told that the real source of his pain was a wisdom tooth—it badly needed to be pulled. Not until the man was accurately diagnosed by a professional could the actual problem be fixed.

No doubt you recognize certain symptoms in your life. You may not know their source, but they have your attention. The One who is the expert of your heart knows what's causing those symptoms. He knew the very moment the problem started, and He holds the answers to its resolution. Whether your words and wonderings gush out in a torrent of questions, or the only prayer you can muster is a sigh of desperation, you are not without hope; God knows what you need.

Present your symptoms to Him and then wait for Him to reveal the diagnosis—and provide the remedy.

Hello God...it's me. Thank You for Your gentle love that reveals our brokenness so that we may find healing in You.

Find the Wonder

O Lord, our Lord, your majestic name fills the earth! Your glory is higher than the heavens.
PSALM 8:1 NLT

Stop for a few moments and look at creation. Gaze at the tiniest snowflake or the vastness of the sky. Does it make you pause in awe of who God is and what He has done? We should be amazed that He would care enough to create flowers that bloom in vibrant colors, animals of all kinds and shapes, planets seen and yet to be discovered. We should live in wonder that He sent His Son to die for guilty, sinful humanity.

Frequently, however, we bring God down to our level. Movies and books attempt to make Him too much like us—with characteristics sometimes bordering on the ridiculous. Yet when we lose our sense of wonder, we lose a sense of the greatness of God. Rediscover the wonder of who God is and what He has done. It should send you to your knees in gratitude.

Hello God...it's me. Will You fill me today with wonder beyond my own ability?

One in a Billion

For You formed my inward parts; You wove me in my mother's womb.
I will give thanks to You, for I am fearfully and wonderfully made.
PSALM 139:13–14 NASB

We fight against monotony. We may feel like we are just one speck on a massive planet filled with billions of other tiny dots. How can we possibly matter to God?

Our God, however, must exult in a certain amount of monotony. While we exclaim at the wide variety of flowers all over the globe, we should also stand in sheer wonder of a field decorated with millions of daisies. Just one flower, duplicated a million times, yet each daisy is created separately and put into its own special place.

Similarly, we are much like all other humans. We exhibit the same general size, shape, and functions. Yet each of us is created by God, different from the next person and lovingly put into the place that God has specially planned for us.

No one on the planet is just like you. You were uniquely designed in your mother's womb. God knows you intimately and intricately.

Monotonous? Boring? Not on your life. You're one in a billion!

Hello God...it's me. Thank You for valuing uniqueness, for valuing me.

Our Wild Longing

He satisfies the longing soul, and fills the hungry soul with goodness.
PSALM 107:9 NKJV

What is the deepest longing of your heart? We often pursue that for which we long. C. S. Lewis, author of the children's series the Chronicles of Narnia, is well known for his use of the German word *Ysehnsucht,* which means "longing" or "intensely missing." This deep longing moves us when we see a beautiful sunset, hear a masterful symphony, or feel a baby's small hand wrap around our finger. God placed this longing within us, and this desire can be satisfied by nothing and no one besides Him. No matter how intensely we pursue other people, places, and things, we "intensely miss" the author of all: God.

The wild longing we all experience will be finally fulfilled when we reach heaven. The most beautiful sunset or symphony is only a shadow of the glory that is to come and the One with whom we will spend eternity.

Filled with longing? Turn to the One who desires to take His place on the throne of your life.

Hello God...it's me. I will not take for granted the fulfillment Your presence brings.

Declare His Glory

Declare his glory among the nations, his marvelous deeds among all peoples.
For great is the LORD and most worthy of praise; he is to be feared above all gods.
1 CHRONICLES 16:24–25 NIV

Oswald Chambers wrote, "If in preaching the gospel you substitute your knowledge of the way of salvation for confidence in the power of the gospel, you hinder people from getting to reality."

The focus of the gospel is the resplendent nature and the magnificent work of God. Methods or doctrines are no substitute for that reality. When Jesus gave His mandate to preach the gospel, it was a simple instruction: if His glory and His deeds are declared, the world will be drawn to Him.

The Hebrew meaning of the word translated "deeds" is literally "action." God takes action in His creation and in the lives of His people. The exuberant response is to talk about it—what He has done, what He is doing, and what He will do.

The salvation of God through Jesus reveals the glory and wonder of God's excellent goodness to us. It is a reality we can always celebrate and a truth that can never be exhausted. He has done wonderful things. Talk about it!

Hello God...it's me. Open my mouth to tell others of the wonderful things that You do.

Years to Come

*In the beginning was the Word, and the Word was with God, and the Word was God.
He was in the beginning with God. All things were made through him, and without him
was not any thing made that was made. In him was life, and the life was the light of men.
The light shines in the darkness, and the darkness has not overcome it.*
JOHN 1:1–5 ESV

To some folks, God is the great watch-maker in the sky who set time in motion and stepped back to watch from a cosmic distance. Others believe He is intimately involved with specific daily concerns. A person's picture of God makes all the difference in the depth of relationship he or she will have with the Creator.

Though we cannot grasp the concept of eternity, we can trust that God is eternal. Our lives on earth are governed by time and bookended by conception and death.

God, however, is outside of time. He existed before hanging the stars and will continue to exist long past our time on this planet.

When we grasp the significance—the *bigness*—of this fact, only then are we ready to trust Him in everything else. When we understand that we can never fully understand, when we trust promises that are beyond our comprehension, then we'll be ready to take God at His word as He walks with us today.

Hello God...it's me. Help me not to stumble over the unanswerable but to trust in You.

The Way Home

The Son of Man came to seek and to save the lost.
LUKE 19:10 NIV

Have you ever become separated from your group in an unfamiliar place, longing to find home? Your heart pumps faster. Your palms grow clammy. Your thoughts run wild.

Lostness is not just a physical reality; it is a spiritual fact too. When we are lost, we need someone to show us the way home. Verbal communication is not good enough; personal help is what we long for—someone to take us by the hand to guide us home.

That's the message of the gospel. God dropped everything to seek out and rescue lost humans. It boggles the mind that God would send His own Son so that a lost humanity would find its way to Him. Yet that's exactly what God did.

Try to find a parallel story in another religion. Can't do it, can you?

The gospel is God finding us and bringing us home.

Hello God...it's me. Thank You for dropping everything to bring me home.

The Tender Shepherd

The LORD is my shepherd; I shall not want. He makes me to lie down in green pastures; He leads me beside the still waters. He restores my soul; He leads me in the paths of righteousness for His name's sake.
PSALM 23:1–3 NKJV

The job of a shepherd involves much more than sitting on a hillside keeping an eye on his flock. A good shepherd knows where to lead his sheep for nourishing food and fresh water. He moves his flock from one place to another along the safest route possible. When one of his flock is missing, he leaves the others in a safe place and doesn't rest until the lost one is found. He protects his helpless lambs from danger.

In Psalm 23 we affirm, "The Lord is my shepherd." What a wonderful image! Believers know that Jesus Christ is our Shepherd. He cares for each of us. No matter what comes our way, our Shepherd will always be present to protect our hearts and minds from danger. When we hurt, He comforts us. When we don't know which way to turn, He guides us. When we lose our way, He leads us home.

Look to your Shepherd today.

Hello God...it's me. Today, will You help me to trust You to meet my every need?

March 23

Living Sacrifice

Therefore, I urge you, brothers and sisters, in view of God's mercy, to offer your bodies as a living sacrifice, holy and pleasing to God—this is your true and proper worship.
ROMANS 12:1 NIV

Albert Einstein said, "Only a life lived for others is worth living." For the believer, the only meaningful, eternal way to serve others is to dedicate that service to God, day by day, for a lifetime.

In the ceremonies of the Jewish religion, an animal without flaw was offered as a sacrifice, and when the act was finished, the animal was dead. It couldn't be sacrificed again. How different is a living sacrifice! We offer the best we have—our gifts and talents, our dedicated minds, our resources and riches—to the Lord with each new day.

Ours is not a service of death, but a vigorous and active involvement. In fact, our lives are one long act of giving ourselves back to God, freely, voluntarily. He is holy and deserves our everlasting praise, our worshipful service.

Hello God...it's me. Show me places I am holding back from You. I want You to have all of me.

A Heart for God

My little children, I am writing these things to you so that you may not sin. And if anyone sins, we have an Advocate with the Father, Jesus Christ the righteous; and He Himself is the propitiation for our sins; and not for ours only, but also for those of the whole world.

1 JOHN 2:1–2 NASB

Failure can be very painful. Even the most highly trained professionals, skilled in competitions of winning and losing, cannot hide the agony of failure on their faces. The higher the hopes—Super Bowl, World Series, or Stanley Cup—the greater is the portrait of loss. When the camera pans the losing team with their blank stares, we see their hearts: "We've lost. It's over. We've failed." Then we observe the winning team with bright smiles on their faces, and we grasp their hearts: "We've won. It's ours. We've succeeded!"

As much as in winning, in losing we can see the true heart of a champion. This is especially true when it comes to our moral failure—when we stumble and sin, we discover our true character. Instead of wallowing in the pain of self-condemnation, the next step for a believer is to turn back to God in repentance. The heart of a moral champion is a heart that longs for God's.

Hello God...it's me. Win or lose, You are looking at my heart. Give me the heart of a champion.

March 25
Duty Calls

Shout joyfully to the LORD, all the earth. Serve the LORD with gladness; come before Him with joyful singing....
Enter His gates with thanksgiving and His courts with praise. Give thanks to Him, bless His name.
PSALM 100:1–2, 4 NASB

What do you think of when you think of your "duty" to God? Some equate *duty* with a long, religious to-do list that gives them little joy. This to-do list mentality hinders their relationship with Christ and wearies them with marching orders that contain words like *should* and *ought*. *I should love others. I ought to praise God.*

Yet a fuller realization of God's goodness and mercy will automatically bring praise and thanks to your lips. It takes the burden out of ministry and sees every act of service as a love offering to our gracious God. In the way that a sparkle in the eyes and a smile on the lips are signs of being in love, our joyful praise of our Savior demonstrates our love for Him.

Have you fully accepted the fact that you are beloved of God? Drink deeply at the well of His presence and you will hear the words of praise and thanks fill up your heart and overflow into your life of service to God.

Hello God...it's me. Will You show me how to instill more praise and honor in my day?

Knowing You

As the deer pants for the water brooks, so pants my soul for You, O God.
My soul thirsts for God, for the living God. When shall I come and appear before God?
PSALM 42:1–2 NKJV

It can be intimidating to realize that someone knows a lot about us, at least until we understand the person's motives and how much he or she cares for us. But when it comes to God the Father, we can take comfort in the fact that He knows all about us. We can rest comfortably in His sovereign knowledge because He knit us together in the womb according to His own unique design. We need not fear God's intimate knowledge of us, for we know His motives and His love for us.

Nevertheless, God doesn't want this to be a one-way relationship. He offers us the chance to get to know Him too. We can never know Him as well as He knows us, but He longs to enter into a deep and intimate relationship with each of us. He wants us to know Him so well that we easily recognize His heart and His will.

Knowing God, understanding His love for others, and contemplating His desire for justice are things we can experience by deepening our relationship with the Father.

Hello God...it's me. I want You to know that I desire a more intimate relationship with You.

Be Who You Is

For we are God's masterpiece. He has created us anew in Christ Jesus,
so we can do the good things he planned for us long ago.
EPHESIANS 2:10 NLT

Mother Teresa loved to say, "The only success is faithfulness." Brennan Manning used to quote an old-time preacher who told him, "Brennan, be who you is, 'cause if you ain't who you is, then you is who you ain't."

God has made each of us what and who we are. And wrapped in the redemptive love of His Son, Jesus, each of us has been created for a life of service and ministry, and for a particular service and ministry that God has specifically intended for us to do.

Every time you use the specific gifts and abilities He has given you, you reveal His imprint. His fingerprints are everywhere in your life, to His glory. So don't try to be anyone besides who you are because the Great I AM loves for you to be you.

His genius is evident in every person ever born, and one beautiful way to pay homage to that unprecedented creativity is to walk the path and do the work He has prepared just for you.

Hello God...it's me. Someone You know so well. Will You show me where I am not being the person You made me to be?

Who Am I Now?

May God himself, the God of peace, sanctify you through and through. May your whole spirit, soul and body be kept blameless at the coming of our Lord Jesus Christ. The one who calls you is faithful, and he will do it.
1 THESSALONIANS 5:23–24 NIV

It's interesting to look back on our lives and review certain decisions and behaviors from the viewpoint of being a more mature adult. As we grow older, we gain insights and experiences that help us make better decisions.

The same applies to the life of the believer—only more so. We all remember the person we were when we were new in Christ: the struggles we had, the sins we wrestled with, the truths we tried to apply to our lives. Yet as we grow in our faith, we notice that we are less like the person we used to be and more like the person we want to become. We're not quite there yet, but we can thank God for bringing us this far.

God didn't give up on us when we were lost in our sin, He didn't become frustrated with us when as new believers our growth was slow, and He still doesn't walk away from us when as more mature believers we still struggle. We can thank God for His presence through it all.

Hello God...it's me. The one You love. Thank You for Your unshakeable, transforming abidance with me.

A Leap of Faith

When Elizabeth heard Mary's greeting, the baby leaped inside her,
and Elizabeth was filled with the Holy Spirit.
LUKE 1:41 HCSB

Watch children on a playground. One will climb up high on the monkey bars. His daddy will stand beneath him and say, "Jump into my arms." Without hesitation the miniature Tarzan will leap into the air and fly into the secure grasp of his father. Five minutes later the little boy will again be at the top of the monkey bars. A stranger passing by might say, "Jump; I'll catch you." But the little lad will not jump. His father he trusts, for he knows that Daddy will never fail him, but everyone else is under suspicion.

As believers, we can take a leap that requires faith—risking all yet risking nothing—for we know our heavenly "Daddy" is there to catch us. Deuteronomy 33:27 says, "The eternal God is your refuge, and underneath are the everlasting arms." Are you ready to leap at the chance to serve Him?

Hello God...it's me. Your daughter. Help me to see You as my Father who will always catch me.

Head and Heart

*Knowledge puffs up, but love edifies. And if anyone thinks that he knows anything,
he knows nothing yet as he ought to know. But if anyone loves God, this one is known by Him.*

1 CORINTHIANS 8:1–3 NKJV

Few people like a know-it-all, but we are happy to have an expert in the IT department fix our computer, an expert plumber fix the leaky pipe, an expert surgeon perform an appendectomy, or an expert accountant handle the books for our business. Their knowledge is invaluable to us.

Yet knowledge can be a stumbling block if it is without virtue. You want experts to fix what you can't, but you also want them to be honest. That experienced but dishonest accountant could siphon funds from your account without you even noticing. Knowledge loses its dignity and becomes an obstacle if it is used for evil rather than for God. Paul wrote that "knowledge inflates with pride, but love builds up" (1 Corinthians 8:1 HCSB).

Pursue knowledge, but let your knowledge be used for God's glory. Let holiness be your guide.

Hello God...it's me. Please help me to use my knowledge for Your glory.

The Cleansing Pain

[Jesus] said to him the third time, "Simon, son of John, do you love Me?" Peter was grieved because He said to him the third time, "Do you love Me?" And he said to Him, "Lord, You know all things; You know that I love You." Jesus said to him, "Tend My sheep."

JOHN 21:17 NASB

The very day after a person has surgery, nurses get the patient on his or her feet for a walk. It's agonizingly painful, but it keeps the blood circulating, lessening the chance of clots and hastening the healing process. Similarly, if someone comes to the emergency room because of an accident, that person's wound is first cleansed of all dirt then doused in antiseptic. This cleansing process is frightfully painful, but it assists the body in warding off infection.

Often in our spiritual lives, we must endure some pain in order to be healed. Saul (soon to be the apostle Paul) was made blind for three days before God restored his sight, thus giving him a lesson in spiritual blindness. Jesus made Peter tell Him *three times* that he loved Him after Peter had denied Jesus three times, thus helping Peter see that Jesus was fully forgiving him.

The pain is part of the plan. God is there, holding you up. Lean on Him.

Hello God...it's me. Show me how to respond when pain is part of the plan.

April 1
Draw Near to God

Come close to God, and God will come close to you.
JAMES 4:8 NLT

We need God; He does not need us. Often we are like a hapless sailor in a boat who throws a rope at a rock, hoping it will provide security and stability. When the rock is lassoed, it's not the sailor pulling the rock to the boat (though it may appear that way); it is the pulling of the boat to the rock.

The closer we get to God, the more real He becomes. He's the rock. If you are physically distraught, He is the lifeline that saves your drowning soul. If you are spiritually famished, He is the umbilical cord that provides nourishment to your starving spirit. If you are emotionally depleted, He is the second wind that enables you to go the distance.

Think of yourself in that boat being pulled to safety by a loving Father.

Hello God...it's me. Thank You for pulling me to safety.

April 2

The Flag of Joy

"I am coming to you now, but I say these things while I am still in the world,
so that they may have the full measure of my joy within them."
JOHN 17:13 NIV

Don't confuse happiness with joy. Happiness is buoyant emotion that results from the momentary plateaus of well-being. Joy is bedrock stuff—the confidence that emerges irrespective of our moods or circumstances; the certainty that all is well, regardless of feelings; the hallmark of God's kingdom dwellers.

An old British educator wrote: "Joy is the flag which is flown from the castle of the heart when the King is in residence." Joy supersedes our circumstances, thanks to our relationship with the King of kings. If Jesus is King—sovereign and in control—then what do we have to worry about? If we live in His presence, we have no reason to fret.

Jesus is joy. He brings joy wherever He goes. Get close to Him. Live in the glow of His life. Be conscious of His presence. Rest in His strong arms.

Hello God...it's me. Let Your joy be the flag flowing high in the castle of my heart.

As Good As Your Word

If a man vow a vow unto the LORD, or swear an oath to bind his soul with a bond;
he shall not break his word, he shall do according to all that proceedeth out of his mouth.
NUMBERS 30:2 KJV

We have numerous catchphrases that express the idea of a person's word being trustworthy. We'll say, "His word is his bond," or "Her word is as good as gold," or "If he says it, then he'll do it." Interestingly, as followers of Christ, our *word* is the Word of God, which of course is always true, always honest, and always just. Understanding this, our own promises, vows, and agreements should be honorable and dependable— part of our Christian ethic.

Numbers 30:2 teaches us, "When a man makes a vow to the LORD or takes an oath to obligate himself by a pledge, he must not break his word" (NIV). This goes beyond saying our wedding vows or swearing in as a court witness. It applies to our every transaction in life. We are to speak truth and live truth because our Savior identified Himself as "the way, the *truth*, the life."

Hello God...it's me. Will You help me to be known as a person of my word?

April 4

Everything or Nothing

I am the vine; you are the branches. If you remain in me and I in you,
you will bear much fruit; apart from me you can do nothing.
JOHN 15:5 NIV

Who are we apart from God? We are everything, or we are nothing. Everything (or so we think)—if we tell ourselves we don't need His help and can rely on our own strength and power. Nothing—if we realize our utter dependence on Him and our place in the created order. Are you willing to admit that you are nothing so that Jesus can be everything to you? Or are you holding on to areas of your life you think you can handle without Him?

Believing in God doesn't always mean we trust Him fully. But He is there for us, if we will accept His grace and appreciate how lost we are without Him. Don't hold on to your life. Let it go, into the loving arms of the Savior.

Hello God...it's me. Today, will You show me what I am trying to handle without You?

A Blind Leap?

Having been justified by faith, we have peace with God through our Lord Jesus Christ,
through whom also we have obtained our introduction by faith into this grace in which we stand;
and we exult in hope of the glory of God.
ROMANS 5:1–2 NASB

Certainly faith involves making an intellectual assent to the truth of God revealed in creation and history. And yet, we can have an intellectual belief in the historical life and death of Jesus but not have *saving* faith—a faith that promises eternal rescue from sin.

Saving faith comes down to Jesus. What do we believe about Jesus's death on the cross and resurrection from the dead? Do we say with our minds and our hearts, "Yes, I believe in Christ and receive what He has done for me"?

At some point, we all have to answer that question. For some, saying yes may feel like taking a leap, a wild jump, in the dark. But it isn't.

We can trust our souls to God because of what Jesus has done for us.

We can say, "Yes! I believe" without fear.

Hello God...it's me. Another day together. More opportunities to trust You.

Seeing God in the Darkness

For his anger endureth but a moment; in his favour is life:
weeping may endure for a night, but joy cometh in the morning.
PSALM 30:5 KJV

The dark night of the soul is a time when God seems distant, when our soul seems lost. But purpose exists in the darkness. In any worthwhile venture, pain precedes gain, hurt comes before health, cleansing precedes completeness. During these dark seasons, God works in our inner being so we will turn from habits that bring destruction to develop a Christ-like character. Like polluted water that flows through a filter, our souls will be purified.

Often when the night is blackest, we feel God has abandoned us. Yet God is working even then. Like the moon hidden by an eclipse, God is present but not visible.

During the dark times, allow God to work. You will see Him again. And, better, you will be cleansed, made right, brought whole.

Hang on. Endure the night. Joy comes in the morning.

Hello God...it's me. Thank You for using the darkness for cleansing me and making me whole.

The Face of Jesus Christ

God, who said, "Light shall shine out of darkness," is the One who has shone in our hearts to give the Light of the knowledge of the glory of God in the face of Christ.
2 CORINTHIANS 4:6 NASB

How amazing it is that God wants you to know His heart. He wants you to know how much He loves you. The Creator of the world, the Holy One who is above and beyond anything you can imagine, wants to know *you*. How do you know the love of God? How do you know the Father's heart? The answer is found in the face of Jesus Christ.

In 2 Corinthians 4, Paul gives a clue to that truth. God has given light in the darkness, and that light shines in our hearts so we can know the glory of God through the face of Jesus. It is Jesus who gives the perfect picture of God. When you know Jesus, you know God.

He wants you to know His heart. He wants you to know how much He loves you. And when you know Him, you can't help but return that love to Him.

Hello God...it's me. Thank You that You have provided a way in Jesus for us to know Your glory.

Humble Leadership

If I then, the Lord and the Teacher, washed your feet, you also ought to wash one another's feet. For I gave you an example that you also should do as I did to you.

JOHN 13:14–15 NASB

It is humbling to think God may call upon us to accomplish major achievements for His glory. Joshua wondered how he *ever* could fill Moses's shoes. Gideon was baffled that he, a low-class laborer, could be summoned to serve as a general in God's army. Paul, who identified himself as "the chief of sinners," was forever astonished to think that God would use him to bring the gospel to the Gentiles. But God was able to use something in them that they didn't see; He brought them to a place of humility and willingness to serve.

God does not seek the services of the pompous. He doesn't need leaders who want fame or power—those are a dime a dozen, and they do nothing for His kingdom. God is constantly seeking those who are willing to serve. Such leaders can, through His Son, change the world.

Hello God...it's me. Will You give me equal measures of humility and God-confidence to boldly pursue Your plan for me?

Prayer Living

Be cheerful no matter what; pray all the time; thank God no matter what happens.
This is the way God wants you who belong to Christ Jesus to live.
1 Thessalonians 5:16–18 MSG

"I'll pray for you." Have you ever said that to someone, and then forgotten to pray? Or have you closed your eyes at Sunday morning worship only to realize it was the first time you prayed all week?

Chances are, we notice if we haven't eaten in a few hours. It would only take a few seconds to discover we were in trouble if we couldn't breathe. Prayer should be the same—we should be unable to get through a day without prayer. We should notice if a few hours have gone by and we haven't been in touch with our Lord.

Prayer is as important as eating and breathing, for it is our lifeline to the One who guides us and walks with us through each day.

Today, practice the presence of prayer. See what happens!

Hello God...it's me. Today, will You help me practice the presence of prayer?

_____

_____

_____

_____

_____

_____

_____

First Things First

Seek first his kingdom and his righteousness, and all these things will be given to you as well.
MATTHEW 6:33 NIV

Those fictional heroes of pop culture—Indiana Jones, Luke Skywalker, and Superman—all had one thing in common: focus. Whenever they were on a mission, they identified their goal, and nothing could distract them from that single target.

They always put first things first. As followers of Jesus Christ, we are on a mission, seeking His will for our lives. When we seek the kingdom of God with a "first things first" mind-set, everything else we need is given to us as well. The beautiful mystery is that the God we seek has the same desire for relationship with us. And Jesus's words in Matthew 6 reveal that very arrangement—that promise of communion.

God asks us to seek Him first so He can supply all of our needs. The sooner we come to Him, the sooner He begins to work everything according to His will and His glory. Our God is a God of love, of mercy and grace. When we put Him first in our lives, all of who He is becomes available in every aspect of our existence. Only He is big enough to give us everything we need.

Why would we ever look anywhere else?

Hello God...it's me. Thank You for giving me the ability to focus.

From "What if?" to "Why not?"

Rejoice in the Lord always. Again I will say, rejoice! Let your gentleness be known to all men. The Lord is at hand. Be anxious for nothing, but in everything by prayer and supplication, with thanksgiving, let your requests be made known to God; and the peace of God, which surpasses all understanding, will guard your hearts and minds through Christ Jesus.

PHILIPPIANS 4:4–7 NKJV

So many of us fret about the *what-ifs*. What if this happens, or that? What if it doesn't happen?

God tells us not to worry about the *what-ifs* but rather to pray about everything. So why don't we do it? *We can't possibly bother God with a problem like ours,* we think. Or we believe we can handle it; we can figure out how to solve it if we only worry about it long enough. Yet the more we worry, the more anxious we become.

Instead, we should trust Christ for today's troubles and those coming up. Otherwise, it's hard to be productive or to stay focused on Christ. Philippians 4:6 implores us to tell God what we need, and to thank Him for what He will do.

Why not give that a try and experience peace, God's way?

Hello God…it's me. Today, I will not be anxious but will tell You immediately of my needs.

April 12

Meaningful Promises

Let us hold unswervingly to the hope we profess, for he who promised is faithful.
HEBREWS 10:23 NIV

The Bible is filled with thousands of promises from God. The most important promise He makes to us is this: He will save anyone who calls upon the name of Jesus Christ. First John 1:9 tells us that if we confess our sins, He is faithful to cleanse us from all unrighteousness. And He promises us that nothing in this world—not even death—will be able to separate us from His love (Romans 8:35–39).

We know God will keep His promises because the Bible also tells us that God cannot lie (Hebrews 6:18). What a blessing! We have assurance that when God says something, He means it.

God will never make a promise that He cannot keep. His promises are astounding, and they are trustworthy. We can stand firm in our faith knowing it is built upon a solid and unchanging foundation.

Hello God...it's me. Thank You for Your rock-solid promises.

Serious about Heavenly Joy

Shout joyfully to God, all the earth; sing the glory of His name; make His praise glorious. Say to God, "How awesome are Your works! Because of the greatness of Your power Your enemies will give feigned obedience to You. All the earth will worship You, and will sing praises to You; they will sing praises to Your name."

PSALM 66:1–4 NASB

What motivated Jesus to die for us? Was it love? The Bible says, "Greater love has no one than this, than to lay down one's life for his friends" (John 15:13 NKJV). Was it obedience to God? Scripture tells us, "[Jesus] humbled himself by becoming obedient to death—even death on a cross" (Philippians 2:8 NIV). Was it to satisfy God's wrath against sin and evil? "God set [Christ] forth as a propitiation by His blood" (Romans 3:25 NKJV).

These verses all help answer the question: why was Jesus crucified on our behalf? Yet the Bible also tells us another reason that Jesus stayed on the cross, though He could have called many angels to His aid—*joy.* "Jesus...for the joy that was set before Him endured the cross, despising the shame" (Hebrews 12:2 NKJV).

If joy is the business of heaven, should it not also be the serious business of earth?

Hello God...it's me. Will You show me how to pursue joy throughout my day?

Amazed by Faith

The officer said, "Lord, I'm not good enough for you to come into my house. Just give the order, and my servant will get well.... "When Jesus heard this, he was so surprised that he turned and said..., "I tell you that in all of Israel I've never found anyone with this much faith!"
MATTHEW 8:8–10 CEV

What could possibly cause Jesus to be amazed? Present at the creation of the world, Jesus experienced breathtaking splendor. When He left the majesty of heaven to enter our world, Jesus was familiar with the miraculous: bringing sight to the blind, feeding the multitudes with a young boy's lunch, and even raising the dead. During His ministry on earth, Jesus encountered the rich and the righteous, the proud and the poor, the official and the outcast. Yet He stood amazed only in the face of one thing—unwavering faith.

The Roman centurion knew the protocol of authority. He knew the hierarchy of power. He obeyed his superiors and demanded complete submission from those under his leadership. He also believed in the authority of Jesus. The man knew Jesus commanded everything seen and unseen with just a word, so he told Jesus that he believed his servant would be healed if Jesus would simply give the command.

And Jesus stood *amazed* at this type of faith.

Hello God...it's me. I want You to know how much I want my faith to amaze You.

Our Offering of Suffering

These things I have spoken unto you, that in me ye might have peace.
In the world ye shall have tribulation: but be of good cheer; I have overcome the world.
JOHN 16:33 KJV

Most of the time, it feels like we're at the mercy of an unmerciful world. How else can we begin to understand the pain and suffering we see all around us?

We may live in an unmerciful world, but we do not have an unmerciful God. He promises to love us and to be with us every moment of our life's journey. Trusting in God doesn't necessarily keep bad things from happening, however. God's Son experienced suffering, so how can we expect any less? When we experience suffering, we are in His company.

He truly understands how we feel.

When we face great suffering, God gives us the precious gift of His Son to walk with us through it. Instead of blinding ourselves with questions about why this had to happen, we can take our sufferings and offer them to Christ as our little share in His sufferings. It's not easy, but it's vital. For when we give our heavy burdens to Christ, He takes them, wraps His arms around us, and guides us through the darkness into the light of His presence.

Hello God...it's me. Thank You for the answer of Your arms around me.

April 16

The Stoop of Grace

God's readiness to give and forgive is now public. Salvation's available for everyone! We're being shown how to turn our backs on a godless, indulgent life, and how to take on a God-filled, God-honoring life. This new life is starting right now, and is whetting our appetites for the glorious day when our great God and Savior, Jesus Christ, appears. He offered himself as a sacrifice to free us from a dark, rebellious life into this good, pure life, making us a people he can be proud of, energetic in goodness.

TITUS 2:11–14 MSG

In the birth of Jesus, God burst upon our sin-darkened world and the whole drama of God's redemptive plan for the human race was personified. The One who created the world came into the world as a humble baby. The incomprehensible became comprehensible. God stooped. Divinity became humanity.

That moment rocked the planet—and the world has never gotten over it. It separated the human calendar, distinguishing B.C. from A.D.

Our nature does not deserve our King's blessing; our actions do not earn His approval. But lovingly God came to us, touched us, blessed us, redeemed us. God stooped.

That action should humbly compel us to respond to Him with worship, affection, and love.

Hello God...it's me. I can hardly believe how good You were in leaving heaven, and what You accomplished for me.

Mosaic

"For I know the plans I have for you," declares the Lord, *"plans to prosper you and not to harm you, plans to give you hope and a future. Then you will call on me and come and pray to me, and I will listen to you. You will seek me and find me when you seek me with all your heart. I will be found by you," declares the* Lord, *"and will bring you back from captivity. I will gather you from all the nations and places where I have banished you," declares the* Lord, *"and will bring you back to the place from which I carried you into exile."*

JEREMIAH 29:11–14 NIV

The history of mankind is full of hatred, bigotry, wars, and bloodshed. Collectively, our conscience is stained.

Knowing how dark and shameful our history is, it's difficult to think that *anyone* is in control of it—much less a benevolent, all-powerful God. Yet Scripture tells us that the book of history is in the hand of God. He has a plan greater than what we can see from our limited perspective. We are like ants crawling around on an enormous mosaic, scoffing, "How on earth could a picture be made of this?" Yet God, who stands outside history, has an intended purpose.

Despite all our flaws, we can take comfort in the fact that God has a great plan for us, one more intricate and beautiful than we can imagine.

We are—we have always been—His passion.

Hello God...it's me. Thank You that Your plan for my life is intricate and beautiful. You are my passion, too.

Knowing Makes the Difference

For the grace of God that bringeth salvation hath appeared to all men.
TITUS 2:11 KJV

Opinions are a dime a dozen. The person with experience always trumps the person with an unsupported opinion. The experienced person knows; the opinionated person guesses. There's a big difference.

Those who have truly experienced God know the loveliness and beauty of a grace-touched and holy life. Deserving judgment, they are the recipients of a second chance (grace) and a special endowment (holiness).

God's holiness sets apart God's grace. God, who is different from us, stooped to be among us. God, who is awesome in power, came in weakness. God, who sits on the throne of heaven, walked on earth as a servant. He is the One we want to experience and emulate. Knowing Him makes all the difference.

Get close to Jesus. His loveliness and beauty will rub off on you in the form of holiness and grace.

Hello God...it's me. I want You to know that I desire Your beauty above my own.

True Belief

Do you see that faith was working together with [Abraham's] works, and by works faith was made perfect?
JAMES 2:22 NKJV

Nietzsche said God is dead. While Nietzsche, an atheist, wasn't interested in embracing the gospel, his words are a good reminder of what can happen when a society sets God aside. People execute their faith and turn their back on the Savior. They stop pursuing God with resolve and passion. Even those who go to church and claim a religion can quickly veer off course if they stop at "belief" but do not let it affect their lives.

Belief is more than just a position or a realization. We were designed for a relationship with Christ and we find our ultimate purpose and meaning in Him. True belief is about the journey through life in relationship with God. True belief is alive and active, affecting your life today and every day.

Hello God...it's me. Let my belief in You be evident in everything I do today.

The Living Word

Whatsoever ye do in word or deed, do all in the name of the Lord Jesus,
giving thanks to God and the Father by him.
COLOSSIANS 3:17 KJV

Nurses and doctors report that when aged saints are on their deathbeds and under heavy sedation, they often will revert to their childhood. They begin to recite memory verses learned during vacation Bible school, or they will sing "Jesus Loves Me" or "This Little Light of Mine." Colossians 3:16 (NKJV) says, "Let the word of Christ dwell in you richly."

Such blessings can happen when we have made the Word of God a living, active, vibrant part of our lives, judging every action, every deed, every thought by what the Lord has instilled in our hearts. David said, "Your word have I hid in my heart." The totality of Christ living in us gives believers a contentment that unbelievers cannot understand. But it is real. It is comforting. It is genuine.

Hello God...it's me. Help me to hide Your Word in my heart and retrieve it on a daily basis.

April 21
Do Not Be Afraid

"Do not be afraid," Samuel replied. "You have done all this evil; yet do not turn away
from the LORD, but serve the LORD with all your heart.... For the sake of his great name the LORD
will not reject his people, because the LORD was pleased to make you his own."

1 SAMUEL 12:20, 22 NIV

The most frequently spoken words in the Bible are "Do not be afraid." The statement appears about seventy times—used by prophets, angels, Jesus, and God, and spoken to calm the natural tendency of the human heart to be fearful. There is certainly a place for reverence and fear in the comprehensive relationship we have with God. He is our Creator after all. Yet it is God's desire to draw us into His love and keep us there.

This is not a halfhearted invitation. This is not a halfhearted commitment. God is "all in," and He asks the same of us. No matter the spiritual condition of our souls, for the sake of His great name, God's invitation is always available. This is a glimpse into the wonder of God's sovereignty.

Through the redemptive work of Jesus, we are all offered this divine option to accept the enfolding love of God's embrace.

Throughout Scripture, God was constantly making His presence known to those who had open and eager hearts. It is no different now. "Do not fear" is an invitation to accept His wonderful love. It is an offer to let go of those things that hinder us from finding refuge in God's loving arms.

Hello God...it's me. Will You help me to seek refuge in You when I am tempted to fear?

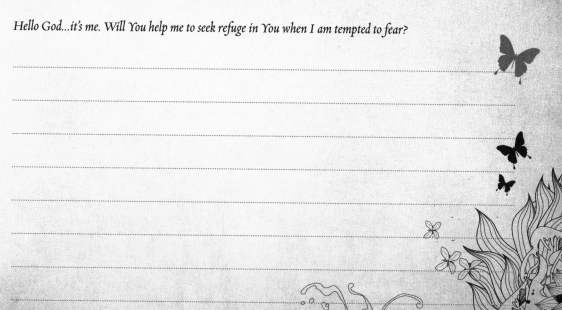

Living in the Normal

Do not get drunk on wine, which leads to debauchery. Instead, be filled with the Spirit.
EPHESIANS 5:18 NIV

The normal believer's life is life in the Spirit. When we come into relationship with Jesus, the Spirit takes up residence. He fills us. He possesses our mind. He controls our heart. We walk in step with Him. We are open to His desires. We think His thoughts.

Our spiritual lives are overcome with God's presence and might, enabling Christ-centered actions. We are under the influence of the Spirit. Instead of doing things only within our own strength and ability, the Spirit empowers us.

This power is greater than our own. It moves us, inspires us, motivates us, encourages us, and anoints all that we say and do, making Christ known.

Be filled with the Spirit.

Hello God...it's me. Please fill me with Your Spirit. Show me if I am quenching Your Spirit in any way.

In His Steps

If you suffer for doing good and you endure it, this is commendable before God. To this you were called, because Christ suffered for you, leaving you an example, that you should follow in his steps.
1 Peter 2:20–21 niv

Who doesn't long for a guide through life—maybe a crystal ball that responds to all of life's questions. Should I take this class? Marry this person? Relocate for this job? Confront this colleague? How easy it would be to wave a hand over the crystal ball and heed its replies.

As humans, we long for such answers. As believers, we need answers that take us the way God wants us to go.

Though we often act like God's will is some mystery that He is trying to keep from us, we don't need magic to figure it out. In reality, God *wants* to show us the way. He wants us to know and follow His will. To do that, we stay close to His Son—we read Scripture, we pray, we do what we already know is right.

The more we understand Jesus, the more likely we are to keep in step with Him.

Hello God...it's me. Will You help me to better hear Your voice, understand Your leading?

Walking in Peace

The peace of God, which surpasses all comprehension,
will guard your hearts and your minds in Christ Jesus.
PHILIPPIANS 4:7 NASB

What would it be like to walk in perfect peace? To do so, we must have peace *with* God before we can have the peace *of* God. In other words, we must know God before we can know peace. And when we are at peace with God, we understand that God is *for* us, not *against* us.

Before we knew God, we were at war. We were the enemy. We were fighting a losing battle. But then, when all seemed lost, Jesus— the Prince of Peace—mediated on our behalf, establishing and guaranteeing eternal peace with God. Once estranged from God, we are now His friends. Once vulnerable, now protected. Once defeated, now victorious. Once downcast, now happy. Once the opposition, now we have joined His forces. We are living on the right side. We live under His watch. We can walk in perfect peace.

Hello God...it's me. Help me to find shelter in You today instead of becoming annoyed and lashing out.

Remarkable Resemblance

Dear friends, we are already God's children, but he has not yet shown us what we will be like when Christ appears. But we do know that we will be like him, for we will see him as he really is.

1 JOHN 3:2 NLT

After the birth of a child, comments like "Oh, she has her mother's nose" or "He definitely has his father's eyes" are common. In reality, it's truly hard to tell when a child is so young. Often there is a variety of opinions. What parents do know for certain in those moments is "This baby is my child." Who that child will end up looking like remains to be seen.

Similarly, who knows how much God's children will end up looking like Jesus on this side of heaven? We are God's children if we have recognized our sin and accepted the grace and forgiveness that are available through Jesus. As our lives here on earth unfold, we will grow up to be—to one degree or another—like Jesus.

What will we ultimately look like when Christ appears? Scripture says only that "we will be like Him." We will resemble our heavenly Father; we will unmistakably be the sons and daughters of God. In the meantime, the longing of our heart should be to grow in purity and wisdom, in grace and kindness.

Hello God...it's me. Help me to be more concerned about my appearance in Your eyes than in others'.

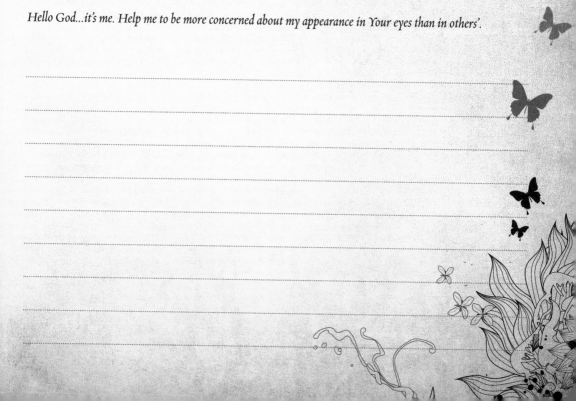

The Greatest

Surely our griefs He Himself bore, and our sorrows He carried; yet we ourselves esteemed Him stricken, smitten of God, and afflicted. But He was pierced through for our transgressions, He was crushed for our iniquities; the chastening for our well-being fell upon Him, and by His scourging we are healed.

ISAIAH 53:4–5 NASB

We think in terms of greatness. Who is the greatest at a particular sport? The greatest president? The greatest musician? The greatest writer? The nominees are nearly endless, depending on who is expressing their opinion. Ask enough people, and the list will only grow.

Two thousand years ago, however, one man singularly became the centerpiece of history. Men devoted themselves to His leadership. A woman poured out a year's wages worth of perfume on His feet. Crowds shouted His praises as He rode a donkey into Jerusalem.

Jesus Christ changed the world more than any other person in history. In His name, people have created awe-inspiring art, initiated wars, and offered up their very lives.

No one can claim to match Him in ability to influence or change a life. How about you? How has the incomparable Jesus changed your life?

Hello God...it's me. You are incomparable. Thank You for Your transforming touch that has changed me, and so many others down through history.

Never Purposeless

*The righteous shall flourish like a palm tree, he shall grow like a cedar in Lebanon.
Those who are planted in the house of the LORD shall flourish in the courts of our God.
They shall still bear fruit in old age; they shall be fresh and flourishing, to declare
that the LORD is upright; He is my rock, and there is no unrighteousness in Him.*
PSALM 92:12–15 NKJV

A man spoke at a rural nursing home. His audience was retired, many of them feeling worthless. But instead of reinforcing their feelings of inadequacy, he enlisted them for action. He needed six people to be prayer warriors for a new missions outreach; four people to read books onto CD for the blind; two women to teach a class to Girl Scouts on needlework and crocheting; and two men to judge a historical essay competition for the local high school.

In its opportunities for service, faith gives all of us—young or old, healthy or impaired— a purpose for living. We may not set any world records, star in any films, or record any hit songs, but there is reason to face each new day with optimism. Life never loses its value, because even as our bodies deteriorate, we can still accomplish great things for Christ.

Hello God...it's me. Thank You that no matter my age, You will always have a plan.

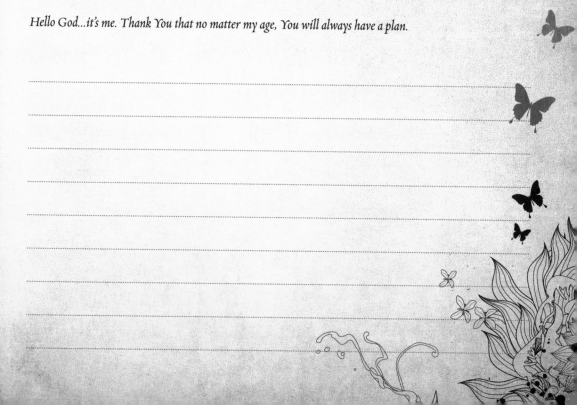

He Is Life

Before long, the world will not see me anymore, but you will see me. Because I live, you also will live.
On that day you will realize that I am in my Father, and you are in me, and I am in you.
JOHN 14:19–20 NIV

It was the great American film director Billy Wilder who said, "Hindsight is always twenty-twenty." Jesus's disciples would have benefited from that understanding. Imagine the emotions, thoughts, and memories swirling within their souls after a few years with Jesus. They had to be scratching their heads at the mysterious things He told them.

But perhaps they weren't surprised. After all, the Son of God had been making bold and puzzling statements all along. Jesus was trying to help them grasp the concept of death and resurrection—His death and resurrection. Twenty-twenty hindsight would soon prove to be their greatest wonder when they would see the risen Lord and recall all that He had said.

As it was for them, it will also be for us. We will see our glorious risen Savior. We will finally know as we are known. We will worship Him because He died to give us life, and we will live forever because our awesome, wondrous God is faithful to all His promises.

Hello God...it's me. Thank You for the day when I will know fully, as I am known by You now.

Ideally Created

*In the same way, let your light shine before others, so that they may see your
good works and give glory to your Father who is in heaven.*
MATTHEW 5:16 ESV

Have you ever felt that you could be more effective for God if only you were more of an extrovert...or you had additional financial resources...or you had the gift of evangelism?

Here's something to consider: we would do well to spend less time trying to be like other people and more time discovering God's plan for us as individuals.

Who are the people God has placed in your life to whom you can show His light? What talents has God given you, and how might He use them to draw others to Himself? What resources has God provided that you could invest in His kingdom?

God made you to fit His plan and purpose for *you.* He has given you a unique circle of influence and a unique approach to being His appointed light in this dark world. Ask Him to show you how.

Hello God...it's me. Thank You for where I am today. Will You give me an opportunity to reflect Your light?

April 30

Tangled in Grace

Each time he said, "My grace is all you need. My power works best in weakness."
2 CORINTHIANS 12:9 NLT

On a December day in 2005, a two-month-old bottlenose dolphin became tangled in the ropes of a crab trap off the coast of Florida. The dolphin was taken to a nearby sea lab for treatment, but her tail eventually flaked off due to the trauma. Amazingly, a team of experts rallied together and developed a prosthetic tail for the dolphin, named Winter. The advancements in prosthesis design that were discovered in helping Winter are now being used to provide better prosthetic limbs to American war veterans. Who would've ever thought that so much good would come from this dolphin's misfortune?

With God there are no impossibilities. What some would see as futility, God sees as an opportunity to display His strength and dispense His grace. He can redeem the most hopeless and desperate of situations to reveal His wisdom and might.

With God on your side, you are never entangled in impossibility or isolation. The Lord will meet you in places of weakness and lavish you with His grace and power.

Hello God...it's me. Thank You for the opportunities that are now disguised as so much less.

May 1

Delighting in God

Delight yourself in the Lord, and he will give you the desires of your heart.
PSALM 37:4 ESV

Christ-followers who serve God out of obligation use words like *ought*, *duty*, *expected*, and *necessary*. These words aren't necessarily wrong or bad when pertaining to the faith, but those who cite these as primary reasons for following Christ have lost a sense of a loving, personal relationship with their Savior. It is like the lover who knocks on the front door of his love's house on Valentine's Day, and when she answers he holds out a dozen long-stemmed red roses and says in a flat tone, "Here. These are for you. It's my duty." How appealing would those roses be?

When we express our love for Christ out of duty alone, we sound similar: "There. I've read my Bible. It's my spiritual duty." Practicing such an obligatory religion when absent a delight in Christ can be loveless and stale. But when we truly delight in Him, when we are drawn to Him in joy, imagine the pleasure that brings to God's heart

Hello God...it's me. I want You to know that I desire to delight in You more. Will You show me how to do that?

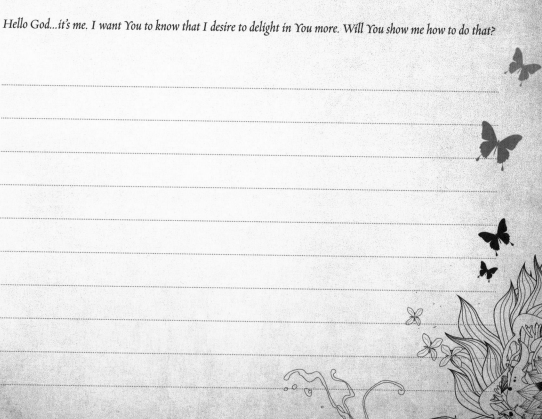

Just Trust

I tell you the truth, if you had faith even as small as a mustard seed, you could say to this mountain, "Move from here to there," and it would move. Nothing would be impossible.
MATTHEW 17:20 NLT

Our universe contains more than 10 billion trillion stars. That's the number 1 followed by 22 zeros. It seems unfathomable. But it's nothing compared to explaining the Trinity—three entities in one, yet one all-powerful being. It doesn't make sense to the human mind, to those of us who are used to finding answers and solving mysteries. We don't like to leave matters unsettled. But some things can't be known this side of eternity. They require unwavering trust in Jesus, without any further explanation. Can we accept that? Do we have a choice?

The Lord knows our desire to seek solutions to life's puzzles. But He is more concerned that we live by faith. If we have the faith of a mustard seed, He said, we can move mountains. He also exhorts us to be still, and know that He is the Almighty.

Hello God...it's me. Give me a desire for You more than the solution.

May **3**

Grappled to God

Having predestinated us unto the adoption of children by Jesus Christ to himself, according to the good pleasure of his will, to the praise of the glory of his grace, wherein he hath made us accepted in the beloved.
EPHESIANS 1:5–6 KJV

"The friends thou hast, and their adoption tried, grapple them to thy soul with hoops of steel," says Polonius in William Shakespeare's *Hamlet*. "Hoops of steel" is powerful imagery. Not only is steel an almost indestructible metal, but Shakespeare uses the plural "hoops" to show the level of commitment to those we "adopt" as friends.

In the wonder of God's redemptive work in Jesus Christ, adoption is available to all who accept it by faith. There is no condition of acceptance. By God's immeasurable grace, we are all free to come to Him as His beloved children. Each of us is invited to call Him Father and to find in Him the love and identity we have sought all our lives.

By His pleasure and the act of His will, God has freely adopted all who believe through Jesus Christ. Praise Him and thank Him for welcoming us into His beloved family.

Hello God...it's me. Thank You for welcoming me into Your family.

May 4

Do You See What God Sees?

I will rejoice greatly in the LORD, my soul will exult in my God; for He has clothed me with garments of salvation, He has wrapped me with a robe of righteousness, as a bridegroom decks himself with a garland, and as a bride adorns herself with her jewels.

ISAIAH 61:10 NASB

Look in the mirror. What do you see? Are your sins written all over your face? Pride? Envy? Lack of forgiveness? Prejudice? Judging? Anger? Bitterness?

Look again and see what God sees. Beauty. Loveliness. Perfection. How can this be? Because when God looks at you, He sees His Son. He sees the shed blood of His beloved One given for you. He sees you clothed in righteousness.

A sixteenth-century hymn says it well: "Jesus, Thy blood and righteousness, Thy beauty are, my glorious dress." What God sees is beauty that is not our own. It was bought with a price. The precious blood of Jesus was shed for believers to be right with God...to be clothed with Christ.

Be beautiful. Wear Christ.

Hello God...it's me. Will You show me how to be clothed in You?

Grace in Humility

Blessed are the poor in spirit, for theirs is the kingdom of heaven.
MATTHEW 5:3 NKJV

Living the way Jesus taught is often in direct contrast to the way the world lives. To be poor in spirit means you understand your own helplessness to stand before a holy God. We recognize that we are nothing apart from the grace of Jesus. What a humbling thought!

If we want to experience the joy of living the way God wants us to live, humbling ourselves is a great place to start. This means giving when it's easier to take, assisting when it's easier to be indifferent, loving others when it's easier to ignore. By being poor in spirit you will be blessed beyond measure and experience God's abiding peace. The rewards might come in this life, and then again, they might not. But God promises that the kingdom of heaven will belong to you.

For the deepest peace, humble yourself and follow Jesus.

Hello God...it's me. Where I am ignoring a need or being indifferent today, will You bring that immediately to my attention?

May 6

The Real Light

The LORD is my light and my salvation; whom shall I fear?
The LORD is the stronghold of my life; of whom shall I be afraid?
PSALM 27:1 ESV

The sun sank below the horizon. The clouds blotted out the stars and moon. Darkness swept over like a canopy. The darkness made the hiker wary—of animals, of losing the trail, of stepping in holes—but he'd come prepared. In his backpack he'd placed a flashlight. During the day, as the sun lit up the man's surroundings, the flashlight was unnecessary. More a burden than a help. A useless accessory. It wasn't until the darkness descended that he turned to it for light.

Like the hiker, we often cannot appreciate the Light of the world until we are faced with dark circumstances. In the blackness, however, we need the light more than anything else. We need the light of hope. We need the light that only God can give.

Are you facing darkness in your life today? Turn on the flashlight of God's Word. Seek His face and let the precious light of His presence fill your life and cast out any darkness. Allow the Light of the world to so illuminate your circumstances that hope replaces doubt and the shadows of uncertainty, darkness, and fear vanish like the night before the approaching dawn.

Hello God...it's me. Thank You for Your Word that is a light to my path.

Be with God

Obeying your instructions brings as much happiness as being rich. I will study your teachings and follow your footsteps. I will take pleasure in your laws and remember your words.
PSALM 119:14–16 CEV

Do you read your Bible? Excellent. Knowing God's Word is essential to our growth; it is true knowledge. As we study and learn the truth of Scripture, our passion for Him will be strong.

Do you attend a good church? Wonderful. Sermons that point us closer to God help deepen our relationship with Him, and spending time with other believers strengthens ourfaith.

There is more to the life of the believer, though. Being alone with Jesus, whether in direct prayer or quietly listening—privately, away from the noise and clatter of this world—is essential to the Christian life. In these solitary moments, we praise Him, thank Him, confess to Him, and tell Him we love Him...when no one else is watching.

Close the door, turn off your cell phone, and be alone with our Lord. Hide His Word in your heart, then return it to Him with joy.

Hello God...it's me. Help me to be more disciplined in spending time alone with You.

Streams of Thought

*The weapons we fight with are not the weapons of the world. On the contrary, they have divine power
to demolish strongholds. We demolish arguments and every pretension that sets itself up
against the knowledge of God, and we take captive every thought to make it obedient to Christ.
And we will be ready to punish every act of disobedience, once your obedience is complete.*

2 CORINTHIANS 10:4–6 NIV

As soon as the words were out of your mouth, you wished you could take them back. You hadn't meant to *think* those things, let alone *say* those things. But now you've done both!

On some days our thoughts are beautiful and clear, like a mountain stream flowing gently between green valleys. All is well with our world and everyone in it. On other days, though, our thoughts are like raging rapids— full of churning turmoil and unexpected dangers. Interactions with people leave us angry, tense. Circumstances force us to navigate the waters of loneliness or sorrow. Situations tempt us to be reckless and reflect on things that are impure or unlovely.

Amid those rough-water days, how essential it is to take all our thoughts captive. Peace is ours when we submit our thoughts to Christ and resist the enemy. Today, let God calm your thoughts with His truth, His light, His love. He's ready to quiet your mind and your heart.

Hello God...it's me. Thank You for how You transform my thoughts and emotions when I surrender them to You.

Let Go

Now to him who is able to do immeasurably more than all we ask or imagine, according to his power that is at work within us, to him be glory in the church and in Christ Jesus throughout all generations, for ever and ever! Amen.

EPHESIANS 3:20–21 NIV

Bringing those we love to God in prayer isn't always an easy task. We see a spouse struggling, a child wandering, a friend hurting—and we want to help. It's our first instinct! Yet sometimes their struggle runs so deep that we can only pray, keenly aware that there is nothing more we can do. The person we are praying for may be blind to God's work. Or uninterested in His answers. Or in too much pain to listen.

It is in those times that we must remind ourselves—minute by minute, if necessary—that God can do far more in a loved one's life through our prayers than we could ever imagine. Just as we trust God to be at work in our own lives, so must we trust Him to be at work in the lives of those we love.

Make it a daily habit to hand over your loved ones to the Lord in prayer. He will never let go of them. He promised. See for yourself in His Word.

Hello God...it's me. Thank You that You never get tired of my often anxious, minute-by-minute requests for the ones I love.

Worth the Wait

"Do not let your heart be troubled; believe in God, believe also in Me. In My Father's house are many dwelling places; if it were not so, I would have told you; for I go to prepare a place for you. If I go and prepare a place for you, I will come again and receive you to Myself, that where I am, there you may be also."

JOHN 14:1–3 NASB

Perfect. Now there's an adjective that rarely describes us. And rightly so. This side of the Fall, we are weak, limited, and sinful. But all is not lost. There is still hope for perfection: heaven. A lot of adjectives could be used to describe it: *beautiful, resplendent, glorious, holy.*

But *perfect* describes it best. Life, eternal life, can't get any better than that.

Here on earth, we're known for our flawed bodies, faulty reasoning, and clumsy reactions, but in heaven we will be perfected. It's worth the wait.

Hello God...it's me. Thank You for Your perfect love that planned heaven for me.

Heart Surgery

"I will give you a new heart and put a new spirit within you; I will take the heart of stone out of your flesh and give you a heart of flesh. I will put My Spirit within you and cause you to walk in My statutes, and you will keep My judgments and do them."

EZEKIEL 36:26–27 NKJV

When the human heart is full of self and sin, it has no room for God. Only the humble heart has ample space for Him.

Do you desire a new heart? How open are you to the Great Physician's recommendations?

To let God perform His work, we must give up our proud self-sufficiency. We never know how He might soften us and change us. Sometimes He uses blessings and answered prayers, overwhelming us with His love. Or He may choose trials, difficulties, and sorrow to polish our faith.

As challenging as this process may be, we can rejoice that God cares enough to heal our hearts—to take them in His hands and restore them to health so that they beat in sync with His heart.

Are you willing to expose your heart to God and let Him remake it? Are you willing to let Him, piece by piece, day by day, create in you a new heart?

Hello God...it's me. Will You heal my heart, piece by piece?

Taking a Backseat Willingly

"Whoever desires to become great among you, let him be your servant. And whoever desires to be first among you, let him be your slave—just as the Son of Man did not come to be served, but to serve, and to give His life a ransom for many."
MATTHEW 20:26–28 NKJV

An elderly mother is in need of care and supervision. But her children are too busy with their own lives. They argue over who should take care of her: "It's your job—you're the oldest." "You live closer to her." "But you have more time." And on and on it goes. The mother goes without the care she needs, and the siblings only get cross with each other.

Another elderly mother is also in need of care. But her children willingly come to her aid and provide what she needs. They are grateful for the chance to care for their mom, even though it may be inconvenient. And the family grows closer together as they express love for one another.

There's quite a difference between those who carry their crosses willingly, and those who do so begrudgingly.

Maybe we all need a reminder about the first being last and the last being first in God's kingdom. Each of us has burdens to bear. No one is immune from suffering. And while we will find an end to our troubles in heaven, we should strive to finish strong here, honoring our Savior and loving others.

Hello God...it's me. Will You open my eyes to see opportunities to serve others today?

May 13

The Wings of God

Whoever dwells in the shelter of the Most High will rest in the shadow of the Almighty. I will say of the LORD, "He is my refuge and my fortress, my God, in whom I trust." Surely he will save you from the fowler's snare and from the deadly pestilence. He will cover you with his feathers, and under his wings you will find refuge; his faithfulness will be your shield and rampart.

PSALM 91:1–4 NIV

If you were raised on a farm, you have possibly witnessed the resolute protection of a mother hen. Whenever a hen senses that her chicks are in danger, she spreads her wings over them and pulls them close. This act of care places her in harm's way but provides safety for her chicks. No matter the risk, she's willing to sacrifice herself for them.

The psalmist compares God to a mother hen. God loves us so much that He opens His arms wide and gathers us in. His loving embrace draws us close, letting us know that we are cherished and protected. He shields us under His wings, and He will gently guide us in the direction He has set out for each of us.

Ultimately, Jesus spread His arms wide and allowed Himself to be sacrificed in order to save us. There is no gesture of love greater than that.

Hello God...it's me. I want You to know how thankful I am for Your unchanging character that gathers and protects.

No One Like Him

God, investigate my life; get all the facts firsthand. I'm an open book to you; even from a distance,
you know what I'm thinking. You know when I leave and when I get back; I'm never out of your sight.
You know everything I'm going to say before I start the first sentence. I look behind me
and you're there, then up ahead and you're there, too—your reassuring presence,
coming and going. This is too much, too wonderful—I can't take it all in!

PSALM 139:1–6 MSG

Who are we without God? What do we have that He has not granted us? Our hearts should be overwhelmed with gratitude every day for the blessings He has given. His mercy on us has been great and completely undeserved. There is no God like our God. He is infinite, omnipotent, omniscient, real. He spoke all of creation into existence yet dresses the wildflowers in beauty. He brought all of humanity to life yet saw you in your mother's womb and knew every day of your life before it was written.

In all of heaven and earth, there is none like God, and no one can love us as He does. That awesome fact should penetrate into our very bones, making us cry out to Him, "Lord, who is like unto You?"

Thank Him today for His mercy and love.

Hello God...it's me. I am humbled, overwhelmed, and baffled by the depth of Your love for me. There is no one like You.

Joy in Heartbreak

Let all those rejoice who put their trust in You; let them ever shout for joy, because You defend them; let those also who love Your name be joyful in You. For You, O LORD, will bless the righteous; with favor You will surround him as with a shield.

PSALM 5:11–12 NKJV

Heartbreak and joy don't seem to go together. Joy is parties and balloons and laughter and loved ones. Heartbreak is just the opposite—loneliness, depression, desperation, pain.

We want life to be easy, don't we? We'll take the joy, thank you; hold the sorrow and tears. Some people are even willing to step into sin in order to pursue some elusive sense of joy. But that's the problem. What the world mistakes for joy is really a lesser, more fleeting contentment—happiness. And happiness is tied to events and circumstances. Joy, on the other hand, can be felt even in the midst of heartbreak.

Joy is a gift of the Holy Spirit, with a purity that allows us to face all of life's ups and downs with a steady undercurrent of peace. We may not feel happy—life is full of pain and trouble—but we can be assured that God is in control. And that makes us safe enough to embrace even the sorrow.

Hello God...it's me. Thank You for the foundation of You, enabling me to weather the storms of life.

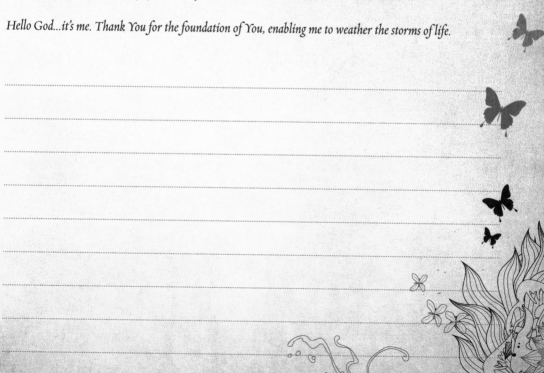

Byways and Back Lanes

Thus says the LORD, "Stand by the ways and see and ask for the ancient paths, where the good way is and walk in it; and you will find rest for your souls."
JEREMIAH 6:16 NASB

Where are the byways and back lanes of your heart? What grows along those paths? Too often they are somberly lit, allowing the darkness to hide the actions or thoughts that would be an embarrassment if seen in the light.

Too often, we slip there. A temptation. An angry outburst. A feeling of hopelessness or helplessness. A desire unfulfilled. We justify our actions and walk down the shadowy path. Only too late do we realize that we have slipped away from the presence of God.

In His presence is light. In His presence the pathway is clear and the way is lit by God's Word, as the psalmist wrote, "Your word is a lamp to my feet and a light to my path" (Psalm 119:105 NKJV).

Close off the byways and back lanes. Stay on the path. God has promised that He will show us the way; we merely need to walk in it.

Hello God...it's me. I trust Your gentle love to pull me back from the back lanes into the light of Your presence.

New Creature in Christ

Therefore if any man be in Christ, he is a new creature:
old things are passed away; behold, all things are become new.
2 CORINTHIANS 5:17 KJV

Forrest Gump said many wonderful things, but "My mama always said you've got to put the past behind you before you can move on" has particular resonance regarding new beginnings.

We've all seen those before-and-after pictures: the "before" picture of the forlorn, ninety-pound weakling; the "after" picture of a smiling Mr. Universe. It looks so easy in all those advertisements for millions of products and procedures. At best, it's a temporary fix on a used model.

"New creature" means *a completely new creation.* The beauty of our "after" picture is glorious and eternal. Think of God creating order from chaos. And what was His opinion of His work? It was good. Through the redemptive work of Jesus Christ, God has done the same with us. Perhaps this is the most wondrous part of the Father's nature: He can make all things new!

Hello God...it's me. Thank You for complete newness in You.

May 18

He Rules the World

His invisible attributes, that is, His eternal power and divine nature, have been clearly seen since the creation of the world, being understood through what He has made.

ROMANS 1:20 HCSB

In this modern age, we sometimes forget how dependent we are on life's basics and necessities. No matter how advanced our technology or how cutting-edge our modern scientific breakthroughs, we still need air to breathe. We still need sufficient water and food to survive. And we still depend completely on our planet, which is perfectly situated within our galaxy in order to sustain life. Without any one of these, we would be doomed.

When we realize that God is completely in control of all of the details of creation, it should make us even more astounded at who He is. As we realize the limitlessness of His power and sovereignty, it should cause us daily to fall on our knees and worship Him.

As we contemplate who God is and all that He has in His power, we should respond to Him in unrestrained devotion and obedience. We serve an incredible, powerful, and majestic God!

Hello God...it's me. Today I will worship You for Your mighty control of the details that sustain life on earth.

Living in the Present

"You are not even fifty years old!" they said. "How could you have seen Abraham?"
Jesus answered, "I tell you for certain that even before Abraham was, I was, and I am."
JOHN 8:57–58 CEV

When we read the Bible, we sometimes get caught up in the historical facts presented in God's Word. The Old Testament is filled with dramatic events that happened thousands of years ago. Likewise, the New Testament recounts many details about the ministry of Jesus and the formation of the early church, events that occurred in history two thousand years ago.

Yet God is not the God of the past or the God of a certain historical period. He is the God of the past, present, and future. His power, guidance, and redemptive plan are current and ongoing.

In the Old Testament, God told Moses to tell the Israelites that "I AM" sent Moses to them. In the New Testament, Jesus told those gathered around Him "before Abraham was born, I am!"

God does not exist in some past historical context, but He exists eternally, eager to interact with us and to be present with us in our lives.

Hello God...it's me. Thank You for Your love that continues to change whoever it touches.

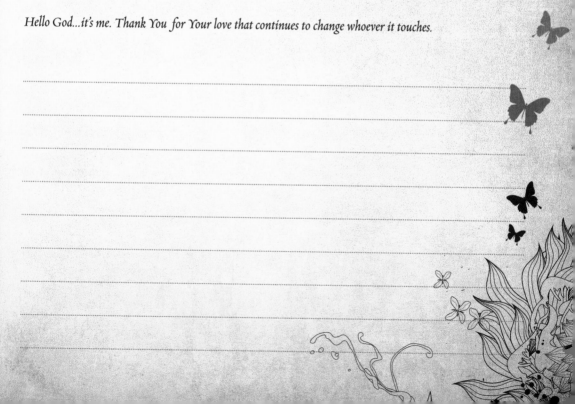

Reading the Right Journal

*You were taught, with regard to your former way of life, to put off your old self,
which is being corrupted by its deceitful desires; to be made new in the attitude of your minds;
and to put on the new self, created to be like God in true righteousness and holiness.*

EPHESIANS 4:22–24 NIV

It's been a rough week. Your kids haven't cooperated, work projects have been frustrating, and friends haven't returned your phone calls. Curling up under a blanket to write in your journal about the week's events seems a perfect way to unwind and de-stress. However, with the penning of each line of your memoir, your sorrow increases instead of decreasing.

Take a different memoir off your memory shelf. In this one, God is the author and main character. Its chapters are filled with stories of God's mercy, grace, and forgiveness. Its pages chronicle His care, provision, and kindness during both joyful and challenging times. The words illuminate God instead of obliterating Him.

The shelf may be a little dusty today, but don't let the cobwebs scare you away. Open up God's memoir—the Bible. You'll be glad you did. You're still part of the story, but in this one, God is on the throne—right where He should be.

Hello God...it's me. Thank You for Your Word, a powerful memoir that shows Your long-desired relationship with us.

May 21

Unlikely Kings

Around the throne were twenty-four thrones; and upon the thrones I saw twenty-four elders sitting, clothed in white garments, and golden crowns on their heads.... And when the living creatures give glory and honor and thanks to Him who sits on the throne, to Him who lives forever and ever, the twenty-four elders will fall down before Him who sits on the throne, and will worship Him who lives forever and ever, and will cast their crowns before the throne.
REVELATION 4:4, 9–10 NASB

The Bible provides two unlikely snapshots of royalty. One focuses on a thief dying on a wooden cross. While the crowd jeered, the thief dared to believe that the man next to him—Jesus—had a kingdom waiting for Him and could take him to an eternal paradise (Luke 23:39–43). The second comes in the fourth chapter of Revelation where a group of believers in heaven cast their crowns before the throne of God. Because of Jesus, the unlikely are made kings in a place they would have no hope of gaining without Him.

Through God's grace, you too will someday bear a crown that no one can take away. Salvation, the guarantee of your future inheritance, clothes you with royal authority like a kingly mantle. God chose you to rule with Him.

On a day when you might feel helpless or powerless, remember that you're royalty—you're a child of the King!

Hello God...it's me. Thank You that You chose me to rule with You.

May 22

One Day at a Time

Come to Me, all of you who are weary and burdened, and I will give you rest. All of you,
take up My yoke and learn from Me, because I am gentle and humble in heart,
and you will find rest for yourselves. For My yoke is easy and My burden is light.
MATTHEW 11:28–30 HCSB

How can we possibly stay on track spiritually in all of life's ups and downs? How can we know that we'll be able to stay faithful to God tomorrow when we have no idea what tomorrow will bring—much less next month, next year?

A Chinese proverb says that the journey of a thousand miles begins with a single step. So it is with life. We do not know what the future holds, but we trust God and walk into it one step at a time. If we are faithful in this moment, and then faithful in the next moment, and so on and so on, then this will build up to a life of spiritual faithfulness.

And what does that faithfulness look like? It is simply coming unto Jesus, staying close to Him, seeking to honor Him in all we do—in the strength He Himself gives.

All of those obedient steps will add up to a life of obedience.

Hello God...it's me. Thank You for Your faithfulness that comes one step at a time.

Don't Look Back

*I press on, that I may lay hold of that for which Christ Jesus has also laid hold of me....
One thing I do, forgetting those things which are behind and reaching forward to those things
which are ahead, I press toward the goal for the prize of the upward call of God in Christ Jesus.*
PHILIPPIANS 3:12–14 NKJV

Lot's wife will be forever remembered as the one who looked back to her detriment (Genesis 19:17, 26). With one last anxious peek at the city she left behind, she turned into a pillar of salt. Her longing for the past ended up destroying her.

Like Lot's wife, how many times have we anxiously glanced back at the "glory days" that we think will never come again? Or maybe our backward gaze is at a past mistake that haunts us.

While the enemy whispers, "Keep looking back," in order to discourage us or push us toward discontentment, the Lord Jesus urges us to look ahead and focus on Him. The apostle Paul reminds us to forget the past and look toward the prize that awaits us: eternal life with the Savior. His blood covers our sins and provides us the hope of glory. We can choose to dwell on that hope now or be destroyed by clinging to the hopelessness of the past.

Which will you choose?

Hello God...it's me. Will You help me to keep my eyes off the rearview mirror and on You?

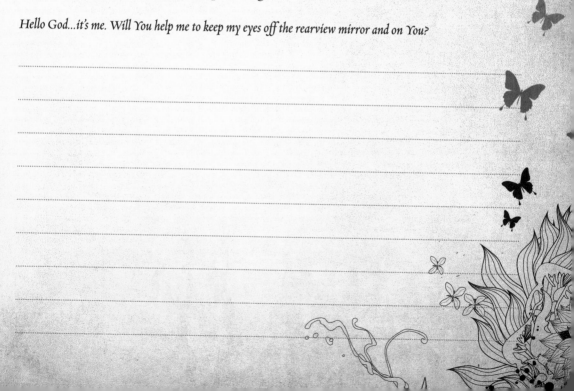

Slow Down and Find Him

*Then He said to His disciples, "Therefore I say to you, do not worry about your life,
what you will eat; nor about the body, what you will put on. Life is more than food, and the body
is more than clothing.... For all these things the nations of the world seek after, and your Father knows
that you need these things. But seek the kingdom of God, and all these things shall be added to you.*
L*UKE* 12:22–23, 30–31 NKJV

We all know people who seem to be always in motion, always working on something, always in the midst of some new project or endeavor. Most of us consider those people to be successful. After all, our society admires and esteems busy people.

Yet in our spiritual lives, we are given a completely different model. God's model for success is not so much focused on movement as it is on attitude. The movement of obedience will come later, but first we must make sure our attitudes—our hearts—are in the right place.

If we want to draw closer to God and His will for our lives, we must pause what we are doing to make time for Him and determine His heart for us. We cannot do this while we are constantly in motion; we can only do this by slowing down through prayer, meditation, Scripture reading, and an earnest desire to become more like Him.

Hello God...it's me. I want You to know I am determined to be still and know that You are God.

May 25

No Posers

I say, walk by the Spirit, and you will not carry out the desire of the flesh.
GALATIANS 5:16 NASB

The Urban Dictionary defines *poser* as someone who "tries to fit in but with exaggeration." You've probably encountered such individuals. They desperately want to blend into the group, but it rarely happens because they are so self-conscious in trying to do so.

Posers mingle about in the Christian world, doing and looking good. In public, they tell us life is great, and their smiles flow freely—for a few short hours. Eventually, though, they must retreat and reenergize, because relying on self-righteousness runs even the best intentions into the ground.

Are you guilty of posing, of putting on a good face? Stop trying so hard. Become consumed with Christ and who He wants to be in your life. Go forward in the confidence that He is with you, and let His Spirit enable you to find your place.

Hello God...it's me. Help me to be consumed with You and who You want me to be.

May 26

Countermeasures

You belong to God, my dear children. You have already won a victory over those people,
because the Spirit who lives in you is greater than the spirit who lives in the world.

1 JOHN 4:4 NLT

Suffering is a universal language. We can't escape pain. Plans go wrong. Troubles come. Our bodies wear out. We live in a fallen world, and sometimes the pressure paralyzes us.

Deep ocean waters can crush a submarine made of thick steel, but little fish with the thinnest layer of skin swim there without a care in the world. Why aren't they crushed? Those fish have an internal pressure that perfectly corresponds to the pressure from the outside. God gives them what they need to swim in the deep places.

When faced with the pressure of suffering, we don't need skin made of steel; we need a power inside us that corresponds to the pressure from outside. That power comes from the presence of Jesus who lives within us.

Surrounded by pressure? Sense the presence of Jesus. Then rest secure in Him.

Hello God...it's me. I can't thank You enough for the power that comes from Jesus in me.

Move Forward

You must continue in the things which you have learned and been assured of, knowing from whom you have learned them, and that from childhood you have known the Holy Scriptures, which are able to make you wise for salvation through faith which is in Christ Jesus.

2 TIMOTHY 3:14–15 NKJV

It is ironic that what seems like failure to us can be turned into a monumental step forward by God. Bodybuilders know that muscle must be broken down by stressing it; only then can it rebuild in a much stronger form. Musicians know that the minor notes in a symphony can add a mysterious tone to the concerto that major notes cannot evoke. Bakers know that when they pinch off a section of dough and let it become "sour," it can serve as yeast to raise a dozen future batches of sweet rolls.

The Lord can advance us in similar ways. Peter denied Christ three times, but this led to all-out devotion. John Mark was sent home from a mission trip, but he matured and became invaluable to Paul. If you fail (and you will), know that God can draw good from the situation. Don't become discouraged. Move forward. God is with you.

Hello God…it's me. Help me to trust You with my failures and keep going.

Doing Little Things

One who is faithful in a very little is also faithful in much,
and one who is dishonest in a very little is also dishonest in much.
LUKE 16:10 ESV

Have you ever heard someone say, "I want to be second place"? How about, "I'd like to get straight Bs on my report card," or "I plan to own a string of second-rate restaurants"? Sounds silly, doesn't it?

No matter how small or seemingly insignificant the task God is asking you to do, it is something He designed you to do for the body of Christ. Maybe God hasn't designed you to be a world-renowned preacher or famous missionary. Maybe inviting your neighbors to dinner, working on the assembly line, or serving in the church nursery are the very things God wants you to do. Are you willing to accept doing those little things, and nothing more, if that is God's will?

Even a little cricket's chirping can be heard from a great distance. Be faithful to do the little things cheerfully and God will be glorified.

Hello God...it's me. Thank You for the little things You have planned for me to do today.

Who Me, Worry?

Don't worry about anything, but pray about everything. With thankful hearts offer up your prayers and requests to God. Then, because you belong to Christ Jesus, God will bless you with peace that no one can completely understand. And this peace will control the way you think and feel.
PHILIPPIANS 4:6–7 CEV

When we face difficult circumstances, it's much easier to be anxious than to hand our worries over to God. Instead of letting go of our troubles, we desperately want to hold on to them—ignoring the amazing offer from the Creator of the universe to take our burdens, if we would only release them to Him. But we seem hardwired to rely on ourselves first and God second—or in some cases, not to lean on Him at all.

In times of difficulty and uncertainty, we should pray and let God do the worrying. This means the next time we are tempted to fret about our finances or relationships, our health or loved ones' safety, our job or anything else, we should let the Lord handle it—and step out of the way. It won't be easy at first. Old habits die hard. But if we are to truly live out our faith and experience other-worldly peace, we must give our worries to God and trust Him to work out all things for our good and for His glory.

Hello God...it's me. Help me to cast my worries onto You the minute they enter my mind.

Love Despite

God demonstrates his own love for us in this: While we were still sinners, Christ died for us.
Since we have now been justified by his blood, how much more shall we be saved from God's wrath
through him! For if, while we were God's enemies, we were reconciled to him through the death of his Son,
how much more, having been reconciled, shall we be saved through his life!
ROMANS 5:8–10 NIV

In the movie *Marley & Me*, John Grogan and his wife adopt a hyperactive, out-of-control Labrador puppy they name Marley. Through the course of the book, Marley eats drywall, takes the dog-sitter for an all-out sprint around town, almost escapes a moving car by climbing out its window, and jumps into the pool of a house that's being shown to prospective buyers. He makes life for the Grogans complicated and sometimes miserable. They are constantly cleaning up Marley's messes and making up for the damage he's caused. They have every reason to be angry with Marley for his misdeeds. But despite all of this, they still love him and keep him in their home.

We constantly mess things up, return to our sin, and do wrong against God and others. He has every reason to be angry with us. Yet, as much as we don't deserve it, God chooses to love us—and continues loving us—despite our shortcomings. It's inexplicable, but true.

Hello God...it's me. With Your empowerment I will love others with the unconditional love that You have for me.

Which Yoke?

*It was I who taught Ephraim to walk, taking them in My arms, but they never knew
that I healed them. I led them with human cords, with ropes of love.
To them I was like one who eases the yoke from their jaws; I bent down to give them food.*
HOSEA 11:1–4 HCSB

We like to do things our own way and often bristle at being told what to do. The Israelites, too, resisted God's commands and often turned from the laws of the Lord. But instead of finding liberation, they merely exchanged one set of regulations for another. They ran from the boundaries of God and His love and became slaves to this world—a heavy yoke that leads only to sin and death.

Jesus tells us to take His yoke and find rest. Does that sound strange? Jesus knows what we might refuse to admit—a yoke is not a device of torture but an implement necessary to do a job effectively and efficiently. A yoke distributes force, enabling more work to come from less effort. A yoke joins a pair, unites a team, and keeps them together so the row is plowed straight. Jesus says to us, "Join My team. We have work to do, and if you stick with Me, you will go faster, farther." His yoke is easy, and His burden is light.

Which yoke will you choose?

Hello God...it's me. Help me to use my talents for Your kingdom. I love the thought of being yoked with You.

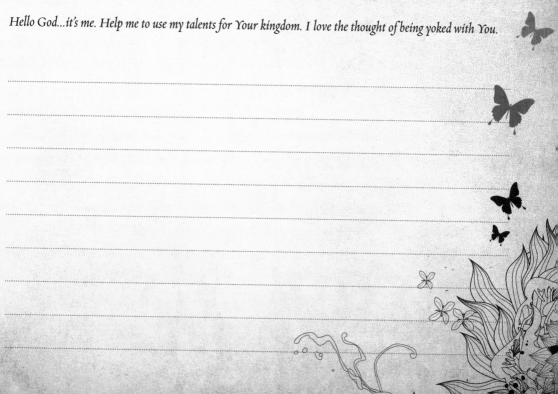

Ultimate Happiness

Seek the kingdom of God above all else, and live righteously, and he will give you everything you need.
So don't worry about tomorrow, for tomorrow will bring its own worries. Today's trouble is enough for today.
MATTHEW 6:33–34 NLT

At face value, we might disagree that there is only one unhappiness. Why, we can recite a litany of things that make us unhappy! Unhappiness seems to come in significant doses every day of our lives. But when we look deeper, beyond our outer circumstances and into the inner recesses of our hearts and souls, we have to ask: what do we do with the deep secrets that cannot be solved by any human intervention?

When we do not love God, we have nothing to cling to; we have no hope. That is why *not* loving God is the only true unhappiness. Without Him, we have nothing. The converse, however, is that in loving God, we find everything we need for this life and the life to come.

Hello God...it's me. Thank You for my deep, secure hope in You.

Love in Action

Love your enemies, and do good, and lend, expecting nothing in return,
and your reward will be great, and you will be sons of the Most High,
for he is kind to the ungrateful and the evil. Be merciful, even as your Father is merciful.
LUKE 6:35 –36 ESV

Mercy is far more than nice thoughts, a kind disposition, sympathetic feelings, or a loving demeanor. Mercy realizes that someone is hurting and gets involved. Just as Jesus took on human flesh and lived among us, experiencing our pain and limitations, mercy gets inside people's skin. The merciful see a need, are moved by that need, and meet that need. Mercy helps the hurting, cares for the sick, brings a cup of cold water to the thirsty, reaches out to the untouchable, forgives the fallen, and is patient with the peculiar.

We are to be merciful because God has shown mercy to us. He has met our needs, eased our ache, and saved our souls— all while sharing our humanness through Jesus. We respond by showing mercy to others. And in that act, we receive even more mercy from God.

Hello God...it's me. Help me to show others Your mercy every day.

More Human

A little while longer and the world will see Me no more, but you will see Me. Because I live,
you will live also. At that day you will know that I am in My Father, and you in Me, and I in you.
He who has My commandments and keeps them, it is he who loves Me. And he who loves Me
will be loved by My Father, and I will love him and manifest Myself to him.

JOHN 14:19–21 NKJV

This side of heaven, believers do not live perfectly. Yet all Christ-followers do have a perfect standing before God, having received "the righteousness of God through faith in Jesus Christ" (Romans 3:22 ESV).

Our position in Christ, however, does not always match our process of living like Christ. We are still very much human with all our foibles, fears, and sinful desires. When a saved saint acts less than saintly, those outside the church cry, "The church is a bunch of hypocrites!" Certainly, more often than should happen, Christ-followers fail to live up to their name. We never deny that we are still human and, as such, can sin like all the rest of humanity. What makes us different is that we have the presence of One in us who transforms us desire by desire, attitude by attitude, and action by action. Through Him we become more human as we become more like Christ in our thoughts, actions, and lives.

Hello God...it's me. Thank You that You transform us desire by desire, attitude by attitude, action by action.

Great Plans

It won't be long before this generous God who has great plans for us in Christ—eternal and glorious plans they are!—will have you put together and on your feet for good. He gets the last word; yes, he does.
1 PETER 5:11 MSG

The school year is finally over, and summer has arrived. That's when every kid loves to hear the wonderful words, "We're going on vacation!" All the homework and early mornings and school lunches fade into memory, and the countdown begins. Half the fun is anticipating the unknown until it is revealed what the trip will hold. There are so many details for parents to take care of—hotels, car tune-up, what do we do with the dog?—but the payoff is amazing. The happy smiles of their little ones say it all.

It's impossible to imagine what our generous, bighearted God has planned for us. We know the timeline: eternity. We know He's infinitely creative, so though our minds can't conceive of the variety, detail, brilliance, and delight that lie in store, we can anticipate the wonder. Time to begin the countdown. He's in control, He has the last word, and it's going to be glorious.

Hello God...it's me. Thank You for the joy of the anticipation of eternity with You.

Right Side Up

You have heard the law that says the punishment must match the injury: "An eye for an eye, and a tooth for a tooth." But I say, do not resist an evil person! If someone slaps you on the right cheek, offer the other cheek also. If you are sued in court and your shirt is taken from you, give your coat, too. If a soldier demands that you carry his gear for a mile, carry it two miles.

MATTHEW 5:38–41 NLT

In his book *The Different Drum*, M. Scott Peck described Jesus's total upheaval of the entire social order that occurred the Thursday before the crucifixion. Jesus was already on top, so to speak, but He lowered Himself and washed His disciples' feet. It was a revolutionary moment where everything was turned upside down. But as far as the kingdom of heaven was concerned, everything about that moment was right side up.

It's the same in Matthew 5. Jesus overturns everything that seems natural to us and says, "Listen to what I say: here's how to really march to a different drummer." Jesus contends that by abiding in Him and His power, we can outlove any revenge, outlast any court case, and outwalk any of this world's expectations. His way is constantly turning perceptions upside down, while setting reality right side up.

That's our God: His solutions are surprising but powerfully perfect.

Hello God...it's me. I praise You for turning perceptions right side up in Your counterculture kingdom.

Word - Watching

The tongue can no man tame; it is an unruly evil, full of deadly poison....
Out of the same mouth proceedeth blessing and cursing. My brethren, these things ought not so to be.
JAMES 3:8, 10 KJV

Our mouths can get us into all kinds of trouble. James cautioned in the Bible that the tongue, though small, can act like a spark that sets an entire forest on fire. Not only do we have the ability to do great good or great harm with our words, but as believers, the things we say will either draw people closer or push them further away from Jesus. If our words don't uphold the message of love that Christ came to bring, then we'll be tearing it down in ways we don't even realize.

Quarreling and fighting don't represent our Lord well. Too often our words short-circuit in our minds and come out before we've thought them through. So take the advice of both James and St. Francis: put a watch on your mouth, and let the words you speak today represent Christ.

Hello God...it's me. Will You help me to be quick to listen, slow to speak, and slow to get angry today?

Seek and Find

I will be your God throughout your lifetime—until your hair is white with age.
I made you, and I will care for you. I will carry you along and save you.
ISAIAH 46:4 NLT

We may laugh at the irony, but it's true: The older we get, the smarter our parents become. When we move into our own lives, experience a few knocks, and then have children of our own, suddenly we begin to understand our parents' worries and fears for us. We understand their rules and restrictions, for now we are far too aware of what's "out there," and we want to protect our children from those threats.

Similarly, as we get older, we may discover that theology increases in relevance as well. Our knowledge and understanding of God grows deeper and wider as we willingly engage the greater issues and study the teachings and writings of those who came before. As we advance in years, we must continue to make it a priority to know the Lord more fully, for He will continue to make Himself known.

Hello God...it's me. Thank You for the unfolding of Your likeness in me that continues as I seek You through the years.

In the Least of These

"And when did we ever see you sick or in prison and come to you?"
Then the King will say, "I'm telling the solemn truth: Whenever you did one of these things
to someone overlooked or ignored, that was me—you did it to me."
MATTHEW 25:39–40 MSG

In 1994, some 3,500 Congressional and international power brokers from over one hundred countries gathered at the National Prayer Breakfast in Washington, DC. They assemble annually to "meet Jesus, man to man," and that year, tiny Mother Teresa of Calcutta had a huge word for these influential leaders.

"Love, to be true, has to hurt," she said. "It hurt Jesus to love us. Jesus makes Himself the hungry one, the naked one, the homeless one, the unwanted one." She asked those attendees to give to "the least of these" until it hurt, because as Jesus taught, to deny love to the obscure, the poor, the despised and afflicted is to deny God.

Jesus's unrestrained grace and goodness is available to *every* sufferer. This is His revolutionary plan—that He who is highly exalted is miraculously present in those who are the least honored.

Honor Him whose heart has no limits. Love others until it hurts.

Hello God...it's me. Let me take Your love to someone who is suffering today.

Dissatisfactions

I say, walk by the Spirit, and you will not carry out the desire of the flesh.
For the flesh sets its desire against the Spirit, and the Spirit against the flesh;
for these are in opposition to one another, so that you may not do the things that you please.
GALATIANS 5:16–17 NASB

Motivational speakers know the secret to motivating change. First, they explain in great detail why your current situation is unbearable. Even if you weren't unhappy before you began listening, you're likely to suddenly find yourself extremely dissatisfied with your life. After the seed of dissatisfaction has been planted, the desire to change easily sprouts from it.

Dissatisfaction does indeed drive us—we want to make changes. And it can be good—a positive exercise that compels us to look at our lives, see what needs to be changed for the better, and then work to make those changes. The challenge is to want the kinds of change that *God* wants for us, allowing *Him* to show us where we need to improve and then letting Him guide us into transformation. Where are you dissatisfied? Take that dissatisfaction to God. He'll show you how to want what He wants for you.

Hello God...it's me. Will You show me how to want what You want for me?

The Greatest Gift

No, in all these things we are more than conquerors through him who loved us.
For I am convinced that neither death nor life, neither angels nor demons, neither the present
nor the future, nor any powers, neither height nor depth, nor anything else in all creation,
will be able to separate us from the love of God that is in Christ Jesus our Lord.
ROMANS 8:37–39 NIV

We take another promotion, seeking status in our work. We build bigger nest eggs, seeing power in our money. We take exotic vacations, seeking adventure in our trips. We relive our past through our children, seeking a lost youth.

We are looking for ourselves as though we were searching for hidden treasure. Yet our gift is the presence of Jesus. Consider His love to us. Despite our faults, He runs to us. Seeing our sin, He forgives us. Knowing we deserve death, He grants us life. Our identity is hidden in the love and mercy of God. In Him, our veneers of self-preservation are sanded off; the scaffolding of stuff to hold us up is removed. We are loved by God. What better gift could you find? Receive it as your own.

Hello God...it's me. Thank You for my new identity, embedded in Your love and mercy.

Only a Glimmer

When I sit in darkness, the LORD will be a light to me.
MICAH 7:8 NKJV

Combat soldiers are disciplined in how to sight an enemy down the barrel of a rifle, gauge the range, and then pull the trigger. But what about at night, when there is no sunshine to make the enemy visible? During the Vietnam War the military developed a special telescope called the Starlight Scope. This amazing piece of technology could amplify the gleam of stars to many times their normal brightness, making it seem like daylight for the soldier looking through it.

As believers we sometimes feel alone, abandoned, and surrounded in darkness. In those times we are tempted to doubt God's promises, God's faithfulness, God's goodness. After all, we don't seem to be experiencing them.

Do not doubt in the dark what God told you in the light, for His words are always and forever true.

Hello God...it's me. When I doubt, please help me to remember the many, many times You have been faithful in the past.

Shine On!

The LORD said to Moses, "Stretch your arm toward the sky, and everything will be covered with darkness thick enough to touch."... During that time, the Egyptians could not see each other or leave their homes, but there was light where the Israelites lived.

EXODUS 10:21, 23 CEV

Moses stretched out his hand and darkness covered Egypt. Not a rosy dusk. Not a sapphire twilight. Not the inky velvet of a star-studded summer night. Darkness so deep you couldn't see an inch into the blackness. Yet all the Israelites had light in the place where they lived. In the midst of the plague of darkness, the light of the presence of the Lord shone on His chosen ones. God's light pierced the darkness, appearing even brighter in relation to the oppression surrounding it.

Darkness covers our world in the form of sin and evil. Many people are lost in darkness so deep that they can't see a way out. But when we shine the light and love of Christ, those around us can't help but notice. Our testimony is a valuable thing, but sometimes, more than our words, more than a choice verse of Scripture, people need to see the presence of the Lord reflected in our life, directing them to the Light of the world. Shine on!

Hello God...it's me. As I lay myself before You, I will trust that others will see Your presence reflected in my life.

The Voice of God

Then He said, "Go out, and stand on the mountain before the LORD." And behold, the LORD passed by, and a great and strong wind tore into the mountains and broke the rocks in pieces before the LORD, but the LORD was not in the wind; and after the wind an earthquake, but the LORD was not in the earthquake; and after the earthquake a fire, but the LORD was not in the fire; and after the fire a still small voice.

1 KINGS 19:11–12 NKJV

When we pray, we should be quiet in order to hear the voice of God speaking to us. But how often is God's voice drowned out by the chaos of our busy lives?

God is the most powerful being in the universe. When He spoke, our solar system and everything on planet Earth came into being. He breathed and Adam lived. With that much power, imagine what might happen if He were to sing or shout! But the Bible says He speaks to us in a still, small voice. Maybe the reason we don't hear God's voice when we pray is that we are surrounded by too much noise. Like the music at a concert when we can't hear ourselves think, the cacophony of everyday life can overshadow God's voice—no matter the volume.

It's time to remove the distractions and dial down the chaos. Listen for God's voice beyond the clamor. It will be a welcome sound indeed.

Hello God...it's me. Please help me hear Your voice through the chaos.

"I Need Jesus and..."

*But seek first his kingdom and his righteousness, and all these things
will be given to you as well. Therefore do not worry about tomorrow,
for tomorrow will worry about itself. Each day has enough trouble of its own.*
MATTHEW 6:33–34 NIV

Hopefully we are aware that we need Jesus, but if we're truly honest with ourselves, don't we sometimes think that we need Jesus AND...a salary large enough to pay the bills...a job that provides a sense of fulfillment...a spouse who nurtures and encourages us?

Perhaps we need to remember when we first came to Jesus—how we eagerly set aside time to meet with Him each day, how we found daily joy in being a new creation. Is it possible that we have known Jesus so long that we have begun to take Him for granted? Have we shifted our focus instead to the ANDs, such as money, career, and family? If we want to experience Jesus anew, we must become aware of the ANDs in our lives and come back to Him as the priority that matters most.

Hello God...it's me. It's all about You. Forgive me where I have taken You for granted.

An Undeniable Treasure

Christ has been raised from the dead, the firstfruits of those who have fallen asleep.
For as by a man came death, by a man has come also the resurrection of the dead.
For as in Adam all die, so also in Christ shall all be made alive. But each in his own order:
Christ the firstfruits, then at his coming those who belong to Christ.
1 Corinthians 15:20–23 ESV

We tend to think of ourselves as common, run-of-the-mill, or average. When we look at the extraordinary gifts and talents of other people, we consider ourselves to be ordinary in comparison. But to God, each of us is exceptional, unequaled, beyond measure.

Because we are specially designed by God, we are incomparable, perfect in every way. God has a special love for each of His sons and daughters, as a father loves each of his children. Each of us is an undeniable treasure, in a class by ourselves, one-of-a-kind, and loved uniquely by our heavenly Father. And through the sacrifice of His sinless Son, Jesus our Lord, we are a cherished member of God's family, destined to spend eternity with Him in heaven.

Jesus Christ died freely for the church, and He loves each of us as if we were the only person on this planet. His shed blood has removed our imperfections. And though we still sin, when God looks at us now, all that's in view is Jesus.

Hello God...it's me. Thank You that not only am I unique in Your sight, but so is Your love for me.

Faithful

My eager expectation and hope is that I will not be ashamed about anything, but that now as always, with all boldness, Christ will be highly honored in my body, whether by life or by death.
PHILIPPIANS 1:20 HCSB

What comes to mind when you think of *success*? Business suits, multimillion-dollar budgets, and a wall full of trophies? Or maybe healthy children, surplus income for travel and leisure, and a thriving ministry? The real secret to success is faith-driven obedience.

Paul knew the gritty reality of obedience. This giant of the faith listed quite a résumé of suffering in 2 Corinthians 11. He knew hunger and thirst. He fought against rivers, bandits, sleeplessness, and cold. Paul was imprisoned, flogged, stoned, and shipwrecked.

He was stripped of his clothing and faced death on several occasions. And he struggled against a thorn in his flesh. Yet Paul boasted in his hardships.

Paul knew that God measures success by a faithful heart. A life committed to God, living His commands, loving His people, and spreading His Word results in the only bottom line that matters—souls saved and the body edified. In God's economy, that's the secret of success.

Hello God…it's me. I look to You to define the success You have in mind for me.

On Board

Is anyone among you suffering? He should pray. Is anyone cheerful? He should sing praises.
Is anyone among you sick? He should call for the elders of the church, and they should pray over him....
The prayer of faith will save the sick person, and the Lord will restore him to health; if he has
committed sins, he will be forgiven. Therefore, confess your sins to one another and pray for one another,
so that you may be healed. The urgent request of a righteous person is very powerful in its effect.
JAMES 5:13–16 HCSB

Clark Kent's alter ego, Superman, had a knack for appearing at just the right moment to rescue the helpless from the brink of destruction. Clark would swap his business suit for a superhero's cape at a moment's notice—once all other possibilities for help had been exhausted. It took an emergency— a crisis—to bring out the rescuing hero.

How different God is! He is not the solution of last resort but the source of immediate help. Always. With all power at His fingertips, He stands ready to save any who will appeal to Him. In fact, He *wants* to be the One who saves. It's not up to us to save ourselves.

We can call out to Him with just a word, asking to be rescued in the moment, or we can spend hours pouring out our deepest concerns. Regardless, He is on board! He saves our souls as surely as He keeps our feet from stumbling on a morning walk.

Hello God...it's me. I just want You to know: You are my hero.

June 18

He Has Visited Us

He said to them, "But who do you say that I am?" Simon Peter answered, "You are the Christ, the Son of the living God."... From that time Jesus began to show His disciples that He must go to Jerusalem, and suffer many things from the elders and chief priests and scribes, and be killed, and be raised up on the third day.

MATTHEW 16:15–16, 21 NASB

It's easier for us to believe something if we can see it, touch it, smell it, or hear it. Something about our human perspective requires tangible evidence in order to believe something with absolute certainty.

Yet as believers living two thousand years after Christ walked the earth, we don't have the luxury of ministering alongside Him on His journeys. We can't walk with Him on the road to Jerusalem or see Him heal the sick or hear Him teach the crowd on the mountainside.

Don't be discouraged! We know that Christ lived among us and died on the cross to forgive us of our sins. Scripture is not the only reference we have for this. Secular historical accounts also record Jesus's life and ministry—and He also appeared to hundreds of people after He rose from the dead. Because of Christ, we can be assured that God is real—and He is as real and alive today as He was two thousand years ago.

Hello God...it's me. Thank You for the faith You confirm inside me.

Unmerited Grace

*(John testified concerning him. He cried out, saying, "This is the one I spoke about when I said, 'He who comes after me has surpassed me because he was before me.'")
Out of his fullness we have all received grace in place of grace already given.
For the law was given through Moses; grace and truth came through Jesus Christ.*

JOHN 1:15–17 NIV

Grace is a magnificent concept that is particularly meaningful to those who follow Christ. Because of grace, our fallen nature and sinful behavior no longer form a barrier between us and God. He bestows His grace upon us without merit—meaning we don't deserve it and can't do anything to attain it.

Yet God's grace is offered to us free of charge. All we have to do is ask for it. His grace is available to us when we are not yet believers in Christ but ask earnestly for Him to enter our hearts, and it's available to us each time we fail but honestly seek His forgiveness. And God's grace never runs out. We can never approach God for grace and hear Him answer, "Sorry, but you have used up your allotment of grace." He continually offers us His abundant, overflowing, undeserved, amazing grace.

Let's live in light of the freeing power of God's unmerited grace in our lives.

Hello God...it's me. How can I adequately express my thanks for Your endless grace?

Our Assigned Cross

Anyone who intends to come with me has to let me lead. You're not in the driver's seat—I am. Don't run from suffering; embrace it. Follow me and I'll show you how. Self-help is no help at all. Self-sacrifice is the way, my way, to finding yourself, your true self.
LUKE 9:23–24 MSG

Jesus told His followers to take up their cross daily and follow Him. Then He explained, "For whoever would save his life will lose it, but whoever loses his life for my sake will save it" (Luke 9:23–24 ESV). For the Christ-follower, taking up our cross means loss.

The Bible assures us that we have been saved by grace; it is not our actions or our circumstances that bring us salvation. But a personal encounter with the Crucified does mean carrying our assigned cross and walking our own path of suffering for Christ in this life. For some, that may mean enduring criticism from friends or loved ones. For others, that may even include persecution or martyrdom. When God allows us the high calling of carrying our cross, will we be as eager to follow the Crucified as when we follow Him as the Rescuer, Strong Tower, and Healer? For all who follow the Crucified, there is no other way home.

Hello God...it's me. Help me to always follow Your footsteps home.

Trusting in the Consequences

Offer the sacrifices of righteousness, and trust in the LORD.
PSALM 4:5 NASB

How many times have we decided to follow through with a request from someone after he or she said, "Just trust me. Everything will be fine"? In doing so, we put our trust in a fallible human being. And those times don't always end favorably for us.

The person making the request may be a friend, a coworker, a relative, or some other trusted person. Nevertheless, we are putting our faith in a person who has motives that are less than perfect and intentions we often know little about. And as humans, their trustworthiness is limited by imperfect knowledge and reasoning ability.

But for the follower of Jesus, what joy and security we have when Christ calls us to trust Him and the truth of His Word. We can completely rest in the fact that regardless of the direction, Christ leads us with perfect knowledge and motives. He will take care of us and give us the strength we need in any situation.

As long as Christ leads us, we have nothing to fear.

Hello God...it's me. I ask You to take away anything in me standing in the way of complete trust in You.

Costly Forgiveness

Put on therefore, as the elect of God, holy and beloved, bowels of mercies, kindness,
humbleness of mind, meekness, longsuffering; forbearing one another, and forgiving one another,
if any man have a quarrel against any: even as Christ forgave you, so also do ye.
COLOSSIANS 3:12–13 KJV

The film *The Passion of the Christ* gives viewers a vivid emotional understanding of Christ's suffering for our forgiveness. In the movie, the events of Christ's crucifixion are portrayed in sights and sounds that are almost beyond what a person can bear to watch!

Attempt to imagine what it was like for the heavenly Father to put His Son on the cross to suffer and die. "Stop it!" we might scream from the perspective of our human justice. "Jesus does not deserve to suffer!" Yet for God the Father, that is the point of Calvary. As a sinless man Jesus did not deserve to die, but He willingly took on our sin. He suffered for our forgiveness.

As beneficiaries of His suffering, should we offer anything less to others? Though we will never suffer as Christ did for us, we must accept in our forgiving others that sometimes we too must bear suffering for the sake of love.

Hello God...it's me. Please prepare me to suffer for the sake of love. I want to be like You.

The Destination

I will bless you with a future filled with hope—a future of success, not of suffering.
JEREMIAH 29:11 CEV

Using a road map or following the directions on a GPS helps us go from point A to point B with relative ease. But when we set off on our own trying to locate a destination using only our sense of direction, we often end up going in circles, backtracking, and generally getting stressed out.

Submission to God is a lot like using a road map. He knows the path we should travel and He's ready to be our guide. We shouldn't try to make the journey on our own—we are not wise enough to get ourselves out of the pitfalls and dead ends that show up as we travel. We need His help!

As we submit to God in all circumstances, we not only reach our destination but we experience contentment and joy in the journey. And through submission, we will one day reach our ultimate destination— kneeling before the throne of God, where true contentment will be ours forever.

Hello God...it's me. Help me to submit to You as my Guide in every area of my life.

The Meaning of Life

In the beginning was the Word, and the Word was with God, and the Word was God.
He was with God in the beginning. All things were created through Him,
and apart from Him not one thing was created that has been created.

JOHN 1:1–3 HCSB

What joy the Creator must have had in creation, the glorious dawn of God's history with us. Jesus was there with God at the very beginning, and all of history looked forward to the day when He would descend to the earth He created in order to save His people from their sin.

Jesus was fully God and fully man. Because He was willing to wrap His divine glory in human flesh, He truly understands the human condition. During His days on earth, He experienced the fullness of humanity—sorrow, joy, temptation, hunger, thirst, delight, pain, laughter, and so much more. And even though we are totally unworthy, He allowed Himself to become the sacrifice to take care of our sins once and for all.

God's story is our story when we choose to accept the gracious gift of Jesus's sacrifice for us. Real meaning in life is found in our Savior.

Hello God...it's me. Thank You that the thrill of living and the meaning of life is in Your hand.

The Parcel

Thank God for this gift too wonderful for words!
2 CORINTHIANS 9:15 NLT

We stare at the parcel on the back porch of life, not wanting to pick it up. Its wrapping is ugly, with no return address. The unwelcome package contains a family crisis, financial woes, or a challenge at work—something that will surely keep our thoughts running in circles and leave us numb. We instinctively know that its contents will bring pain and sorrow or anxiety and grief.

Yet God often wraps His choicest deliveries in those unwanted packages. Unexpected provision, deeper faith, more lasting friendships, unfathomed blessings.

Even if you're in survival mode today, stay open. We have a creative God. You may be afraid to check underneath all the wrapping, but He knows exactly what is coming to your back door—and He's got you covered. Hang on to Him as you pick up the parcel.

Hello God...it's me. I want You to know that I am walking into today, expecting Your goodness.

June 26

What's Cookin'?

We continually ask God to fill you with the knowledge of his will through all the wisdom and understanding that the Spirit gives, so that you may live a life worthy of the Lord and please him in every way: bearing fruit in every good work, growing in the knowledge of God, being strengthened with all power according to his glorious might so that you may have great endurance and patience, and giving joyful thanks to the Father, who has qualified you to share in the inheritance of his holy people in the kingdom of light.

COLOSSIANS 1:9–12 NIV

Brisket in the slow cooker. Soup simmering on the stove. Barbecue in the smoker. With time, a few simple ingredients can become a masterful dish that would delight any palate.

Our growth as a believer is like those savory dishes—and we already have the ingredients. We just need to mix them together and start cooking. The main ingredient, salvation in Christ, is already in the pot. The rest of the ingredients are in the pantry waiting for you.

Jars and boxes marked with labels like justice, mercy, love, truth, holiness, faithfulness, goodness, grace, and wisdom fill the shelves.

What's on the menu for your spiritual growth today? God offers all we need for life and godliness. Allow who He is and what He is doing to gradually work itself out in your life today, like the aroma of a delicious, slow-cooked meal.

Hello God...it's me. Thank You for the variety of good things You pour into my life to restore me.

A New Level

*If any of you lack wisdom, let him ask of God, that giveth to all men liberally,
and upbraideth not; and it shall be given him.*

JAMES 1:5 KJV

We don't tend to look at difficulties and opposition as opportunities. Instead, we see them as excuses to quit, to give up, to determine that we must have been on the wrong path, misread the signs, didn't understand what we thought was God's guidance.

At times, it's true that the roadblocks are God's way of stopping us. At other times, however, those roadblocks are opposition from our enemy, and our job is to hear God calling us higher, calling us to climb over the roadblocks and continue on His path.

The difficulty, of course, is determining which is true—where is this roadblock from and what should we do about it? Ask God. He will give you the wisdom to discern whether to let the roadblocks guide you onto a new path, or whether to climb right on over them! When you seek God's guidance, He will give you power and blessings for the road ahead.

Hello God...it's me. Thank You giving me discernment to navigate the roadblocks today.

Hope Beyond the Grave

By the sweat of your brow you will eat your food until you return to the ground, since from it you were taken; for dust you are and to dust you will return.

GENESIS 3:19 NIV

Our life here on earth appears as a vapor and then disappears. Our body is on a funeral march to the grave. It's a difficult reality for us humans to grasp. We avoid death as much as possible—we are all about life and living.

Genesis 3:19 reminds us that we are God's creations, only temporarily on this earth, our bodies eventually returning to the dust from which we were created. It's not great news—and yet God does not leave us there. We have hope through God's mercy and grace.

Because Jesus conquered death, those who belong to Him will conquer death also. In the short time we have on earth, we should be enthusiastic and grateful for what Jesus did for us at Calvary. The cross provides the only way to eternal life.

Hello God...it's me. Thank You that Your Word proclaims that we are more than conquerors through Him who loved us. What a beautiful promise.

June 29

Toss That Mountain

So Jesus answered and said to them, "Have faith in God. For assuredly, I say to you, whoever says to this mountain, 'Be removed and be cast into the sea,' and does not doubt in his heart, but believes that those things he says will be done, he will have whatever he says. Therefore I say to you, whatever things you ask when you pray, believe that you receive them, and you will have them."
MARK 11:22–25 NKJV

Mountains can be a beautiful sight when they're stretching over the horizon in all of their purple or snowcapped majesty. But when the only mountain you see is a problem you can't solve, words like *impossible* come to mind, instead of *beautiful*. In the face of such a seemingly insurmountable situation, you consult your resources—only to find that they are dwarfed in comparison. What will you do?

If you're facing a mountain-sized problem, Jesus invites you to give that mountain a toss. Impossible, you say? Not for God. Moving mountains is His specialty. All He requires from us is trust. Trust in God is the great mountain mover. When we believe that He has our best interests at heart and delights to hear from His children, we can pray with confidence that God will answer and provide everything we need.

Why not exchange your doubt for the rest that trusting God provides?

Hello God...it's me. I believe that You can and will move the mountains in my day and throughout my life.

A Satisfied Soul

"If you are thirsty, come to me and drink! Have faith in me, and you will have life-giving water flowing from deep inside you, just as the Scriptures say." Jesus was talking about the Holy Spirit, who would be given to everyone that had faith in him. The Spirit had not yet been given to anyone, since Jesus had not yet been given his full glory.
JOHN 7:37–39 CEV

When you're thirsty, cotton-mouth parched, water is what you want and need. Scientists have told us that we can survive for only a matter of days without water. Being thirsty reminds us that we need to drink; therefore, our thirst helps keep us alive.

Another thirst is crucial in keeping us spiritually alive. That is the thirst of our souls. This soul-thirst recognizes when we have let our lives become arid deserts, wandering far from the fountain of life. With only sand around us, we look for the oasis, the soul-quenching satisfaction that only God can give. Jesus invited soul-thirsty people to come to Him: "If anyone thirsts, let him come to Me and drink" (John 7:37 NKJV).

Only in Him will our souls find complete satisfaction. Only through His Spirit can we know precisely and perfectly the One who is the eternal source for a fully satisfied soul.

Hello God...it's me. Thank You that the satisfaction You give isn't partial, but complete.

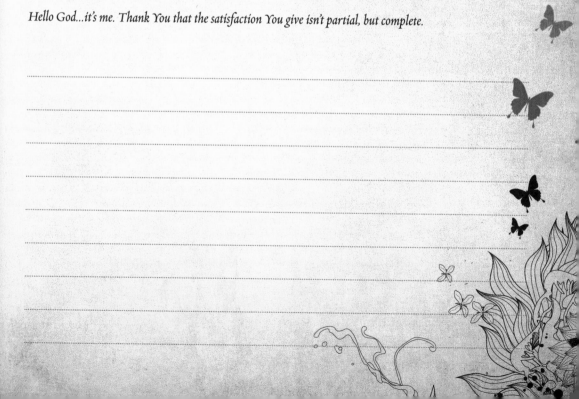

July 1

More

Whoever loves money never has enough; whoever loves wealth is never satisfied with their income.
This too is meaningless. As goods increase, so do those who consume them.
And what benefit are they to the owners except to feast their eyes on them?
ECCLESIASTES 5:10–15 NIV

More money, more status, more vacations, more stuff for our kids. There is no end to the "more" society tells us to want.

Our churches also deliver the message that we need more. More Bible knowledge, more ministry programs, more music choices, more activities for our kids.

Though shouts of "More is better! If you get it, you will finally be happy!" echo in our ears, contentment in the things of this earth lies perpetually out of reach. The one pursuit that will truly provide contentment is pursuing more of God Himself. More love of Him, more passion felt for His name, more time spent alone in His presence.

More of Him is truly more of everything else our heart longs for.

Find contentment even today by lingering in His presence for just a while longer.

Hello God...it's me. Today, help me take time to linger a little longer in Your presence. I want more of You.

Fingerprints of God

Then God said, "Let us make man in our image, after our likeness. And let them have dominion over the fish of the sea and over the birds of the heavens and over the livestock and over all the earth and over every creeping thing that creeps on the earth." So God created man in his own image, in the image of God he created him; male and female he created them. And God blessed them.

GENESIS 1:26–28 ESV

The fingerprints of God are upon all souls. In the Garden of Eden, God scooped up dirt from the ground to form the first man, Adam. Into the man God breathed life and proclaimed it very good. Every person since has value as God's crowning achievement.

What makes us prized by God ahead of the eagle with its grandeur, the ant with her diligence, the lion with his majesty, and all His other creatures? The distinction lies with God who said, "Let us make mankind in our image, in our likeness" (Genesis 1:26). As humans, we have the distinction of the only beings in all of creation who were made in the image of God.

As ennobling as it is to bear God's likeness, far nobler is having the very Spirit of God dwelling in us. On this side of heaven we are jars of clay dusted with the fingerprints of God as His chosen vessels in Christ, redeemed to display His glory!

Hello God...it's me. Help me to believe that I am Your crowning achievement, and to treat others like they are too.

Richer and Deeper

You are glorious and more majestic than the everlasting mountains. Our boldest enemies have been plundered. They lie before us in the sleep of death. No warrior could lift a hand against us. At the blast of your breath, O God of Jacob, their horses and chariots lay still. No wonder you are greatly feared! Who can stand before you when your anger explodes? From heaven you sentenced your enemies; the earth trembled and stood silent before you. You stand up to judge those who do evil, O God, and to rescue the oppressed of the earth.

PSALM 76:4–9 NLT

One of the hardest parts of reading is diving deeper into the text. Literature classes are difficult for most students because they're prone to simply skim over the material. That's why professors push their classes to evaluate every word, sentence, and paragraph—it's the only way to find the symbolism and discern the author's intent.

Though God is richer and deeper than any text will ever be, we are too often content with complacency in our relationship with Him. God, the Creator of the universe and the Lover of our souls, is yearning for us to shed our ambivalence—to give up the obligatory gestures and *enter in*!

To enter into an intimate relationship with Him. From that vantage point, we will be so invigorated that we won't be able to keep ourselves from worshiping Him.

Hello God...it's me. Help me to get rid of my complacency and worship You.

Becoming More Like Christ

There is therefore now no condemnation to those who are in Christ Jesus,
who do not walk according to the flesh, but according to the Spirit.
For the law of the Spirit of life in Christ Jesus has made me free from the law of sin and death.
ROMANS 8:1–2 NKJV

Most of us can remember the day or even the hour we accepted Christ as Savior. Regardless of the details surrounding our conversion, it was a wonderful experience when our sins were forgiven and our eternal home was determined.

But Christ's death and resurrection did more for us than just spare us from eternal damnation; His saving power is also alive and at work in our daily lives. While we were yet dead in our sins, we could not experience the freedom that life in Christ provides. This freedom gives us victory over our sin and the ability—through the Holy Spirit—to daily live in communion with our heavenly Father.

This freedom also prepares us for an ever deeper relationship with Jesus, a relationship that daily draws us closer to Him and changes our desires and objectives to align with His.

Never lose sight of the journey of freedom and faith that follows salvation.

Hello God...it's me. Where I am falling down in my journey of freedom, please draw me closer to You;
empower me to overcome.

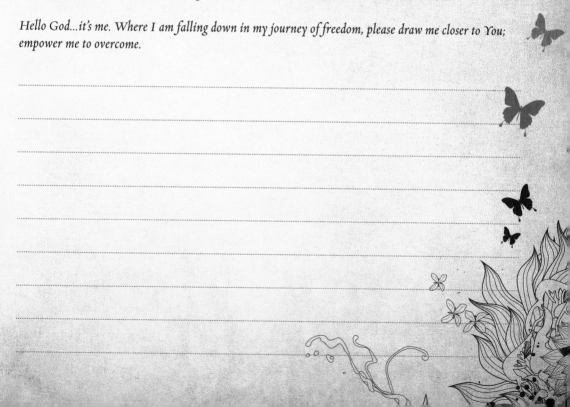

A Long Commitment

Dear friends, if we feel at ease in the presence of God, we will have the courage to come near him.
1 JOHN 3:21 CEV

Life is so temporal and fleeting. Throughout the history of humankind, we see that our lives are but a mere speck. Many spend their allotted years chasing after physical pleasures and accomplishments that neither satisfy nor leave a lasting mark.

Yet those who have faith in Christ are blessed, for we are promised eternal life. More than that, we are also promised that we will experience the very presence of Christ in our daily lives. As we continue to seek Him, He will reveal more and more of Himself to us. And if we commit ourselves to Him and His work, He will ensure that our labor on this earth will not be in vain.

So let us throw off whatever sins, habits, or other earthly barriers constrain us, and attach ourselves completely to Christ's presence. Let us seek His vision for our life, filled with love for our neighbors, service to our fellow man, and allegiance to whatever Christ lays on our hearts.

Hello God...it's me. Will You reveal to me a clearer vision for my life?

Stay Faithful

Joseph's master took him and put him in prison, the place where the king's prisoners were confined. But while Joseph was there in the prison, the LORD was with him; he showed him kindness and granted him favor in the eyes of the prison warden. So the warden put Joseph in charge of all those held in the prison, and he was made responsible for all that was done there. The warden paid no attention to anything under Joseph's care, because the LORD was with Joseph and gave him success in whatever he did.

GENESIS 39:20–23 NIV

The Bible is filled with the stories of people who remained faithful during tough times. Remember the story of Joseph in the Old Testament? From a young age Joseph knew he was special. His dad favored him above all of his brothers, and God favored him by allowing him to dream of the future. Even so, he was thrust into some truly awful circumstances.

His brothers sold him into slavery.

His boss's wife accused him of attempted rape.

He spent years in an Egyptian prison.

Yet Joseph remained faithful to God. With God's blessing, Joseph became second-in-command of all Egypt.

What are you going through today? Tough times take a lot out of us—physically, emotionally, and spiritually. At the time when bad things happen, we might not feel like God even notices. But we can follow the example of Joseph: keep dreaming and be faithful to God, even in the tough times.

Hello God...it's me. Thank You for the example of Joseph. Make me as faithful as he was in the difficulties I face.

Come and See!

Come unto me, all ye that labour and are heavy laden, and I will give you rest.
Take my yoke upon you, and learn of me; for I am meek and lowly in heart:
and ye shall find rest unto your souls. For my yoke is easy, and my burden is light.
MATTHEW 11:28–30 KJV

Once upon a time, people who wanted to cheat others by selling balms and pills that promised much but delivered little traveled alone and moved from place to place to make a dishonest living. Nowadays, they bark at us from the nearest television or Internet banner advertisement. They clamor for our attention: "Come here! You must see this!" Too often people fall for the flashy ads and spend their hard-earned money on empty promises.

Someone else in our world is calling out to us: "Come hither!" But what God promises delivers more than we can imagine. He calls us to bring our burdens to Him so that He can give us rest and peace. He promises to give us life that matters, life that works. He promises to take the bad things and turn them good. He promises to be with us now and forever.

Hello God...it's me. Thank You for Your love that calls for us to lay our burdens on You.

The Quickening

GOD, your God, will cut away the thick calluses on your heart and your children's hearts, freeing you to love God, your God, with your whole heart and soul and live, really live.
DEUTERONOMY 30:6 MSG

Guitarist Brian "Head" Welch's metal band, Korn, sold more than 35 million albums worldwide. He had the world's idea of a dream life—and thick calluses on his heart. But in time, something changed. It started with a softening—an invitation to church. Then came the quickening, then enlightenment, and then purity.

"I hit rock bottom," he has said. "I sank to the lowest gutter I could ever think of. I prayed Matthew 11:28—'*I'm* weary. *I'm* burdened. *I* need rest for my soul. Search me right now. Search my heart.' And *instantly*, I got the love from God coming into me, and then it came out of me. It was so powerful. It changed me."

He experienced a callus-cutting that frees a person to really live. "And then," said Welch, "you're exactly where you need to be. The question about life is answered."

How does God do it—reach into the heart, cut away the burden and weariness, and put in love? Only He is able. He is the Liberator who frees the whole heart to love Him.

Hello God...it's me. Thank You for Your desire and ability to touch and change my heart.

Immersed in God

Stay joined to me, and I will stay joined to you. Just as a branch cannot produce fruit unless it stays joined to the vine, you cannot produce fruit unless you stay joined to me. I am the vine, and you are the branches. If you stay joined to me, and I stay joined to you, then you will produce lots of fruit. But you cannot do anything without me.
JOHN 15:4–5 CEV

We spend a lot of time and money creating beauty for ourselves—whether through our bodies or in our surroundings. We may spend far less energy, however, on beautifying our souls. Yet that is where our beauty—or lack of it—really shines through.

You don't see your soul in the mirror, but it is hinted at there. Look deep behind the eyes; notice the expression of your mouth, the worry lines on your forehead. Those hints reveal what is happening in your soul.

Do you want a beautiful soul? Immerse yourself in the things of God. Stare at the stars. Gaze into the face of a baby. Spend a special day with a friend. Sit quietly and consider God's hand in your life. Journal your prayers. Read His Word just because. Before long, the beauty of God's handiwork within will filter outward and beautify your world.

Hello God...it's me. Let my face reflect a heart in love with You.

God Knows What He Is Doing

We know that for those who love God all things work together for good,
for those who are called according to his purpose.
ROMANS 8:28 ESV

Mourners filled the church. The casket held a young man—a man who had been devoted to God. He knew and lived the goodness of God. He demonstrated that goodness to his family, his church, his neighbors. Wherever he went, God's goodness spilled out to touch others. What was God's purpose in allowing this life to end so soon?

If you are asking God what He is doing and why, know that His Word makes His goodness plain. He has reasons we know nothing of, and a perfect plan that He brings to completion in His time.

Even in what spells tragedy to us, God can be trusted to know what He is doing. For this young man's family—and for us in our own times of trial—the days of grief will be hard, the bumps in the road will hurt, and the holes in our hearts will be vast. But the goodness of God will flow through them if we will trust in Him.

Hello God...it's me. Thank You for Your plan for my life, and Your timing for every season.

Why Pray?

Listen to my words, Lord; consider my sighing. Pay attention to the sound of my cry,
my King and my God, for I pray to You. At daybreak, Lord, You hear my voice;
at daybreak I plead my case to You and watch expectantly.
PSALM 5:1–3 HCSB

God tells us in His Word to pray about everything. Yet He already knows everything. So what is the point of prayer?

Compare it to a child who comes to a parent with a request. When we pray, we are that child—humbling ourselves before our heavenly Father, admitting our limitations, trusting His desire to provide, and acknowledging His resources.

In the process of approaching Him, in asking Him to take care of us, in making our responses known, *we* mature. We grow in our understanding of both ourselves and God. And we learn to trust as well.

God commands us to pray, and pray specifically, because He knows it is good for us. Our loving Father wants to help us mature in our faith through the spiritual discipline of prayer. He knows that prayer brings us closer to His heart.

Hello God...it's me. Thank You for all the benefits You've built into prayer that go beyond Your answer.

The Cross

Then, accompanied by the disciples, Jesus left the upstairs room and went as usual to the Mount of Olives. There he told them, "Pray that you will not give in to temptation." He walked away, about a stone's throw, and knelt down and prayed, "Father, if you are willing, please take this cup of suffering away from me. Yet I want your will to be done, not mine." Then an angel from heaven appeared and strengthened him. He prayed more fervently, and he was in such agony of spirit that his sweat fell to the ground like great drops of blood.

LUKE 22:39–44 NLT

Sharing doesn't come easily. We learn to say, "It's mine," early and then say it all too often. Even the most well-meaning Christ-followers can find their hearts hardened when someone asks for something.

What if Christ had been like that, saying no to His Father's plan for the ages? There would have been no cross—and no salvation.

But Jesus was always thinking of others, from making sure guests at the wedding in Cana had enough to drink to ensuring that Peter didn't sink into the Sea of Galilee.

The ultimate example of Christ's selflessness was Calvary, of course. The cross stands as the offer of salvation to all humanity. No one person owns it. It belongs to all.

Hello God…it's me. If I am holding something back from You, will You reveal that to me?

Resetting the Treadmill

Very early in the morning, while it was still dark, Jesus got up,
left the house and went off to a solitary place, where he prayed.
MARK 1:35 NIV

Work, school, family, community. There are some days when an underlying rhythm seems to keep it all together in a smooth flow. On other days, though, all those commitments seem to be cycling on a treadmill that speeds up with each mile we run.

Speed has become the taskmaster in this digital age. We move so fast and handle so many tasks on any given day that we hardly even notice any of our accomplishments. Worse, our connection with God starts to slip. The light of His work in our lives rushes by in an unrecognizable flash.

Still, Jesus is calling. He beckons us to a speed of His design and perfection. He invites us to reset our pace to keep Him in our line of vision, just as He did with His Father. As Jesus talked and prayed with God, He was refreshed for ministry and prepared for His Father's pace.

Take some time to refuel, refresh, and regroup today. Hit the "reset" button on your treadmill. Jesus is waiting to help you move in step with Him.

Hello God...it's me. I ask for Your help today in keeping in step with You.

The Measure of a Soul

Who is wise and understanding among you? Let him show by good conduct that his works are done in the meekness of wisdom.... For where envy and self-seeking exist, confusion and every evil thing are there. But the wisdom that is from above is first pure, then peaceable, gentle, willing to yield, full of mercy and good fruits, without partiality and without hypocrisy.

JAMES 3:13, 16–17 NKJV

The word *measure* comes from the same Latin root as our English word *moderate*. When we take our own measure, when we make a modest, honest appraisal of the state of our souls and adapt accordingly, then we walk in wisdom. That wisdom in turn leads to lasting happiness.

What if we made it a discipline to spend time before God once a week, taking the measure of our soul? What if we asked ourselves just two pointed questions—and gave ourselves and God some honest answers?

Are we truly seeking God or seeking to act like our own god?

Have we elevated people or objects above God, making them idols?

Let us resolve to be people who routinely take the measure of our souls and walk in wisdom.

Hello God...it's me. I want to worship only You. Please show me when I am elevating someone or something over You.

Risky Business

We have this treasure in jars of clay to show that this all-surpassing power is from God and not from us. We are hard pressed on every side, but not crushed; perplexed, but not in despair; persecuted, but not abandoned; struck down, but not destroyed. We always carry around in our body the death of Jesus, so that the life of Jesus may also be revealed in our body. For we who are alive are always being given over to death for Jesus' sake, so that his life may also be revealed in our mortal body.

2 CORINTHIANS 4:7–11 NIV

What do we seek most in life? Most of us want to do well—and there's certainly nothing wrong with education and honorable service and quality work and receiving kudos for those things. Few of us, however, are out trying to get scars.

This is not a call to jump into any number of extreme sports sure to give us physical scars. But it *is* a call to do something risky. It's a call to do the things that will bring glory to God, regardless of how much they might hurt.

Far too often, safety sits at the top of our priority list and hides God's agenda for our lives. God is looking for people who are willing to live dangerously and be risk takers for the honor and glory of His name.

In the end, He'll be looking for scars that show we have taken the risk to sacrifice ourselves in service to Him. What will He see on you?

Hello God...it's me. Help me to be a risk taker for Your glory.

July 16

Don't Touch That!

We know that all things work together for good to them that love God, to them who are the called according to his purpose. For whom he did foreknow, he also did predestinate to be conformed to the image of his Son, that he might be the firstborn among many brethren.
ROMANS 8:28–29 KJV

A child can be obstinate. She wants to touch the pan on the stove, but you tell her no because it's hot and it will burn her hands. As soon as you turn away, she walks back to the stove and reaches for the pan again. You remove her from the danger and discipline her, explaining that it's for her own safety and urging her to obey.

We adults aren't that different from children. We make the same mistakes over again, and we sin today in the exact way we swore we wouldn't sin yesterday. Because God knows what's best for us, He sometimes has to warn us; He sometimes has to do something forceful to get our attention. In the moment, His correction might seem "mean" to our wayward minds, but take a step back—get away from the emotion of that instant—and you'll see He was really protecting you.

Our futures are at stake, and God wants us to overcome our temptations, our failures, our straying wills so that we may wholeheartedly embrace all that He has waiting for us ahead.

Hello God...it's me. Knowing Your lovingkindness and desire for my success, I welcome Your correction.

Idle Hands

Act like people with good sense and not like fools. These are evil times,
so make every minute count. Don't be stupid. Instead, find out what the Lord wants you to do.
EPHESIANS 5:15–17 CEV

"Idle hands are the devil's workshop," our parents used to tell us when we were little and complaining of boredom. They encouraged us to find something to do or they would find something for us—which usually entailed some kind of chore. Keeping busy can be valuable, but what happens if even our busyness is no more than wasting time?

The world is filled with distractions that make us feel like our hands are anything but idle, yet we have little of value to show for it. If God didn't desire for us to relax, He would have never committed an entire day to it. However, there is also a reason that He didn't commit every day to rest. We must continually remind ourselves that the time we have in this world is limited. Of course we can rest and have fun, but we must beware of wasting too much of that precious resource that God has granted us.

Hello God...it's me. Will You help me to use my time wisely today?

July 18

Home

These all died in faith, not having received the things promised, but having seen them and greeted them from afar, and having acknowledged that they were strangers and exiles on the earth. For people who speak thus make it clear that they are seeking a homeland. If they had been thinking of that land from which they had gone out, they would have had opportunity to return. But as it is, they desire a better country, that is, a heavenly one. Therefore God is not ashamed to be called their God, for he has prepared for them a city.

HEBREWS 11:13–16 ESV

Home. Often the word invokes images of smiles and warmth, of acceptance and love. Home is where we come after a long day in the work world. Home is where students come after a long day at school. We still may have a home to return to even after we've grown up and moved away and made our own homes in other places. Home is where we are able to be who we are and know that we will be loved anyway.

As wonderful as our home is, as believers we look forward to something better—heaven itself, our eternal home. We haven't yet been there, and we can't even really imagine what it will be like. But something deep inside tells us that heaven will be perfect because our God who loves us is preparing a place for us there. He invites us to join Him in this eternal home so that we can be with Him always—accepted, loved, and perfect.

Hello God...it's me. I want You to know how much I am looking forward to spending eternity with You. I know You are looking forward to it, too.

The Light of the World

The true light that gives light to every man was coming into the world.
JOHN 1:9 NIV

Twilight. The French call it *l'heure bleue*—the "blue hour"—that brief and magical interlude when it's neither day nor night, when the sky is neither completely lit nor completely dark. It is the ambience of painters and photographers. But that diffused light also obscures reality. It's vague, dim, uncertain. You can misread the signs and turn down the wrong street—a dangerous street. You can easily be deceived.

The apostle John lived in the twilight years after Jesus's death. Jerusalem had fallen to the Romans. Uncertainty was rampant. But Christ struck a match that would not go out. So John began his 823,000-word argument that Jesus is the true light—the eminent and excellent light that pierced the darkness from the beginning of time, the light that eradicates ambiguity and ignorance and deception. The only light.

Jesus borrows His shining glory from neither dusk nor dawn, neither man nor angel. He is the Light of the world. Bask in Him.

Hello God...it's me. Thank You for inviting me to You, the Light of the world. You have changed everything for me.

On the Wings of Love

With good will render service, as to the Lord, and not to men, knowing that whatever good thing each one does, this he will receive back from the Lord, whether slave or free.
EPHESIANS 6:7–8 NASB

"Slaves, obey your masters." We read that Bible verse and our eyes skim over it. *That doesn't apply to me; I'm not a slave,* you might think. Let's not miss the wisdom and the truth found in this verse. While we may not be slaves, we still have people in our lives whom we can, and should, work to please.

Do you report to a demanding superior? Respect his place of authority over you and submit willingly. Do you have an unbelieving spouse? Serve him wholeheartedly, as if you were serving the Lord. Do you volunteer on committees or ministries under challenging leaders? Work with diligence and integrity whether they are watching or not.

Our love for Jesus should be more than a private experience, held tightly to our breast. Let your love for Jesus take flight on the wings of respect and honor, service and love, sincerity and integrity toward all those who are in authority over you. Through your actions, they may see the light of Christ in you and come to know Jesus, the One who has all authority in heaven and earth.

Hello God...it's me. When I am annoyed or tempted to react in a way that dishonors You, will You take my hand and lead me the other direction?

Sweet and Tender Love

Lord, Your faithful love reaches to heaven, Your faithfulness to the clouds.
Your righteousness is like the highest mountains; Your judgments, like the deepest sea. Lord,
You preserve man and beast. God, Your faithful love is so valuable that people take refuge
in the shadow of Your wings. They are filled from the abundance of Your house; You let them drink
from Your refreshing stream, for with You is life's fountain. In Your light we will see light.
Psalm 36:5–9 HCSB

How do we know that God loves us—really? At times we may wonder. We look around at a suffering world and question if God really cares. We face moments of frustration and doubt if God really loves us. When we deal with times of intense grief, we wonder if God notices. But when the days are light and happy we think, *Ah yes! Now I know God loves me.*

God loves us as deeply in the times of hurt and pain and suffering as He does in the good days. He is always present, never changing, always constant. As mere human beings, we have a limited perspective and cannot begin to understand the sweet and tender love that God has for us.

Whether we feel it or not, God loves us. Whether we understand it or not, God loves us. Whether we return it or not, God loves us.

Today feel it, sense it, know it—God's sweet and tender love for you.

Hello God...it's me. Creator of my heart, could you help me feel more of Your love today?

The Shade of the Cross

Then [Jesus] said unto them, Yet a little while is the light with you.
Walk while ye have the light.
JOHN 12:35 KJV

What a delight it is on a blistering hot day to sink beneath the spreading limbs of a tree and partake of its shade. Under the shadow of the tree's branches, we are physically refreshed by the cooler temperature and protection from the sun's hot rays.

We can also find spiritual relief beneath the spreading limbs of another tree. This tree is the cross—the ultimate heat blocker. The shade of the cross guards us from the scorching winds of the world and its false pleasures that lure us off God's chosen path and beckon us toward the destructive fire of judgment.

Just before His crucifixion, Jesus reminded His disciples that His death on the cross would draw people to Him. Through His death, Jesus promised that He would supply the ultimate rest for our souls—the power to overcome temptation.

Are you feeling the heat today? Come into the shade of the cross and be eternally refreshed in His presence.

Hello God...it's me. I just want You to know that I love the fact that You are concerned about my rest.

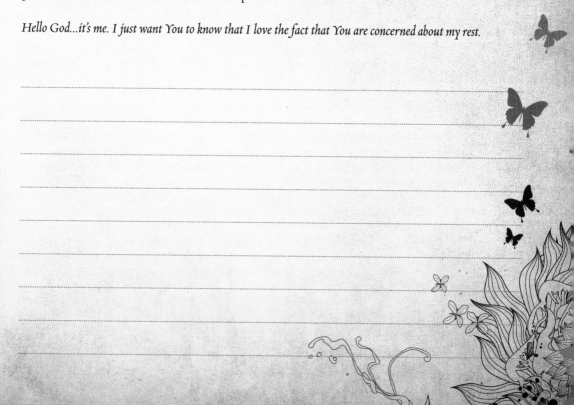

Thank God for the Cross

*So Jesus, knowing all the things that were coming upon Him, went forth and said to them,
"Whom do you seek?" They answered Him, "Jesus the Nazarene." He said to them, "I am He."
And Judas also, who was betraying Him, was standing with them.*
JOHN 18: 4–5 NASB

We need only read slowly and carefully the familiar accounts of Christ's crucifixion in the four Gospels to be overwhelmed by His sacrifice for us. He was innocent of all crimes, yet fake charges were leveled against Him and false witnesses lied about Him. A lead-tipped whip tore apart His back. A crown of long, sharp thorns was crushed into His scalp. A heavy cross was placed on His shredded back to carry to His own crucifixion. Nails dug into His wrists and feet.

Didn't the Jews know that this was their promised Messiah? Didn't the soldiers recognize that this was no ordinary man? Obviously not. But Jesus, knowing who He was and why He came, willingly submitted to all of the torture. He suffered and died and conquered death so that we too could have the final victory.

Hello God...it's me. How can I thank You enough for all the pain that You endured for me?

The Pursuit

*[Jesus] said to him, "You shall love the Lord your God with all your heart
and with all your soul and with all your mind. This is the great and first commandment."*
MATTHEW 22:37–38 ESV

God says to us, "Seek My kingdom first." It is a command that affects every detail of the day, and those who respond obediently are blessed. But more often than not, we reply, "I'm tired." "Maybe later." "Can't it wait?"

Yet there is hope for us if we will invest ourselves in this most important of pursuits. Seek His kingdom first. How? By unrelentingly pursuing God. Read what He has written in the Scriptures. Doggedly press into each verse and ask, "What is God telling me? How should I respond?" Tenaciously look for God in His creation, in your trials, in the faces of those He would have you love today.

Do you pursue God with all your heart? With all your soul? With all your mind? Following hard after God is the pursuit of a lifetime. Make it your primary one.

Hello God...it's me. Will You show me what seeking first Your kingdom looks like in my day today?

Answering God's Call

Therefore, since we are surrounded by such a huge crowd of witnesses to the life of faith, let us strip off every weight that slows us down.... And let us run with endurance the race God has set before us. We do this by keeping our eyes on Jesus, the champion who initiates and perfects our faith.

HEBREWS 12:1–2 NLT

How often, within the first few minutes of meeting someone, have you been asked, "What kind of work do you do?" It's not surprising, really, since in our culture, a person's work is closely tied to their identity.

However, the definition of *vocation* is "a calling"—something well beyond just a job. While God clearly designed us with abilities and interests that help us flourish in certain lines of work, we must not lose sight of the fact that answering His call is far more than finding the right career. Answering God's call means saying yes to His offer of salvation and then investing all that we are, all that we do, and all that we have in living each day for Him.

That calling gives purpose and meaning to life. *That* calling answers all the whys of our existence—and even gives us a reason for getting up and going to work each day.

How will you answer God's call today?

Hello God...it's me. Thank You for Your full investment in me. Help me to invest everything I am in You.

Light in Dark Tunnels

For You will light my lamp; the LORD my God will enlighten my darkness.
For by You I can run against a troop, by my God I can leap over a wall.
PSALM 18:28–29 NKJV

Imagine walking down the stairs into a windowless basement after a storm has knocked out the electricity. You see shadows and hear noises you can't identify—at least until you flip on a flashlight.

We feel much this way when we encounter times of darkness in our lives. Chronic illness, broken relationships, unemployment—everything seems confusing. Is there anything to do but just huddle in the dark, asking God why we are there and begging Him to get us out?

Yes. Look to Him as your Light. Seek His face and let Him guide your steps.

Remember, God knows about each situation in your life. He has promised to be your constant Light, dispelling the shadows and leading you through the frightening places, one step at a time. You can walk confidently through the darkness because He is your trustworthy guide. There's no need to despair, because nothing is too dark for God. He is with you, and He knows the way through.

Hello God...it's me. Today I will seek Your face to receive Your guidance.

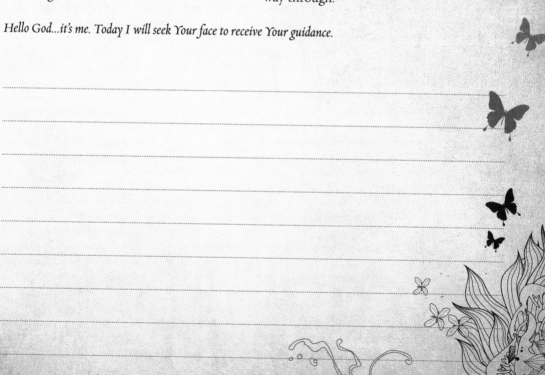

Anything, Anyone, Anytime

I am sending you to Pharaoh. You must lead my people Israel out of Egypt."
But Moses protested to God, "Who am I to appear before Pharaoh?
Who am I to lead the people of Israel out of Egypt?" God answered, "I will be with you."
EXODUS 3:10–12 NLT

You may be a lover, not a fighter. But chances are you've still resorted to "boxing"— that familiar tendency to put others in a box: *I can't visit that church member in the hospital; that's the pastor's responsibility. Why pick up my mess in the church? The janitor gets paid to do it. I'm not going to serve on the worship team; that's the music minister's job.*

We miss so much when we put limitations on ourselves or other members of the body of Christ. But we especially miss out when we try to limit God Himself. God can work through anything or anyone at any time. Remember Balaam's donkey? It spoke words of warning. Remember Moses? God called him from a burning bush. Remember Daniel? God shut the lions' mouths. Remember the earthquake that freed Paul from prison? God did that too.

Fortunately, God will not be put in a box. Trust Him to do the impossible, even with you. He may just break you out of your own box even as He is breaking free of the one you've put Him in.

Hello God...it's me. Thank You for the unique way You relate to each one of us.

The Miracle of Second Birth

Flesh gives birth to flesh, but the Spirit gives birth to spirit.
JOHN 3:6 NIV

The biological mechanisms by which pregnancy takes place make conception a marvelous thing to consider. Life begins when one microscopic sperm cell from a man takes a perfectly unobstructed path during a specific window of time and fertilizes one tiny egg inside a woman's fallopian tubes. The newly formed embryo is then transported into the woman's uterus, demanding precise movements inside her that she cannot dictate. Then, the woman's womb must be receptive to the embryo that has worked so hard to arrive there.

And that is just the beginning. After all of this comes nine equally amazing months of pregnancy, then the birth!

The Bible says that those who believe in the name of the Son of God will experience spiritual birth. Jesus did more than we could imagine to make new birth possible, some of which we know and some of which we do not. But Jesus did all the work, then preserved in writing what was necessary for us to believe. And in believing, we have life—wonderful spiritual life in Christ.

Hello God...it's me. Thank You for Your miraculous power in making us brand new in You.

Our Uncontainable God

*The God who made the world and everything in it is the Lord of heaven and earth
and does not live in temples built by human hands. And he is not served by human hands,
as if he needed anything. Rather, he himself gives everyone life and breath and everything else.*
ACTS 17:24–25 NIV

For centuries there has been an ongoing debate over God versus science, as if they were mutually exclusive. Three hundred years before Jesus, the Epicureans held that matter was eternal and that the world was formed by a fortuitous concourse of atoms. And as recently as this decade, physicists have formulated the M-theory, to describe the behavior of fundamental particles and force, and to even account for the very birth of the universe.

There is nothing new under the sun when it comes to the debate. If the Lord of the heavens and the earth could be put in a test tube—or a temple—then He would not be God.

Why do we think we can contain God? It's possible to harness the wind for power or the sun's rays for energy, but we cannot isolate, control, or make God dependent on our definition of Him.

We are finite creatures. We cannot explain God, but we can marvel at the wonder of His great and astonishing power. A power that leaves man's understanding in the dust.

Hello God...it's me. I love that You are greater than my understanding.

A Rich Feast

*Since we're free in the freedom of God, can we do anything that comes to mind? Hardly.
You know well enough from your own experience that there are some acts of so-called freedom
that destroy freedom. Offer yourselves to sin, for instance, and it's your last free act.
But offer yourselves to the ways of God and the freedom never quits*

ROMANS 6:15–16 MSG

Do you find yourself settling for scraps, like scavenging birds on the beach? Or have you pursued the deeper delights of intimate relationship with Jesus Christ? The gift of grace remains free and available to all who come, but its price is beyond what anyone could pay.

In the freedom we are given to fail, God's grace also grants us forgiveness. But receiving this gift with a relaxed attitude toward sin demonstrates little appreciation for the price Jesus paid to make reconciliation possible.

While enjoying the gift of grace today, consider the cost of your forgiveness. Allow this understanding to prompt a deeper commitment to following Jesus, who makes grace free.

Hello God...it's me. I want You to know that I don't take for granted the price You paid for my forgiveness.

Giving Him Our All

"After a long time the master of those servants returned and settled accounts with them. The man who had received five bags of gold brought the other five. 'Master,' he said, 'you entrusted me with five bags of gold. See, I have gained five more.' His master replied, 'Well done, good and faithful servant! You have been faithful with a few things; I will put you in charge of many things. Come and share your master's happiness!'"
MATTHEW 25:19–21 NIV

Perhaps one of the most difficult lessons of the Christian faith is that this life is temporary, yet what we do in it has eternal consequences. Jesus said, "For whoever desires to save his life will lose it, but whoever loses his life for My sake will find it" (Matthew 16:25 NKJV). Scripture is full of examples of this. The same principle holds true when it comes to how we treat others and what we give them spiritually.

We have been blessed with an eternal reward far outweighing what we deserve—our salvation in Christ. By giving away the love and care that Christ has given us, we know that our efforts will not only have consequences on this planet but will also have eternal results. Giving Him our lives and our passions ensures that they will be used for greater gain.

Let's be eager to share what we have been given, knowing that Christ has greater plans for it than we could ever imagine.

Hello God...it's me. Help me to continually be eager to share what You've given me, even when I can't see the bigger picture that You have planned.

Mine!

So then faith comes by hearing, and hearing by the word of God.
ROMANS 10:17 NKJV

One of the first words a child learns to say is "Mine!" At an early age, we greedily hold on to toys and treasures that we want to keep all to ourselves. And we never outgrow our desire to claim what's ours. We jealously guard our family time or our leisure time. We keep a tight grip on our possessions. We hold our wallets close when churches and charities make appeals.

This tendency to mark what's ours sometimes extends to faith. We talk about owning our faith. But faith is a gift from God just as life itself is. As the apostle Paul explains, our faith comes through hearing the Word of the Lord.

Romans 10:17 and Ephesians 2:8 remind us that salvation is a gift offered to us from God. Through the acceptance of this gift, God looks at you and says, "Mine."

When you belong to God, everything you have is His: your possessions, your time, yourself. Why not offer all to God today?

Hello God...it's me. Thank You for Your desire to call me Your own. Everything I have is Yours.

A Life of Purpose

For everything there is a season, and a time for every matter under heaven....
What gain has the worker from his toil? I have seen the business that God has given
to the children of man to be busy with. He has made everything beautiful in its time.
ECCLESIASTES 3:1, 9–11 ESV

As a teenager, you decide you want to go to college. So in high school, you get a part-time job in a fast-food restaurant and make the best grades you can to help you get into and pay for your college tuition. When you are accepted into college, you study hard to achieve the best university grades and take every opportunity to add to your résumé so that you can be hired for your dream job. Finally in your desired career, you work up the ladder to better positions and more pay to put away for retirement. You work your whole life so you can eventually stop working and end your days in relaxation.

If this is life, what's the point?

With God, life has purpose. You are on an adventure and a mission. Looking through the lenses of your spiritual life, you have the privilege of being able to see your life the way God does and discovering how He makes everything in your life work together for His purpose.

Hello God...it's me. I will go to You for guidance in all my choices in my life. I want Your adventure!

Letting Go of the Grudge

Thou shalt not avenge, nor bear any grudge against the children of thy people,
but thou shalt love thy neighbour as thyself: I am the LORD.
LEVITICUS 19:18 KJV

You spent hours painstakingly painting those stripes in the kitchen. In your eyes, the wall looked perfect—even stripes, straight lines, and subtle color changes. However, your spouse and others in the family didn't agree. When our efforts are rejected by others—whether in something minor, like painting a wall, or something much more significant—disappointment and frustration well up within us. It's easy to feel misunderstood, inconvenienced, or insulted.

Holding on to those feelings sets the table for "grudge soup" in our soul as heavy as the soup's hot iron pot. And the longer we let the soup simmer, the heavier and hotter that pot gets.

We don't have to hold on, though. Give your grudges to God today. He can handle the weight and the heat. And then let Him pour soothing balm over those tired hands. Let Him fill your heart with a new, savory meal of grace and forgiveness that nourishes you and others.

Hello God...it's me. Search my heart for any grudges I am holding that I am not aware of. I want to give those to You.

Radical Love

You have heard the law that says, "Love your neighbor" and hate your enemy. But I say, love your enemies! Pray for those who persecute you! In that way, you will be acting as true children of your Father in heaven.
MATTHEW 5: 43–45 NLT

If you've made up with a friend or family member after a heated argument, you know the blessing of reconciliation. But consider the challenge of being reconciled to an enemy. Getting over the hump of hatred or misunderstanding would take a radical love—the kind of love only God has. While we were still His enemies, He took upon Himself the impossible burden of reconciling us to Himself through Jesus's death. Not content to merely leave us His "non-enemies," God also adopted us as His children.

There's always room for one more child in God's family. All He asks is that we open our hearts to allow for an outpouring of His radical love. His is the kind of radical love that doesn't play favorites and never denies admission to anyone—even to those who hurt Him.

When you were most in need of love, God offered it. Are you willing to do the same for someone else today?

Hello God...it's me. Today, will You help me to show Your love to someone who needs it?

Eye of the Beholder

Aren't five sparrows sold for two pennies? Yet not one of them is forgotten in God's sight.
Indeed, the hairs of your head are all counted. Don't be afraid; you are worth more than many sparrows!
LUKE 12:6–7 HCSB

Flying high above the clouds in a passenger jet makes it possible to see mountain ranges, large cities, and a patchwork quilt of countryside farmlands. From thirty-five thousand feet we can barely make out the colors of the landscape, much less the details of individual people. And if that's the view through a tiny airplane window, imagine what God's view of the entire earth must be like!

Kind of a simplistic view of God, isn't it? We have a picture in our mind's eye of God looking down on humanity from lofty heights. But the reality is that God is always in our midst. Unlike the limited perspective from the windows of a 747, God's view of each one of us is unobstructed, clear, and deeply personal.

To God, we are not insignificant dots in a faraway landscape. We are His sons and daughters. Take the time today to thank Him for His personal involvement in your life.

Hello God...it's me. Thank You for sitting enthroned above the earth, and yet knowing every detail about me.

A Beggar's Kingdom

I promise you this. If you don't change and become like a child, you will never get into the kingdom of heaven. But if you are as humble as this child, you are the greatest in the kingdom of heaven. And when you welcome one of these children because of me, you welcome me.

MATTHEW 18:3–5 CEV

Everywhere you look, people are busy trying to build their own "kingdoms" of power and influence. They strive and sacrifice to make a name for themselves. Desperate to prove their independence, these men and women exhaust themselves chasing worldly success and self-sufficiency.

Yet even seemingly noble intentions reflect insidious pride. God offers us so much more than the delusion of success—He offers His kingdom, on His terms. We must come helpless and humble, knowing that we cannot gain His kingdom on our own; we only obtain it when we humbly accept Christ's love and sacrifice on our behalf. We come as beggars, and then we are given an esteemed place in God's kingdom as His adopted children.

Don't be too proud to accept God's charity. Only when we become beggars will we experience the riches of God's grace.

Hello God...it's me. I come to You humbly, recognizing my own helplessness, ready to receive from You today.

Time for Change

One day when large groups of people were walking along with him, Jesus turned and told them, "Anyone who comes to me but refuses to let go of father, mother, spouse, children, brothers, sisters—yes, even one's own self!—can't be my disciple. Anyone who won't shoulder his own cross and follow behind me can't be my disciple."

LUKE 14:25–27 MSG

Choosing to follow Jesus Christ doesn't mean that your life will be free from trials; it means pursuing Him no matter what trials you encounter. Our greatest heroes of the faith were men and women who suffered as they served God. Why do we think Jesus's call to carry our cross daily has changed?

Jesus said that in this world we will have trouble. We can let the struggles of this life cause us to get angry and sulk. Or we can pursue God in the midst of our trials, asking Him to help us endure them faithfully.

We might still find this life full of thistles and thorns, but if we are God's servants, the Holy Spirit will bring us through it. He will help us change those trials to become God's tools to do work beyond what we can imagine.

Hello God...it's me. I acknowledge and look to Your strength today to overcome.

Loosen Your Grip

Blessed are your eyes because they see, and your ears because they hear.
For truly I tell you, many prophets and righteous people longed to see what you see
but did not see it, and to hear what you hear but did not hear it.
MATTHEW 13:16–17 NIV

Do you cling to the God you've always known? Maybe He's the God your parents and Sunday school teachers taught you about when you were young. He might be the very same God you trusted for salvation at a tender age. You are comfortable with this God and the ways He speaks. Being grounded in the knowledge of such a personal God is likely the best blessing you have been given. But if your understanding of God remains the same throughout your life, your growth will be stunted.

God never changes. His attributes remain exactly the same in proportion and number for all eternity. But to a soul open to deeper understanding, God reveals more of Himself. Where is He working that broadens your understanding of Him? Look, see, and understand that He is much more than you can comprehend. You will never reach the end of knowing Him.

Hello God...it's me. I ask that You reveal Yourself to me today in a new way.

Unlimited Access

Having therefore, brethren, boldness to enter into the holiest by the blood of Jesus, by a new and living way, which he hath consecrated for us, through the veil, that is to say, his flesh; and having an high priest over the house of God; let us draw near with a true heart in full assurance of faith, having our hearts sprinkled from an evil conscience, and our bodies washed with pure water.
HEBREWS 10:19–22 KJV

In the Old Testament, the curtain in the temple prevented God's people from seeing into the Most Holy Place where His presence dwelt. But the New Testament records that when Jesus died on the cross, the curtain ripped in two, signifying our unlimited access to God through Christ.

You may easily assent to this amazing truth—you may even get it intellectually—but do you act on it? Do you enter God's presence throughout your day? Do you see Him, know Him, live with Him ever in your midst? Or do you hang your own curtain that prevents you from enjoying Him?

Perhaps we have allowed our self-focus to become a barrier that keeps us from God. It's possible to even become too self-sufficient to want to be with God—or too full of self-pity.

God wants us to see Him and live with Him and draw life from His smile. Look up. Because that curtain was torn by Jesus, you can see God smiling.

Hello God...it's me. Will You show me when I am starting to take my eyes off You and help me move my heart closer to Yours?

Pop Quiz

Now the deeds of the flesh are evident, which are: immorality, impurity, sensuality, idolatry, sorcery, enmities, strife, jealousy, outbursts of anger, disputes, dissensions, factions, envying, drunkenness, carousing, and things like these, of which I forewarn you, just as I have forewarned you, that those who practice such things will not inherit the kingdom of God. But the fruit of the Spirit is love, joy, peace, patience, kindness, goodness, faithfulness, gentleness, self-control; against such things there is no law.
GALATIANS 5:19–23 NASB

A car cuts you off and you miss your exit. You will be late for your job interview. You finally arrive and rush up the elevator, only to realize you left your résumé at home. Someone in your small group gossiped, telling your embarrassing struggle to close friends.

Your in-laws gave you money for your birthday. You buy something special with it, only to find that your check for the water bill has bounced, and the bank fees leave you with nothing for groceries.

Time to sing the blues, or time to trust the Lord? You know the *right answer* is to trust Him through it all. God may be using this test to find out whether you love Him more than your friends, your job opportunity, or your bottom line. It is in this moment—during the test—that we find out what's in our hearts.

What's in yours?

Hello God...it's me. Will You help me to trust Your control when I'm feeling stressed today?

Standing Firm in the Storm

Likewise the Spirit helps us in our weakness. For we do not know what to pray for as we ought, but the Spirit himself intercedes for us with groanings too deep for words. And he who searches hearts knows what is the mind of the Spirit, because the Spirit intercedes for the saints according to the will of God.
ROMANS 8:26 –27 ESV

In the middle of a storm, the weeping willow sways instead of snapping. As raindrops puddle at the base of its trunk, the tree absorbs the water and stands strong.

At times, the force of the storm threatens to overcome us. When we are diagnosed with cancer, we lose a job, or a friendship ends, we often ask, "Why me?" instead of "Why *not* me?" In those moments, we may not be able to see how we'll ever keep from breaking. After all, the winds and the rain are so strong.... But God is greater, and He knows. He will be our stronghold.

God wants to work in you and your circumstances today. You may not understand the forces you're up against, but you can trust in His sovereignty. Believe in His omnipotence. Look expectantly for His faithfulness. He is holding you up.

Hello God...it's me. Today, I anticipate Your faithfulness and trust that Your arms are always beneath me.

Do You Have the Time?

I pray that the perception of your mind may be enlightened so you may know what is the hope of His calling, what are the glorious riches of His inheritance among the saints, and what is the immeasurable greatness of His power to us who believe, according to the working of His vast strength.

EPHESIANS 1:18–19 HCSB

Do you want to spend more time with God? Perhaps you want to read your Bible and pray, but you're just too busy. An old song by Harry Chapin laments how the busyness of a father keeps him from spending time with his son. When the father is older and regretting lost time, he attempts to make up for it by spending time with his adult son. But his son has no time to give. He's simply too busy.

Our heavenly Father is always there for us whenever we call on Him. He's even there watching over us when our lives are so busy we don't have time to think!

Make time for God today and every day. Spend time in prayer, in praise, in person with Him. Don't come to the end of your life full of regret that you could have spent more time learning, growing, and sharing God's love.

Hello God...it's me. Slow me down today so I can give You the priority that You deserve.

Greater Than Glory

This is how God showed his love among us: He sent his one and only Son into the world that we might live through him. This is love: not that we loved God, but that he loved us and sent his Son as an atoning sacrifice for our sins. Dear friends, since God so loved us, we also ought to love one another.

1 JOHN 4:9–11 NIV

Our God is too great for us to imagine. His majesty and power surpass our understanding. How can we, as limited as we are, possibly understand the glory of a deity who creates solar systems with nothing but a word?

Yet there is an even deeper aspect to God—a marvelous impossibility that confounds our attempts to explain it. Why would the Creator of the universe shed His glory and be born into squalor? What could possibly drive Him to become obedient to death?

It is the same thing that drives a mother to drop everything for the sake of her child, the same strength that compels a man to take a bullet for his friend. Why is God's greatest glory shown in His willingness to save us? Because there is only one thing as great as God's glory: His infinite, all-expansive, uncontainable love.

Hello God...it's me. Will You fill me with Your self-sacrificing love today, so I may show my loved ones and others what You are like?

Individual Preferences

By faith Abel offered to God a more acceptable sacrifice than Cain, through which
he was commended as righteous, God commending him by accepting his gifts.
And through his faith, though he died, he still speaks.
HEBREWS 11:4 ESV

Ask college students how they ended up attending their school, and you'll receive a variety of responses. Some students will say their parents graduated from there. Some will say they followed siblings or sweethearts. Others will talk about scholarships or desired fields of study.

Similarly, Christians have a variety of preferences for forms of worship and ministry. Some people like the worship style of their parents' congregation, while others prefer more modern music. Some serve God in simple, everyday acts of service, while others serve God in more visible, exciting ways.

Trying to force our modes of worship and preferences of ministry on others will only backfire. Traditional hymns may be used to worship God, and Christian rock may stir others to worship God as well. Private devotional time may be one person's favorite time of the day, whereas another may look forward to preaching or leading a group Bible study.

As long as God is the focus for worship that is in spirit and truth, that's all that counts.

Hello God...it's me. Thank You for being a God who is pleased with more than one form of worship.

August 15

Self-Surrender

If then you were raised with Christ, seek those things which are above, where Christ is, sitting at the right hand of God. Set your mind on things above, not on things on the earth. For you died, and your life is hidden with Christ in God. When Christ who is our life appears, then you also will appear with Him in glory.

COLOSSIANS 3:1–4 NKJV

Jesus wants every piece of us. He doesn't merely want our good deeds here or there. He wants more than our weekly church attendance and spotty prayer life. He wants every ounce of us—not only our outward actions but also our inner being with all of its desires, thoughts, and dreams.

The marathon runner decides every morning to get up, lace well-worn shoes, and open the door for yet another run. He puts aside his desire for another hour of sleep and stays focused on his goal. He receives a reward for those daily decisions when he crosses the finish line ahead of those who decided to take a day off and sleep in.

Giving up control of self requires a conscious decision each morning. As we give Christ control of our lives, He kills our natural self and replaces it with His life.

When that last piece of self is handed over in surrender to Christ, you will be living a new life, the best life ever.

Hello God...it's me. Will You help me surrender myself to You in my daily decisions today?

The Holy Spirit's Care for Us

The Spirit Himself testifies with our spirit that we are children of God, and if children, heirs also, heirs of God and fellow heirs with Christ, if indeed we suffer with Him so that we may also be glorified with Him.
ROMANS 8:16–17 NASB

All of us experience periods of difficulty and pain in our lives—times when we wonder what God has in store for us. These times can also feel particularly lonely, as we seem to struggle by ourselves to determine the path God has prepared for us.

Yet in these painful times, as well as during periods of comfort and satisfaction, we must never forget that the Holy Spirit continues to indwell our hearts. He lives in us as One who cares deeply about everything in our lives.

His indwelling serves an eternal purpose, as well. For at all times in our lives, the infinite Holy Spirit is guiding us, caring for us, and ultimately deepening our connection to Him as our physical bodies become His holy temple.

Don't underestimate the refining and care the Holy Spirit is undertaking in your daily life. Know that His ceaseless love is unmatched, and He will never leave His people.

Hello God...it's me. Thank You for Your constant care for me, that Your refining work in me continues even today.

August 17

Why We Pray

Commit thy way unto the Lord; trust also in him; and he shall bring it to pass.
Psalm 37:5 KJV

What benefit is there in presenting requests to a God who already knows the future? If He knows all things and can do all things, doesn't He have an answer before the words even leave our lips?

We pray not because prayer changes our circumstances, but because it changes our plea. As we plead with the Judge, the relationship becomes personal. He works out our circumstances in other matters and we draw closer to Him, thankful for His wisdom and provision. As we pray and seek Him, the Judge becomes our Friend.

The fires of waiting refine our prayers even further. We pour out our hearts to God and He encourages us, comforts us, and teaches us. Our friendship with Him deepens and strengthens. We begin to understand Him so well that we know His desires in general— and for us, specifically.

The more we pray, the more our prayer requests change. Once we wanted what *we* wanted, now we want what *God* wants for us. Our childish desires now echo the will of our Father in heaven.

Hello God...it's me. Thank You for changing me through my very words to You.

The Word

*The word of God is living and active and sharper than any two-edged sword, and piercing
as far as the division of soul and spirit, of both joints and marrow, and able to judge the thoughts
and intentions of the heart. And there is no creature hidden from His sight,
but all things are open and laid bare to the eyes of Him with whom we have to do.*

HEBREWS 4:12–13 NASB

The Bible is often called the Word of God because it is God's words to us. So often people cast about wishing that God would tell them what to do, looking for a sign in the sky, wanting God to speak to them, complaining that God is so unknown and unknowable. All the while, however, they have access to everything God wanted to say to us, neatly packaged in His Word.

The Bible is God's full revelation to us, telling us everything we need to know to live this life and to have access to heaven in the next. God's Word tells us what the problem is (sin) and how God dealt with it (sending His Son). It tells us how to respond to God's gift of salvation and how to live in ways that will please and honor Him.

When we read the Word of God, we hear His words to us. It's really just that simple—and that astounding!

Hello God...it's me. I want You to know how grateful I am for Your Word.

The Ultimate Walking Partner

I sought the LORD, and he answered me and delivered me from all my fears.
Those who look to him are radiant, and their faces shall never be ashamed.
PSALM 34:4–5 ESV

You were expecting to receive empathy and comfort, but instead you heard laughter. Now you want to run and hide. It seemed like a safe moment to share your fears. You thought others could relate and even offer support. Instead, your heart was trampled by ridicule, and embarrassment reddened your face.

Turn to the Lord. Without laughing or smirking, He always listens as you tell Him your deepest fears. He knows what you are going through. He has experienced it all— dusty roads stung His eyes, those closest to Him rejected Him, and spasms of pain shook His body. In His humanity He relates to what we're going through, and in His divinity He offers us the ultimate comfort.

When uneven terrain makes us wobbly, He steadies us. Against relentless winds, He helps us stand firm. And in the face of a steep path that looks insurmountable, He gives expert guidance. Take your fears to God today. Invite Him to help you find a way through them. He's ready to walk with you.

Hello God...it's me. I accept Your hand today, ready to walk through the day with You.

What the World Needs

Love does no harm to a neighbor; therefore love is the fulfillment of the law.
ROMANS 13:10 NKJV

Over and over again, Scripture presents flesh-and-blood characters essentially asking, "What's the meaning of life?" That's also the question that most of humanity has been asking since the dawn of time. To that universal question, Jesus responded by calling people to love God and to love their neighbors as they love themselves. And Romans 13:10 is another reminder of the answer to mankind's question: *love* is the meaning of life.

What may not be apparent, however, is that love involves more than being devoted to the holy but unseen God. It involves caring for our neighbors too (read: family, coworkers, church members, neighbors, other team parents, etc.)—even the ones who are hard to like. Thankfully, God's Spirit in us and with us is a transforming presence: He enables us to love with God's love, to treat people the way we want to be treated, and to extend mercy in the same way that God has been merciful to us. We fulfill all of the Old Testament law when we love the way He loves us.

Hello God...it's me. Thank You for Your transforming presence in me, enabling me to love with Your love.

The Future Is Now

Because Jesus was raised from the dead, we've been given a brand-new life and have everything to live for, including a future in heaven—and the future starts now!
I PETER I: 3–4 MSG

"We talk about heaven being so far away," said Dwight L. Moody. "It is within speaking distance to those who belong there."

The future starts now. *Now.* It's not speculative. It's not an empty promise. It's a daily, powerful, *living* hope that became active at the moment of Christ's resurrection.

God loves His people and has given us life. When the world seemed cold and broken, our faithful God sent the promised Savior to redeem it. When Jesus left for His heavenly throne, He sent the compassionate Holy Spirit to restore it. The Holy Spirit whispered His Word to His scribes to constantly renew it.

The Father is in the business of redeeming, restoring, renewing *everything* until it is healed and whole. It's proof of His abiding love.

Yes—a future in God's brilliant heaven is worth living for. But the future is now. Embrace the hope. Live it now.

Hello God...it's me. Thank You for the healing and restoration that You breathe into me even this side of heaven.

Anchored

He said to me, "My grace is sufficient for you, for my power is made perfect in weakness. " Therefore I will boast all the more gladly about my weaknesses, so that Christ's power may rest on me. That is why, for Christ's sake, I delight in weaknesses, in insults, in hardships, in persecutions, in difficulties. For when I am weak, then I am strong.

2 CORINTHIANS 12:9–10 NIV

A flash of lightning and a clap of thunder announce the beginning of a storm. A boat far from shore drops its anchor and waits. Winds howl; waves roar and rise as the storm intensifies. More clouds roll in. The sky grows darker with the sun hidden. The wind and the waves attack the boat, and it rocks back and forth, as if to be torn apart by the elements. But the anchor rests safely beneath the surface, far below the rough waves. It holds the boat in place, stabilizing it in the storm, keeping it secure.

When we face life's storms, however bleak and rocky, we must place our trust in God and make Him our anchor. He has not promised a life free from storms or problems or questions. But He has promised us that He will go with us.

So in life's storms, let's cling to the anchor of God's abiding presence to stay afloat and remain secure in Him.

Hello God...it's me. Thank You for the promise of Your steadfast presence with me today.

Making Our "for Instances" for Real

"Either make the tree good and its fruit good, or else make the tree bad and its fruit bad;
for a tree is known by its fruit.... For out of the abundance of the heart the mouth speaks."
MATTHEW 12:33–34 NKJV

"Do what I say, not what I do" may work for earthly fathers, but it won't fly with the heavenly Father. With Him, our words must always be congruent with our behavior. Otherwise, they are just useless chatter.

But when our advice matches our actions, then we honor God and show respect to others. We set a good example for fellow believers and also keep nonbelievers from discrediting our faith and denouncing us as hypocritical. Not living out our biblical principles is a huge strike against us in their eyes—and is an affront to Jesus, who set the ultimate example of putting beliefs into action. He wants us to trust Him to live His life in us, encouraging us to make our "for instances" for real.

Hello God...it's me. Will You enable me today to make my advice match my actions?

Your Offering

Do not store up for yourselves treasures on earth, where moths and vermin destroy, and where thieves break in and steal. But store up for yourselves treasures in heaven, where moths and vermin do not destroy, and where thieves do not break in and steal. For where your treasure is, there your heart will be also.
MATTHEW 6:19–21 NIV

When it's time to collect items to give away or to sell at a garage sale, we think about the things we don't need: that extra coffeemaker someone gave us, that picture frame gathering dust, those books we never read. But we keep a vise grip on the things we think we need the most—the items of most value to us. Ironically, some of those things end up at the next garage sale.

Jesus advised His disciples to let go of the things on this earth and to transfer their grip to the things that aren't of this world. The possessions of heaven can't be lost or stolen here on earth. Offering ourselves and our belongings to God is a way of storing up treasure in heaven. It also helps us to hold things loosely in this life. We came into this world with nothing and we can take nothing we have in this world into the next.

What will you offer God?

Hello God...it's me. Will You help me transfer my grip today to the things that matter most?

The Measure of God

I lift you high in praise, my God, O my King! and I'll bless your name into eternity.
I'll bless you every day, and keep it up from now to eternity. God is magnificent;
he can never be praised enough. There are no boundaries to his greatness.

PSALM 145:1–3 MSG

Miles and meters. Light-years and leagues. Newtons and knots. From the tiniest particle to the tallest mountain, all of creation is considered and calculated by scientists and mathematicians. From the far reaches of our galaxy to the physical bodies we inhabit, everything is reduced to a number or a measurement and recorded for academic study.

Infinite and omnipotent. Everlasting and eternal. Almighty and I AM. While many of the details of creation can be captured in a book or on a computer screen, the Creator Himself cannot be measured. His very name defies description. He is without measure, without end, without boundaries or limitations. The God who is the beginning and the end is not bound by the restraints of time. The omnipotent God is not hampered by the unknown. The Creator who is the first and the last holds all of creation in His hands.

Nothing is too difficult for our God or beyond His capabilities. Great is the Lord and worthy of praise!

Hello God...it's me. I praise You today for being all-powerful, all-knowing, and holding creation in Your gentle hands.

The Power of Faith

Now faith is the assurance of things hoped for, the conviction of things not seen.
For by it the people of old received their commendation. By faith we understand that
the universe was created by the word of God, so that what is seen was not made out of things
that are visible.... And without faith it is impossible to please him, for whoever would
draw near to God must believe that he exists and that he rewards those who seek him.

HEBREWS 11:1–3, 6 ESV

Ever wish you knew a real-life superhero—one who could leap tall buildings at a single bound like Superman? Wouldn't you keep that superhero's phone number at the top of your cell phone contacts list when life's problems loom larger than tall buildings? Yet the power of an imaginary superhero doesn't come close to the power of our very real God, accessed through the power of faith.

Perhaps you have days when your faith seems powerless. Even now you might long for the kind of faith embodied by the biblical heroes described in Hebrews 11. Yet a tiny bit of faith in a big God is all you need. A tiny bit of faith is all that many of the people in the Bible had. But our God can do a lot with just a little bit.

The power of faith is the power of God. It invites you to draw nearer to God, who is the only superhero you will ever need.

Hello God...it's me. Thank You that You do not have a requirement on the size of our faith before You act.

Endless Possibilities

Jesus answered again and said to them, "Children, how hard it is for those who trust in riches to enter the kingdom of God! It is easier for a camel to go through the eye of a needle than for a rich man to enter the kingdom of God." And they were greatly astonished, saying among themselves, "Who then can be saved?" But Jesus looked at them and said, "With men it is impossible, but not with God; for with God all things are possible."

MARK 10:24–27 NKJV

"Who then can be saved?" the disciples once asked Jesus. In response, Jesus reminded them of the truth that still stands today: "With men this is impossible, but with God all things are possible" (Matthew 19:25–26 NKJV).

No matter how hard we try, we cannot save ourselves. Left to our own devices, we will fail every time. God tells us to have faith, but we doubt. God says to believe, yet we question. God commands us to trust, but still we hesitate. God understands our limitations, so He grants us the faith. He supplies the belief. He earns our trust.

How amazing that not only does God tell us the qualities He wants us to possess, but then He places the seeds of those traits within our hearts and waters them. He knows our weaknesses and gives us everything we lack. We need not do anything on our own. We are fully supplied for every decision, every journey, and every task by the One who has no limits.

Hello God...it's me. Thank You for planting in my heart the seeds of the traits You want me to possess. Everything comes from Your hand.

Knowing Our Potential

Whether, then, you eat or drink or whatever you do, do all to the glory of God.
1 CORINTHIANS 10:31 NASB

We accomplish countless goals in our lives. Whether we sing, write, paint, play a sport, work with numbers, teach, or play a musical instrument, we should thank God daily for the abilities He has given us, for we realize that who we are is God's gift to us.

What we do with these gifts from God is, in turn, our gift back to Him. Will we use our abilities selfishly, seeking to enrich ourselves or to take advantage of others? Or will we humbly use our gifts to bring glory not to ourselves, but to our God?

When God formed each of us, He created us with a purpose in mind. We can trust that God knew our potential, even before the moment of our conception, so we can use what we are to give Him glory. There is no greater gift we can give to God than becoming what He always meant for us to be.

Hello God...it's me. Thank You for the great plan You have in my name, and the passion You have for me to achieve it all.

Not Who I Used to Be

I pray that God, who gives peace, will make you completely holy. And may your spirit,
soul, and body be kept healthy and faultless until our Lord Jesus Christ returns.
The one who chose you can be trusted, and he will do this.

1 THESSALONIANS 5:23–24 CEV

One of the most remarkable things about the believer's life is the progression we make from where we once were to where we are now. Just as our bodies mature physically, our faith also matures spiritually. The longer we know Christ, the more we become like Him.

That doesn't mean we ever attain perfection while we are on earth, but as we continue our spiritual journey, our lives should demonstrate a gradual progression of becoming more and more like the One who saved us. As we grow closer to Him, Christ empowers us to resist temptation, to adopt His heart when it comes to caring for others, and to do countless things for His glory that we never could do in our own power.

Christ is changing us—even when we aren't aware of it or can't always see it—to become more like Him. Rejoice that you no longer are who you once were.

Hello God...it's me. Thank You for the change that is happening in me today, making me more like You.

The Problem of Pain

These things I have spoken to you, that in Me you may have peace.
In the world you will have tribulation; but be of good cheer, I have overcome the world.
JOHN 16:33 NKJV

People seek pain relief in many forms today: aspirin, ibuprofen, prescription muscle relaxers…. And those are just for physical pain. To alleviate emotional pain, some try to medicate themselves in other ways: alcohol, legal and illegal drugs, work, relationships, hours spent trolling the Internet. Still the pain lingers like an unwanted guest. But pain is usually the symptom of an underlying problem. Unless the problem is dealt with, the symptom of pain will remain.

Jesus assured His disciples that they would face the pain of persecution and suffering—symptoms of living in a fallen world. But He also gave them some good news: Jesus never met a problem He couldn't overcome. Yes, His followers would go through deep waters. But they would not be alone and defenseless. Jesus would be with them.

None of us will pass through this life pain-free. But the ultimate pain reliever still is, and always will be, Jesus.

Hello God…it's me. When I am in the midst of pain, thank You for the comfort of Your presence.

Prone to Wander

It was our weaknesses he carried; it was our sorrows that weighed him down.
And we thought his troubles were a punishment from God, a punishment for his own sins!
But he was pierced for our rebellion, crushed for our sins. He was beaten so we could be whole.
Isaiah 53:4–5 NLT

Sheep always need a shepherd. These defenseless animals require someone to guide them to water, to lead them to edible pastureland, and to help them avoid harm. When they stray—and some will—they need a firm hand to guide them back to the fold.

Does that behavior sound familiar? No wonder psalmists like David and prophets like Isaiah compared people to helpless sheep. While such a metaphor might cause us to feel sheepish, it is apt when we consider the times we've wandered away from God. Straying doesn't always mean a big step. Sometimes the little decisions we make—"God says to do *this*, but I want to do *this*"—can be a step that leads us in the wrong direction.

Jesus is our "good shepherd" (John 10:14 NKJV). He is an expert at caring for His flock. Because of His humanity, He understands our propensity to stray. Because of His deity, He was the perfect sacrifice for sin. When we stray, He gently guides us back to the fold.

Hello God...it's me. I want You to know how grateful I am for not only Your guidance, but Your gentleness that comes with it.

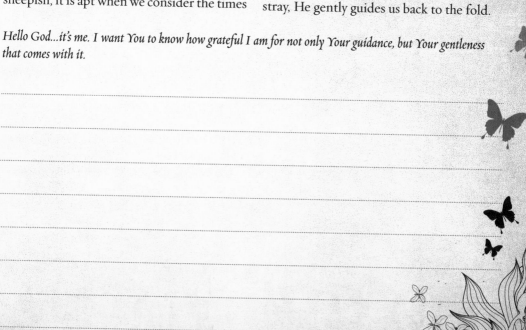

September 1

It Belongs to God

Do not lay up for yourselves treasures on earth, where moth and rust destroy and where thieves break in and steal, but lay up for yourselves treasures in heaven, where neither moth nor rust destroys and where thieves do not break in and steal. For where your treasure is, there your heart will be also.
MATTHEW 6:19–21 ESV

We make a mistake when we look around at our stuff and see it as "ours," when we congratulate ourselves for what we continue to accumulate. We ought to hold this "stuff" loosely, for it is never really ours.

In a very real sense, every penny we earn comes from God. Our ability to work, our job itself, and the salary we earn are all God's gracious gifts to us. What we earn is not our money; it's God's money, lent to us. What will you do with what God has entrusted to you? What would please God and honor His kingdom? Remember that Jesus said, "For where your treasure is, there will your heart be also" (Matthew 6:21 KJV).

Everything we have—friendships, skills, cash—comes from and belongs to God. Knowing this, we should seek to honor the Lord in how we use His gifts. Instead of seeing them as things to use for our agendas, we should see them as God's and use them for His purposes and pleasure.

Hello God...it's me. Thank You for the gifts You give to me, as well as my ability to enjoy them.

Please Forgive

When they came to the place called The Skull, there they crucified Him and the criminals,
one on the right and the other on the left. But Jesus was saying,
"Father, forgive them; for they do not know what they are doing."
LUKE 23:33–34 NASB

"I'msorrywillyoupleaseforgiveme?" mumbled the five-year-old to his big sister for the third time that day. He had accidentally stepped on her chalk drawing in the morning, spilled his drink all over her sandwich at lunch, and then broken her favorite toy while playing with it that afternoon. He was so remorseful that, every time he asked, she willingly forgave.

The little boy was learning a valuable lesson. Each time he messed up, his sister had to start over—new drawing, new sandwich, fixed toy. Yet each time, she loved him enough to forgive. Because she was willing to forgive, he saw the importance of forgiving others.

Forgiveness doesn't come naturally. It isn't always easy. Forgiveness requires self-sacrifice and humility. It lets go of the need for revenge. It releases the past so that you can move forward.

Jesus is our example. He said, "Father, forgive them, for they do not know what they do" (Luke 23:34 NKJV) about murderers.

Hello God...it's me. Today, I will place any desire for revenge in Your hands and ask for Your help to forgive.

Bear One Another's Burdens

Praise the God and Father of our Lord Jesus Christ, the Father of mercies and the God of all comfort. He comforts us in all our affliction, so that we may be able to comfort those who are in any kind of affliction, through the comfort we ourselves receive from God. For as the sufferings of Christ overflow to us, so through Christ our comfort also overflows.

2 CORINTHIANS 1:3–5 HCSB

Dick and Rick Hoyt love marathons. They run as a team, father and son. The 2009 Boston Marathon was their one-thousandth race. That isn't the only remarkable thing about them, though.

Dick Hoyt is almost seventy years old, and Rick Hoyt has had cerebral palsy since birth. Dick pushes his son's wheelchair every inch of every race. Rick depends on his father, but Dick gets a whole lot of encouragement from his son.

We need one another. People around us are hurting, and sometimes the pain can become overwhelming. At those times, we need to put our hurts on the back burner so that we can help others. Then, when the time comes, they will give us a place to lean as well.

And in front of us is the glory of the finish line.

Hello God...it's me. Thank You for the benefit and even healing we receive by helping others.

Do Not Merely Listen

If you look carefully into the perfect law that sets you free, and if you do what it says and don't forget what you heard, then God will bless you for doing it.

JAMES 1:25 NLT

Browse any Christian bookstore and you might get the feeling that following Jesus is a difficult and complex proposition. Thousands of books line the shelves in sections labeled "Christian Living," "Women's Interest," and "Study Materials." One book tells you to follow Jesus through a specific method, while another book outlines a different set of requirements. You might be overwhelmed by all the plans and steps and doctrines and programs that various authors have dictated as paths to following Christ.

But the gospel is simple: *declare with your mouth and believe with your heart that Jesus is the Son of God.* God doesn't make the faith walk a mystery with puzzles to solve or codes to break. He tells us in His Word all He desires of us and for us, and then He says, "Do what it says."

Jesus condensed the Bible to two directives: love God and love your neighbor as yourself. When we worship and revere God for His position as our Creator and Redeemer and when we treat others the way we would like to be treated, the gospel is winsome.

Hello God...it's me. Thank You for the uncomplicated life You desire us to live: following Your example of love.

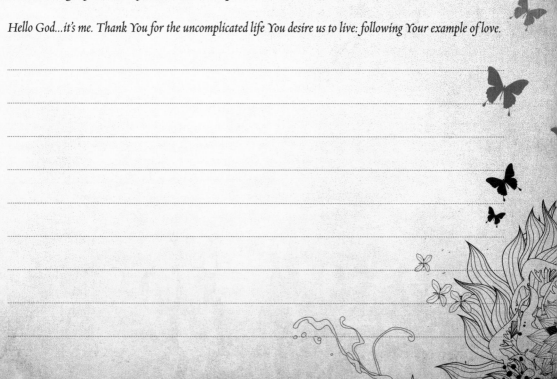

When Life Isn't Fair

Then Peter came to Jesus and asked, "Lord, how many times shall I forgive my brother or sister who sins against me? Up to seven times?" Jesus answered, "I tell you, not seven times, but seventy-seven times."
MATTHEW 18:21–22 NIV

When we hear of such human atrocities as death camps at Auschwitz, the killing fields of Cambodia, or tribal cleansing in Rwanda, we see the fragility of human justice in an evil world. On a much smaller scale, perhaps someone takes your parking place, a colleague gets the accolades for your hard work, or your life savings are cut in half by a recession. Or maybe you've been devastated by a spouse's betrayal or physically injured by violent crime.

When we encounter circumstances like these, we cry, "It's not fair!" We feel that we have a right to be treated fairly, and we are often angered by the injustice in this world.

In some way, at some level, when we are treated unfairly, we need to make the same decision as those who suffer human atrocities: either bitterness or forgiveness. It is not about getting our right to justice; that is God's job. It is about forgiving others as the Lord has forgiven you.

Hello God...it's me. Thank You that I can trust both Your justice to handle unfairness, and Your power in me to forgive.

In Their Defense

Provide justice for the needy and the fatherless; uphold the rights of the oppressed and the destitute.
Rescue the poor and needy; save them from the power of the wicked.
PSALM 82:3–4 HCSB

Many celebrities are known by their causes. They host benefits for those who suffer with AIDS, rock concerts to help the victims of earthquakes or floods, and telethons to raise money and awareness of diseases. Raising money for the plight of the helpless is in vogue today.

Jesus had a soft spot for the poor and needy too. But He did much more than host a benefit concert or raise money. He got eyeball-to-eyeball with them and their suffering. He touched the leper, healed the blind, and spoke with the widow, the adulterous woman, and the Samaritan at the well.

His approach was unpopular. It was scandalous. It was radical.

Jesus calls His followers to follow His example to help the poor and defend the defenseless. Will you adopt an orphan or befriend a homeless individual? Will you clean up after disasters or volunteer in a soup kitchen, food pantry, or shelter? Raising money helps fund causes for the poor, but it is only when we get personal, when we look into their eyes and touch them, that we love the poor the way Jesus loves them.

And that's radical.

Hello God...it's me. Will You show me how I can get personal—how I can reach out and touch those who need You today?

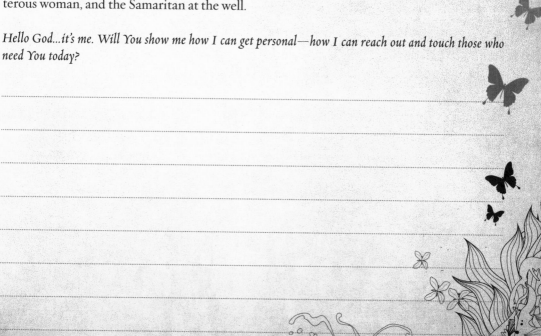

Patience

*Whatsoever things were written aforetime were written for our learning,
that we through patience and comfort of the scriptures might have hope. Now the God of patience
and consolation grant you to be likeminded one toward another according to Christ Jesus:*
ROMANS 15:4–5 KJV

As Christians, when we think about the consequences of our sin, we are quickly—and thankfully—reminded of the saving work of Christ in our lives and how we won't have to pay this penalty. Through His saving grace, Christ demonstrated an incredible love for us.

Christ is also incredibly patient toward us. Some of us run away from Him, some of us regularly stumble into sin, and others of us struggle with faith. Nevertheless, Christ continues to patiently wait for us, helping us overcome our hurdles and drawing us closer to Himself.

With Christ's patience demonstrated in our lives, should we not also be stirred to demonstrate patience toward those around us? How can we who have received such loving patience not look kindly and graciously toward those who have offended us?

Our Christ-infused heart should stir within us a deep and abiding love for others.

Hello God...it's me. Help me to show patience today, especially to those who offend me.

The Mercy of Grace

For the grace of God has appeared, bringing salvation...instructing us to deny ungodliness and worldly desires and to live sensibly, righteously and godly in the present age, looking for the blessed hope... of our great God and Savior, Christ Jesus, who gave Himself for us to redeem us from every lawless deed, and to purify for Himself a people for His own possession, zealous for good deeds.

TITUS 2:11–14 NASB

Grace is unmerited divine assistance. It has been called "amazing" for good reason.

Grace took root in the Garden of Eden, sprouting hope amid the thorns of first sin. Grace followed the Israelites in and out of captivity, to foreign lands, and through the wilderness. Grace took the form of a wooden ark, a scarlet thread, and a kinsman redeemer.

Grace came to the world clothed in the flesh of a helpless infant. Grace took the form of a carpenter's son. Grace walked the earth, touched hurting souls, and healed the sick. Grace gave one life as a ransom for many and secured our salvation. Grace provides a way out. Grace gives a second chance...and a third. Grace restores what the locust has eaten. Grace secures the salvation of the one who would believe. Grace turns a sinner into a saint. Grace is the embodiment of God's enduring faithfulness and love. That's what is so amazing about grace!

Hello God...it's me. Will You let my heartfelt response to Your amazing grace guide my every interaction today?

Our Omnipotent God

God is our refuge and strength, an ever-present help in trouble.... There is a river whose streams make glad the city of God, the holy place where the Most High dwells. God is within her, she will not fall; God will help her at break of day. Nations are in uproar, kingdoms fall; he lifts his voice, the earth melts. The Lord Almighty is with us; the God of Jacob is our fortress.

PSALM 46:1, 4–7 NIV

Popular movies portray God as capricious or even mock Him as weak and uncaring. As a result, people often consider God as a distant but doting figure, not really paying much attention to the world or its inhabitants.

But God's Word tells a different story. We serve a God whose voice can melt the earth. His right hand upholds the universe. He speaks, and creation rushes to obey. He knows *everything*. There is nothing we can hide from Him. He will not be mocked without consequence. And we cannot outwit, outrun, or outdo Him in any way.

Yet this magnificent God—this all-powerful Creator of heaven and earth—stoops to embrace us. He is the unquestionable King of everything...but He is also our Father. Knowing this, we approach His throne boldly, secure in our position as coheirs with Christ; but let us never forget that we approach a *throne*.

Hello God...it's me. Help me to portray an accurate picture of You to those around me today.

Living Proof

O, that you would rend the heavens and come down, that the mountains would tremble before you!
ISAIAH 64:1 NIV

Paul Simon once described faith as "an island in the setting sun," but added that "proof, yes, proof is the bottom line for everyone."

The prophet Isaiah wanted proof—he wanted to hear God speak. More than seven hundred years had passed since Mount Sinai's summit erupted in fire. Lightning flashed, the ground shifted, the air was supercharged with electricity...and Moses emerged with two stone tablets. God came down. God had spoken.

But not in Isaiah's lifetime. And Isaiah desperately wanted God—*begged* God—to show His mighty power, to demonstrate His glory, to *do something* in the land of Judah. His people wanted a visible display. They longed for proof.

Isaiah's lament is also ours. When circumstances feel out of control today, we lament: "Show Yourself...prove You are real." We scream it. We cry it. We whisper it in the dark. But God chooses how and when to reveal Himself. His is a plan of faithfulness—of living within the gap of proof and promise.

Hello God...it's me. Thank You for Your ability to reveal Yourself without being seen.

September 11

You Can't Hide

Write this letter to the angel of the church in Sardis. This is the message from the one who has the sevenfold Spirit of God and the seven stars: I know all the things you do, and that you have a reputation for being alive—but you are dead.

REVELATION 3:1 NLT

X-rays. MRIs. Telescopes. Microscopes. Modern technology reveals the intricacies of the atom and the vastness of the universe. Nothing is too small, nothing too large. It's all visible. There is nowhere to hide our secrets. Scary thought, isn't it?

Yet we think we can hide from God. We've convinced ourselves that somehow activities done under the cover of darkness are not known to the Father of Light. That attitudes held in the inner recesses of our hearts will not be known by the One who knit us in our mother's womb.

The Pharisees—the religious leaders in Jesus's day—thought they were exempt from exposure. Read Matthew 22 for a scathing exposé. The seven churches in Revelation thought that somehow their actions were unknown to the Lord. Read Revelation 2–3, which fully discloses their sins. To each church Jesus says, "I know...."

Jesus sees all and knows all. He would prefer an authentic struggler to a religious hypocrite.

Hello God...it's me. Thank You for Your desire for my honesty, even when it isn't pretty.

An Acting Love

God is love. When we take up permanent residence in a life of love, we live in God and God lives in us.
This way, love has the run of the house, becomes at home and mature in us, so that we're
free of worry on Judgment Day—our standing in the world is identical with Christ's.
There is no room in love for fear. Well-formed love banishes fear. Since fear is crippling, a fearful life—
fear of death, fear of judgment—is one not yet fully formed in love. We, though,
are going to love—love and be loved. First we were loved, now we love. He loved us first.
I JOHN 4:17–19 MSG

Actions are purposeful maneuvers, the results of desire and longing, by-products of the need to accomplish something. A potter acts by molding clay into a vase. A captain acts by steering his ship out to sea. A construction worker acts by hammering nails into wood. A mother acts by feeding her hungry child.

In 1 John 4, God's love is not only a verb—an action—it is a power with its own will. His will.

His perfect love drives out fear. When God's children accept this powerful, perfected love, they can care for others with the same purposeful intent with which God has reached out to them. His love truly depends on who He is. God Himself is love.

Hello God...it's me. Thank You that You embody love, and You release the stranglehold of fear.

Anything but Easy

*If ye forgive men their trespasses, your heavenly Father will also forgive you:
but if ye forgive not men their trespasses, neither will your Father forgive your trespasses.*

MATTHEW 6:14–15 KJV

In a child's world, arguments happen all the time over lost or broken toys and even mean looks. Before long, kicking and screaming ensue, and everyone ends up in tears. Usually, though, after a time-out, apologies are made and the incident is forgotten.

If only adult issues were that simple to resolve! In the adult world, differing opinions derail office projects and business partnerships. Marriages turn sour over disagreements. Misunderstandings separate families for generations. Spats divide close friends, turning them into adversaries.

Jesus spoke in Matthew 6 about the importance of forgiveness. Not only does a lack of forgiveness affect others, but it also hinders our own spiritual walk. If Christ willingly forgave us despite our many sins—if He could hang on a cross that *we* nailed Him to and ask God to forgive us—surely we can offer that same grace to others. Love and forgiveness do not wait to be earned.

Hello God...it's me. I ask for Your help to forgive like You did.

Truly Free

We know love by this, that He laid down His life for us; and we ought to lay down our lives for the brethren.... Little children, let us not love with word or with tongue, but in deed and truth.
1 John 3:16, 18 nasb

When Charles Colson wrote these words, he was in prison. His father had died, his son had just been arrested, and his fellow Watergate prisoners had recently been released.

And then he received a phone call from a friend. This man and three others had been meeting with Colson weekly, supporting him in his emerging faith. They ended each weekly session together on their knees in prayer.

That day on the phone, Al Quie, a high-ranking politician in Congress and one of the most respected public figures in Washington, said he would petition President Ford to let him serve the rest of Colson's sentence so Colson could be with his family during this difficult time. Within hours the other men made the same offer. That night, overwhelmed with the deep love of Christ expressed through these friends, Charles Colson completely surrendered his life to God and finally felt truly free, despite being in prison.

Have you tasted the freedom that Jesus offers? When the Son sets you free, you are free indeed.

Hello God...it's me. Thank You for the power of Your love that brings surrender and makes us whole.

Spontaneous Love

As the Father has loved me, so have I loved you. Abide in my love. If you keep my commandments,
you will abide in my love, just as I have kept my Father's commandments and abide in his love.
These things I have spoken to you, that my joy may be in you, and that your joy may be full.
JOHN 15:9–11 ESV

We all enjoy receiving gifts from friends and loved ones. We look forward to birthday gifts, Christmas gifts, and presents we receive on anniversaries and other special occasions. But especially treasured are those "just because" gifts that come on ordinary days, simply to show that a loved one is thinking of us. Spontaneous gifts represent the love of the sender—someone demonstrating his or her love by giving something away.

A heart filled with Christ's love is eager to show that love in any number of ways. As we experience more and more of Christ's love, our hearts are filled and we are eager to pour out that love to others at the first awareness of a need.

This love has no limits, as Christ demonstrated to the world when He died on the cross. His love, now living and moving in us, should daily overflow our hearts to comfort and restore a broken world. While this demonstration of love is often planned, many times it bursts forth spontaneously because our hearts are so full of Christ that His love simply spills over into others' lives.

Hello God...it's me. Please let Your love overflow from me to touch others as I go about my day today.

Be a Lighthouse

Speak the things which are proper for sound doctrine: that the older men be sober, reverent, temperate, sound in faith, in love, in patience; the older women likewise, that they be reverent in behavior, not slanderers, not given to much wine, teachers of good things.

TITUS 2:1–3 NKJV

In the eighteenth and nineteenth centuries, lighthouses were widely used to warn ships of hazardous coastlines and shoals. In dark and treacherous weather, the constant beam from the lighthouse helped guide ships into safe harbors and kept them from wrecking. The development of the Fresnel lens in 1822 made the beams of lighthouses shine over greater distances, making them even more effective.

Older believers should be like lighthouses to those around them. No matter how long you have been a Christian, you can be a lighthouse for a younger believer. Like a lighthouse, you can shine as a constant example of God's light and can warn those around you of spiritual dangers that will wreck their lives.

The Holy Spirit is the light source that makes you effective and sure. Trusting in the Lord turns on the light switch. Go on and shine that light. Let the Holy Spirit use it to guide others safely to the Rock that is Jesus.

Hello God...it's me. Please remove anything in me that would keep me from being a constant beacon of Your faithfulness.

Our Life's Work Becomes a Prayer

Dear friends, you always followed my instructions when I was with you. And now that I am away, it is even more important. Work hard to show the results of your salvation, obeying God with deep reverence and fear. For God is working in you, giving you the desire and the power to do what pleases him.

PHILIPPIANS 2:12–13 NLT

How many times do we feel like our efforts are in vain? We work so hard at something, yet the result we desire or the outcome we endeavor to bring about just doesn't appear. Our lives are full of moments such as these— either personally, in our jobs, or in some other aspect of our lives.

For those who claim faith in Christ, we can rest assured that when we commit our actions to Him, the results will be fruitful. Maybe success doesn't automatically appear each time we commit something to Christ, but the effort we apply—done in cooperation with him—becomes Christ-infused.

When we commit our lives to serving Christ, our work no longer centers just on us, but it becomes part of something larger, more significant...something eternal. When we commit our life to God and focus on Him as we complete our tasks, every effort becomes a prayer. By cooperating with Christ's will, our life's work is no longer in vain.

Hello God...it's me. I just want You to know, I am committed to serving You and trusting that You will bring about Your plans for my life.

How Refreshing

Your love has given me great joy and encouragement, because you,
brother, have refreshed the hearts of the saints.
PHILEMON 1:7 NIV

A tall glass of cold water after mowing the lawn. A dip in the lake on a sweltering summer afternoon. A long shower after cleaning out the attic all day. Refreshing. Each of us have felt the relief they bring.

Somehow the simple joys can be the perfect answer to our momentary need. How sweet it is to pour that glass of water for another thirsty worker. To offer refreshment to someone else is to share in the great connection of being human.

There are times when our spirits are dry too. We get discouraged or bitter or sad, and it seems impossible to reach for the help we need. That's when the wonder of God's plan can be seen so plainly: God recharges His people through each other. When one believer extends an encouraging word or pitches in to help another, the result is beautiful. The disheartened one is invigorated to take the next step, the discouraged one refreshed—like a parched desert traveler after a drink from a well.

The Lord has given us one another. It's how He works. It's how we work best too.

Hello God...it's me. Thank You for the gift You've given us of one another.

Only in Weakness

This is nothing else but the sword of Gideon the son of Joash, a man of Israel!
Into his hand God has delivered Midian and the whole camp.

JUDGES 7:14 NKJV

Gideon farmed. Moses led sheep. Martha bustled and served. The disciples fished.

Then God came calling.

God used Gideon to grow an army. God told Moses to lead His people. Jesus told Martha to sit and learn. The disciples left their nets and fished for men.

God removed each of them—and many others—from their comfortable, ordinary existence and propelled them into a ministry opportunity that stretched them beyond their natural talents. They learned new skills. They went new places. At times while they served God out of their weakness, they stumbled and He caught them. God put them into circumstances that forced them to depend on Him.

Security and aptitude often breed autonomy. But God knows that dependence and uncertainty foster reliance, and reliance fosters relationship. So He often calls us out of our comfort zones to learn that it is only through *His* strength that we are made strong and only through *His* provision that we accomplish great deeds.

Hello God...it's me. Thank You for bringing me closer to You by orchestrating circumstances that require my dependence on You.

Backstage with God

When you help someone out, don't think about how it looks. Just do it—quietly and unobtrusively.
That is the way your God, who conceived you in love, working behind the scenes, helps you out.
MATTHEW 6:3–4 MSG

Being a stagehand is not a glamorous job. It usually involves working nights and weekends for little if any pay and no recognition. It's an unsung, behind-the-scenes vocation.

So why would anyone want to be a stagehand? To be part of that theatrical environment. To help set the scene, realize a vision, showcase someone who can wow the audience every time. If you're a really good stagehand, you might get to overhear an audience member say, "How did they *do* that?"

That's what a wildly creative God does for His people. He works backstage to get the details right—scenery, lights, sound, props, rigging, special effects—so that when you take the stage of life, you'll be able to fulfill the dreams He has called you to.

God set the world in motion and conceived us in love. The work God does in our lives—and the way we are to live with each other—is not simply a performance for applause, but His grace and compassion. An act of love. Our amazing God is working behind the scenes every day of our lives.

Hello God...it's me. I want to thank You now for all the things that You have done for me behind the scenes.

September 21

God's Embrace

God is our refuge and strength, an ever-present help in trouble....
The Lord Almighty is with us; the God of Jacob is our fortress.
Psalm 46:1, 37 NIV

Concerts. Churches. Festivals. Football stadiums. What do they have in common? Huge crowds. Ironically, though, at any of these events, it's possible—easy, even—to feel alone. It's no secret that humans can feel lonely anywhere. Most of us will go to any length to make a connection. Some of us seek it through romance, others through popularity, and still others via social networks or online games. Connecting is one of our most desperate longings, and we'll strive for it wherever we can get it.

But there's a problem: no matter where we try to find it, true connection will elude us if we seek it in anything but God. For a time, these intimacy substitutes will satisfy, but inevitably they will leave us unfulfilled.

With God, however, we are never alone. As our Comforter, He is close to us, arms stretched out, ready to hold us. Embrace Him. He won't let go.

Hello God...it's me. Help me to seek intimacy with You. I know You will draw close to me when I draw close to You.

By His Hands

In the beginning was the Word, and the Word was with God, and the Word was God.
He was in the beginning with God. All things came into being through Him,
and apart from Him nothing came into being that has come into being.
JOHN 1:1–3 NASB

Looking at the magnificence of the Grand Canyon or the wonder of Victoria Falls, perhaps you can easily picture a big God who created such breathtaking beauty. Gaze upon your own hands, whether thin fingered or work roughened. Could your hands create such wonders?

Jesus could. Though Jesus was a carpenter with calloused hands, the apostle John proclaimed Him to be the One by whom all things were made. Jesus Christ was both man and God. By His word the beluga whale and the butterfly sprang into being. And during His incarnation, the power of creation was evident in His hands—the very hands of God—as He miraculously turned water into wine, calmed the raging sea, and turned one boy's meager lunch into a feast for well over five thousand people.

The next time you look at your hands, consider what Jesus, the eternal creator and sustainer of all things, can do with them.

Hello God...it's me. Thank You for Your calloused carpenter's hands that also created the beauty of all the outdoors.

Prayers of an Aching Heart

In the same way the Spirit also helps our weakness; for we do not know how to pray as we should, but the Spirit Himself intercedes for us with groanings too deep for words; and He who searches the hearts knows what the mind of the Spirit is, because He intercedes for the saints according to the will of God.

ROMANS 8:26–27 NASB

Every Christian experiences pain, weakness, and tragedy. In those times we may find it difficult to pray. It's not that we don't want to pray; in times of distress, we know we need God more than ever! But when our heart is breaking, prayer sometimes seems impossible. We may turn toward God, but in our anguish we can't even form the words to express our sorrow.

God provided the Holy Spirit to be our comforter. In those times when our heart is aching and our vision clouded by confusion and grief, the Spirit comes close to us and wraps us in the soothing embrace of God's presence. When we are overwhelmed beyond words, the Spirit takes our unformed prayers to God on our behalf.

When your heart is breaking, remember that God is near to comfort you.

Hello God...it's me. Thank You that Your Word says You are the One who comforts me. I love that You desire to hold me.

Follow Me

Those who love their life in this world will lose it. Those who care nothing for their life in this world will keep it for eternity. Anyone who wants to be my disciple must follow me, because my servants must be where I am. And the Father will honor anyone who serves me.
JOHN 12:25–26 NLT

"Follow Me." Two simple words uttered by a passing Jewish teacher called the fishermen, two brothers, a tax collector. All who heard Jesus's command followed without question. Did the disciples know who He was? Did they know where they were going? Surely the disciples couldn't have predicted that they would follow Him to heal the sick. They couldn't have known they would follow Him as He fed the multitudes with a little boy's lunch. They couldn't have guessed that the man they followed would teach them a new covenant, wash their feet, and take their place on a cross. Yet they followed anyway.

They healed people in His name. They fed generations with the Bread of Life that they carried far and wide. They recorded His teachings, spread the gospel of love, and remained faithful even unto death.

All this the disciples learned by serving God, loving their neighbor, and remaining faithful to Jesus's two-word invitation: "Follow Me." And He gives us the same invitation today. Love God. Love others. Follow Jesus.

Hello God...it's me. Show me what it means to follow You today.

Fountain of Love

We love Him because He first loved us.
1 JOHN 4:19 NKJV

In Victor Hugo's *Les Miserables*, a priest opens his home to a man named Jean Valjean, giving him food and shelter—only to have Valjean steal a silver plate and cup and run away. When Valjean is caught by the police, they ask the priest to confirm that Valjean stole the items. Instead, in a surprising act of grace, the man of God declares they were a gift and asks Valjean why he forgot to take the candlesticks that went with the set. Valjean, staggered by such kindness, is forever changed. And from that day forward,

he vows to lead a life of honesty, generosity, and graciousness.

It took only one act of self-sacrificing love to radically alter the life of that criminal. But for some people, one self-sacrificing act by the Son of God isn't enough. They want more "evidence" before they'll turn from their ways.

What about you? Have you come face-to-face with God's boundless, incomprehensible love? Have you let it change your life?

Hello God...it's me. Let me never pass up an opportunity to show someone Your grace.

Beauty from Weakness

I can do all things through Him who strengthens me.
PHILIPPIANS 4:13 NASB

We humans are prone to weakness. Our mortal bodies are susceptible to disease and injury, while our emotions and priorities can easily get out of control.

Hymn-writer Fanny Crosby was familiar with frailty. Blind from infancy in an era when blindness could mean an institutionalized existence, no one imagined God had plans for her to become a famous songstress.

Part of the life of a believer is the calling God places upon us, and often that calling seems impossible. But God uses our weaknesses to draw us to Him. For when He requires something of us beyond our ability, we are forced to depend on Him and only Him to complete the task. Our emotions and priorities cannot be relied on, nor can our physical bodies.

When we completely surrender, He will use our weaknesses, our blindness—all our frailties—to make us something beautiful for the kingdom of God.

Hello God...it's me. Thank You that my weaknesses draw me closer to You, and You will use them for Your glory.

20/20 Faith

If anyone builds on that foundation with gold, silver, costly stones, wood, hay, or straw, each one's work will become obvious, for the day will disclose it, because it will be revealed by fire; the fire will test the quality of each one's work. If anyone's work that he has built survives, he will receive a reward. If anyone's work is burned up, it will be lost, but he will be saved; yet it will be like an escape through fire.

1 CORINTHIANS 3:12–15 HCSB

Take a walk down the street on a sunny afternoon, and you'll be squinting in the sun's glare before you know it. Putting on sunglasses enables you to keep going, but your view will still be changed. The scenery becomes dimmer. Details are shadowed. Peripheral vision is narrowed. Yet at least you will no longer be blinded by the sun and hindered from enjoying the day.

Putting on the lens of faith is what enables us to keep traveling on the journey of life. It may be hard to see our destination, blinded as we are by earth's circumstances, but faith allows us enough clarity that we can continue on our way. And then, when we get to heaven, what brilliance we will behold! We'll no longer need the aid of faith; our vision will be clear and complete...everything in high-definition!

Persevere on your journey today. Ask God to help you see what you need to see so that you can glimpse a hope and promise for your future.

Hello God...it's me. Will You give me a greater vision of what You have planned for me?

The Darkest Night

In the same way, the Spirit helps us in our weakness. We do not know what we ought to pray for, but the Spirit himself intercedes for us through wordless groans. And he who searches our hearts knows the mind of the Spirit, because the Spirit intercedes for God's people in accordance with the will of God.
ROMANS 8:26–27 NIV

A young woman lay in her bed. Sleep had eluded her for hours as she tossed and turned. She knew what was keeping her awake: her mind couldn't stop thinking about her problems at work, her shallow relationships, and, even worse, her complete lack of faith that God still cared about her. But then the moonlight shone through the blinds and illuminated her face, reminding her—as silent tears streamed down her cheeks—that the Light of the World still watched over her.

Life is sometimes like the night: with seemingly no end to the darkness, just solitude and loneliness. Problems appear larger than life, and cries to God seem to go unanswered. Paul explained in Romans 8 that at our weakest point, the Holy Spirit will speak for us, communicating what we ourselves do not know we need. After all, who knows our hearts and our needs better than the One who created us?

Hello God...it's me. I want You to know that I am determined to trust You in the darkness.

Competing Goals and Loyalties

Therefore, since we have so great a cloud of witnesses surrounding us, let us also lay aside every encumbrance and the sin which so easily entangles us, and let us run with endurance the race that is set before us.

HEBREWS 12:1 HCSB

As men and women of faith, our top priority should be our walk with God. But there are many other things that compete for our attention—family, career, financial obligations, relationships. How do we manage our relationships and responsibilities without letting them distract us so much that we lose sight of God?

It is good to examine our goals and loyalties honestly and determine if we need to eliminate some of them. As you identify your priorities, ask yourself:

Am I focused on achieving something that keeps me from spending time devoted to growing in my faith?

Am I loyal to someone or something that is pulling me away from God?

Sometimes we must say no to the good in order to say yes to the best. Today, be a man or woman of faith. Determine to put God first.

Hello God...it's me. Today I will not let what is good compete with what is the best.

Resting in God's Best

So humble yourselves before God. Resist the devil, and he will flee from you.
JAMES 4:7 NLT

Submission is a four-letter word in our current culture. We resist anything or anyone limiting our personal freedoms, and we equate submission with weakness.

But submitting to God's plan for us and, yes, even to His rules in the Bible, doesn't mean that we are weak. On the contrary, Christians are strong—we stand firm in the faith and defend our beliefs while dressed in the full armor of God. Even the most stouthearted warriors follow the commands of their leader. The Bible teaches that the most courageous thing we can do as soldiers of the Almighty is to submit to the leadership of our Commander in Chief.

The Lord is the foundation of our faith and the source of all meaning. When we follow in His steps and do things God's way instead of our own way, we receive His blessing and peace.

Above all, our Lord Jesus submitted to His Father's will. Shouldn't we do the same?

Hello God...it's me. Thank You for showing me what submission looks like with Jesus. I ask Your help in walking in submission to You.

Become What You Are

He who had received five talents came and brought five other talents, saying,
"Lord, you delivered to me five talents; look, I have gained five more talents besides them."
His lord said to him, "Well done, good and faithful servant; you were faithful over a few things,
I will make you ruler over many things. Enter into the joy of your lord."
MATTHEW 25:16, 20–21 NKJV

It seems like there's a new smartphone or electronic gadget out every other week. Each incarnation features some fascinating upgrade—only to be outdone in a few months by another version with even more bells and whistles.

We too often think that way about ourselves: We figure we constantly need upgrades. We say that we'll wait to serve until we're "more prepared," we'll get involved in a church "once we find one that we like," and we'll give to missions "when we have more money."

Don't wait. Serve now. Get involved now. Give now. God has already released the resources for the task. He has given you the gifts you need. Use what you have, and God will take care of the rest.

As you are faithful to become what you are, one day you will hear His precious words: "Well done, My good and faithful servant."

Hello God...it's me. Thank You that You have already given me the gifts I need and released the resources for my tasks. Please help me to start today.

October 2

God's Eternal Plan

How blessed is God! And what a blessing he is! He's the Father of our Master,
Jesus Christ, and takes us to the high places of blessing in him.
EPHESIANS 1:3 MSG

Every human heart yearns for a sense of purpose in life. Just below the surface of our consciousness lie such questions as: "Is what I am doing significant?" "Who cares about what I do?" "What really matters in life?"

It might surprise you to learn that Solomon, a man who had achieved astounding success as king of Israel, also struggled with his own significance. Despite all his earthly achievements, he mused, "Vanity of vanities...all is vanity" (Ecclesiastes 12:8 ESV). If a man as wise and wealthy as King Solomon struggled to find purpose in life, where does that leave the rest of us who will never attain such a lavish, royal existence?

We can trust in God's Word, which says that we do have a purpose. According to God's eternal plan, He predestined us for adoption as His sons and daughters through Jesus Christ. He designed each of us with a unique purpose—to love Him and serve Him.

Hello God...it's me. Help me to feel the significance You put on the little things I do today.

He Can Do the Impossible

*So Sarah laughed to herself, saying, "After I am worn out, and my lord is old,
shall I have pleasure?" The LORD said to Abraham, "Why did Sarah laugh and say,
'Shall I indeed bear a child, now that I am old?' Is anything too hard for the LORD?
At the appointed time I will return to you, about this time next year, and Sarah shall have a son."*
GENESIS 18:12–14 ESV

Sometimes we think that we know what's best for our lives. We make plans and do our best to prepare ourselves for the outcome we want to attain. Yet when our plans go awry, we realize that we don't know what's best for us. Only God does. And sometimes His plans take us through the territory of the impossible. More than likely the Old Testament patriarch Abraham didn't imagine that he would be changing diapers at the ripe old age of one hundred. But God knew what was best for them. Sarah's response of laughter when she learned of God's decision to give them a child in their old age showed that she doubted God could do the impossible. But He could—and He did. Do you trust God to not only know what's best for you but also to do the impossible? Are you willing to journey with Him even if He changes your plans and takes you to a place you once thought impossible?

Hello God...it's me. Increase my faith to see the possibility of the impossible.

His Loving Arms

Be strong and courageous, do not be afraid or tremble at them,
for the LORD your God is the one who goes with you. He will not fail you or forsake you.
DEUTERONOMY 31:6 NASB

Think back to a time when you promised someone that you'd always be there for them. Maybe it was a pinky swear when you were just a child, or perhaps you wrote something to that effect in your best friend's senior yearbook. Where is that relationship now? How long has it been since you saw that person...or even thought about him or her?

God said that He will never leave us and never forsake us. We must understand that He made that promise to last forever, through all generations. No matter what circumstances we may face, God will always be right beside us, guiding, protecting, and loving us.

You can believe God's promise that He will always be with you. And when you feel the loving arms of our ever-present God, your life will be transformed.

Hello God...it's me. Thank You that no circumstance I face today will take me away from Your arms.

Go Ahead and Ask

Ask, and it will be given to you; seek, and you will find; knock, and it will be opened to you. For everyone who asks receives, and he who seeks finds, and to him who knocks it will be opened. Or what man is there among you who, when his son asks for a loaf, will give him a stone? Or if he asks for a fish, he will not give him a snake, will he? If you then, being evil, know how to give good gifts to your children, how much more will your Father who is in heaven give what is good to those who ask Him!

MATTHEW 7:7–11 NASB

We may think we've hit the prayer lottery when we consider the words of Jesus, saying, "Ask, and it will be given to you" (Matthew 7:7 NKJV). Like a kid in a candy store, we might eagerly ask for this, this, this, and some of this. After all, we have a green light, thanks to the Savior and the knowledge that God delights in His children's prayers.

Yet God reserves the right to answer prayer however He pleases. He does not always say yes to our requests. He's best pleased when His people persist in prayer, rather than insist on a certain answer.

Prayer is an open door to God's ear and heart. Neither is ever closed to His child's softest plea or grimace of pain. No need is considered too great or too insignificant. So, go ahead and ask and keep on asking. According to God's purpose and time frame, He will answer.

Hello God...it's me. Help me to never lose the anticipation of Your answer to my prayers.

The Old Rugged Cross

Therefore, since we have a great high priest who has ascended into heaven,
Jesus the Son of God, let us hold firmly to the faith we profess. For we do not have a high priest
who is unable to empathize with our weaknesses, but we have one who has been tempted
in every way, just as we are—yet he did not sin. Let us then approach God's throne of grace
with confidence, so that we may receive mercy and find grace to help us in our time of need.
HEBREWS 4:14–16 NIV

It seems unusual, doesn't it? That an instrument of death is considered to be a source of life? Yet that is exactly what the cross of Jesus is to us. The cross, cruelly created as a form of torturous execution and used often by the Roman Empire to keep its subjects in line, was the place where our Lord gave His life for us. Because of that death—and only because of that death—we are given new life. His sacrifice paid the price for our sins and brought us into a relationship with the holy God.

And now we have access to God. We can "come boldly to the throne of grace, that we may obtain mercy and find grace to help in time of need" (Hebrews 4:16 NKJV). Our prayers are alive and welcomed in God's throne room because of what Jesus did for us. Without the cross, we would have no recourse, no prayer, no one to hear and help.

Thank God for the cross—the source of all our life.

Hello God...it's me. Let my life be a prayer of gratitude for what You endured at the cross for me.

Armed and Ready

Put on the whole armor of God, that you may be able to stand against the wiles of the devil. For we do not wrestle against flesh and blood, but against principalities, against powers, against the rulers of the darkness of this age, against spiritual hosts of wickedness in the heavenly places. Therefore take up the whole armor of God, that you may be able to withstand in the evil day, and having done all, to stand.
EPHESIANS 6:10–13 NKJV

Where do you go to find the ammunition needed for today's battle? With evil spiritual forces rallied against us and an unkind world counteracting us in every way, we would perhaps excuse ourselves for going AWOL (or at least for staying far from the front lines). We feel we do not have the munitions we need; we feel outgunned and outnumbered.

But we are never outdone when we have properly prepared for battle through a life of quiet, personal worship. Only in the hidden times with God—when we stand in awe before Him in worship, when we are lost in wonder at His power and grace, when we are captivated by His majesty and holiness and draw close to Him—only then are we prepared for the battle. Finally, my brethren, be strong in the Lord and in the power of His might.

Hello God...it's me. Don't let me lose sight of the importance of worship. You are so worthy.

The Right Medicine

A man was going down from Jerusalem to Jericho and fell into the hands of robbers. They stripped him, beat him up, and fled, leaving him half dead. When [the priest] saw him, he passed by on the other side. In the same way, a Levite...passed by on the other side. But a Samaritan on his journey came up to him, and when he saw the man, he had compassion. He went over to him and bandaged his wounds.... Then he put him on his own animal, brought him to an inn, and took care of him.

LUKE 10:30–34 HCSB

When we accidentally injure ourselves in the middle of a busy day, sometimes there's barely enough time to slap on a bandage—let alone examine it, clean it, or apply any medicine—on our way to the next task.

Isn't it good to know that the Lord doesn't take that approach with us? As the Great Physician, He cares just as much about the cause of our pain as He does the symptoms.

No matter what your wound or source of pain, call on the Great Physician today.

He still makes house calls! Fair warning, though—He'll be thorough. He won't just affix a bandage to the problem. He'll want to evaluate, assess, and examine your life. Then, with skill and precision, He will write the perfect prescription for a comprehensive treatment that will lead to your healing.

What in your life is injured today? The doctor is in, and His appointment book is open.

Hello God...it's me. Thank You for not only revealing my injuries but placing Your gentle hand on me and healing them as well.

Patience in the Journey

I charge you before God, who gives life to all, and before Christ Jesus, who gave a good testimony before Pontius Pilate, that you obey this command without wavering. Then no one can find fault with you from now until our Lord Jesus Christ comes again. For at just the right time Christ will be revealed from heaven by the blessed and only almighty God, the King of all kings and Lord of all lords.

1 TIMOTHY 6:13–15 NLT

"Are we there yet?" It's the question every child asks during a family road trip. Even adults check their GPS to find out "How much longer?" Yet, no matter how much information we have about road conditions, traffic, and construction, the answer is always an estimate.

Aren't we fortunate to have a more reliable source for the timing of our lives than a man-made satellite in the sky—especially when the timing isn't what we expected or hoped for?

Are you waiting on God today for something? Take heart. God never slumbers or sleeps. He is working—even if visibility is poor and you can't see what He's up to. He is trustworthy. Look to Him. Talk to Him about the challenging road conditions, the heavy traffic, the construction sites that are causing detours in your life. And as you ask Him for help, let Him guide your doubts and pain into wisdom, strength, and patience for your journey. He knows the way.

Hello God...it's me. Help me bring the details of my journey today to You and trust You to guide me even through doubt and pain.

Running the Race

Not that I have already obtained this or am already perfect, but I press on to make it my own, because Christ Jesus has made me his own. Brothers, I do not consider that I have made it my own. But one thing I do: forgetting what lies behind and straining forward to what lies ahead, I press on toward the goal for the prize of the upward call of God in Christ Jesus.

PHILIPPIANS 3:12–14 ESV

In the face of shin splints, overwhelming thirst, exhausted muscles, and suffocating heat, it's amazing that any marathoner ever finishes those 26.2 miles. Even more remarkable is the winning attitude these runners have, for it would be easy to quit halfway through when the finish line seems a continent away. Half of the battle in running, experts say, is mental.

Life itself is a marathon, with a finish line seemingly nowhere in sight much of the time. Mundane tasks like answering the phone, cleaning, or cooking supper make each day drag on. Even more tiring are the times when emergencies happen, when all hope appears lost, when we want to quit in hopes of escaping unwanted situations. The key to perseverance when the road gets too hard is to keep our eyes focused on Jesus, who is cheering us on at the finish line.

Hello God...it's me. I want You to know that I am determined to keep my eyes on You throughout my day today.

October 11

A Beautiful Sight

One thing I have asked from the LORD, that I shall seek: that I may dwell in the house of the LORD all the days of my life, to behold the beauty of the LORD and to meditate in His temple.
PSALM 27:4 NASB

What's the most beautiful sight you've ever seen? Was it the ocean or the mountains, a cherished possession, or perhaps your spouse on your wedding day? People are clearly captivated by beauty and seem to enjoy making lists of people, places, and things considered "most beautiful," from *People* magazine's annual "Most Beautiful People" issue to the Internet rankings of most beautiful cities in the world.

God has equipped each of us with a desire for beauty. Yet beauty by society's definition is an ever-shifting commodity. What was beautiful thirty years ago may not be deemed beautiful today. The most beautiful sight is one we haven't yet fully seen: God Himself. Through the eyes of faith we can glimpse His presence in His creation and in His Word, but one day we will finally be able to gaze upon our Lord in all His beauty and splendor. No matter what standard of beauty society imposes on its people, God will always be superior.

Craving beauty? Come and fill your gaze with the most beautiful sight in the universe.

Hello God...it's me. I want You to know that I can't wait for the day when I see You in all Your beauty and splendor.

The Difference Makers

I know the best thing we can do is to always enjoy life, because God's gift to us is the happiness we get from our food and drink and from the work we do.
ECCLESIASTES 3:12–13 CEV

Creativity fuels every aspect of our lives. Whether in the food we eat, the houses we live in, or simply our everyday wanderings, the spark of invention thrives within all of us. This area of our creativity is where God's work flourishes in us. Whether we are changing the world or changing ourselves, the ideas and designs that help us achieve these goals come through God's natural gifts to us. In using those gifts we reveal God to the world.

Intelligence is a tool that God gives us to make our world function, and talent is the brush He gives us to make it beautiful. With everything we create, we represent our Creator. This great gift endows us with unimaginable responsibility but also enables each of us to make a difference in the world. We are all important because God is acting within each of us. When He is within us we become the best possible version of ourselves.

What will you do to make a difference today?

Hello God...it's me. Thank You for speaking to me through "my own" ideas and designs, and that through fulfillment of these designs I can reveal You to the world.

October 13

Nourish Your Soul

Finally, brothers and sisters, whatever is true, whatever is noble, whatever is right, whatever is pure, whatever is lovely, whatever is admirable—if anything is excellent or praiseworthy—think about such things.
PHILIPPIANS 4:8 NIV

Can a human body survive on junk food? The answer is, technically, yes; your body can eke existence out of abysmal nourishment, even if all you consume is food with the nutritional value of a paper bag. However, as any dedicated athlete can tell you, feeding solely on cheeseburgers and potato chips will weaken your body and sap your strength. Junk food may taste good for a time, but it inevitably fails to satisfy because it cannot feed your body properly.

Why then do we feast our minds and souls on spiritual junk? We are meant to fill ourselves with holiness, yet we let our minds consume the "empty carbs" of gossip, lies, pornography, blasphemy, slander, and cursing.

Make it a priority to nourish your soul by consuming *good* food for your spirit and mind today, and spend time focusing on our infinitely fulfilling God.

Hello God...it's me. I want You to know that I am determined to nourish my soul today by staying away from gossip.

What God Is Like

The LORD descended in the cloud and stood there with him as he called upon the name of the LORD.
Then the LORD passed by in front of him and proclaimed, "The LORD, the LORD God,
compassionate and gracious, slow to anger, and abounding in lovingkindness and truth;
who keeps lovingkindness for thousands, who forgives iniquity, transgression and sin."
EXODUS 34:5–7 NASB

In a time when the people of Israel misunderstood God the most, God gave Moses a rare gift: the proclamation of His name. He placed Moses in a safe place and then allowed His presence to pass before Moses, helping Moses understand just what He was like: gracious, merciful, slow to anger. God's decision to show His goodness to Moses came as a result of Moses's request to see God's glory (Exodus 33:18–23). While Moses went to talk with God, the people assumed that God and Moses had abandoned them. But they were wrong.

How many times have we explained or viewed God through the lens of our human limitations? He is the God without limits. We grieve God when we believe He won't continue to forgive because *we* can't fathom forgiving someone the ninetieth time for the same offense. As God helped Moses see, He never changes. He is always gracious. He is always merciful. And He is always slow to anger.

Hello God...it's me. Thank You for being the God without limits.

Take and Eat

Oh, how I love Your law! It is my meditation all the day.... How sweet are Your words to my taste, sweeter than honey to my mouth! Through Your precepts I get understanding; therefore I hate every false way.
PSALM 119:97, 103 –104 NKJV

At times God seems so mysterious, but He has revealed more of His thoughts to us than we may realize. He imagined the entire universe and crafted the creation to give evidence of His character. We see part of God's thoughts every day when we look out our window or in the mirror. More importantly, though, God has given us the ability to know His thoughts through His written Word, the Bible.

The Bible is an invaluable resource to us. It takes us beyond creation and science to the concept of who we are in relation to God. In the pages of Scripture, God has made Himself an open book in which He tells us of His love, His desires for us, and His plans for the future. He loves revealing Himself to us and is never happier than when we seek Him.

Open the book. Read it with reverence and care. Taste it. Digest it. It is food for your soul.

Hello God...it's me. Creator of the Universe, thank You for Your desire to reveal Yourself to me.

Unchanging

Jesus Christ is the same yesterday, today, and forever.
HEBREWS 13:8 HCSB

Life is filled with times of transition and change. The celebration of a wedding is followed by the adjustment into a new home, a new family, and a new name. The joy a mother experiences as she watches her young child proudly head off to kindergarten is mixed with the bittersweet feelings of change.

It is possible to have peace amid all the transitions of life because our heavenly Father never varies. While situations and people change around us, God never changes.

Our heavenly Father is unshakable and unchangeable. Scripture assures us that God is immutable—He is the same yesterday, today, and tomorrow. He is the solid rock we can rest against. And when we reflect on His unchanging nature, we can find stability. As we lean on Him, the tension in our shoulders dissipates. Our muscles relax. We find peace.

Whatever changes you're facing today, lean on your unchanging God. Peace is waiting.

Hello God...it's me. I want You to know how grateful I am for Your unchanging, stabilizing peace.

Lessons from Losing

Then [Jesus] said to Thomas, "Put your finger here; see my hands. Reach out your hand and put it into my side. Stop doubting and believe." Thomas said to him, "My Lord and my God!" Then Jesus told him, "Because you have seen me, you have believed; blessed are those who have not seen and yet have believed."

JOHN 20:27–29 NIV

Failure. We don't like the word anywhere near us. We don't want it in ourselves, in our children, in our home, in our workplace. We all long for success.

A study of top university athletes revealed that more than 60 percent came from wealthy families. After extensive interviews, researchers discovered that these students became involved in a sport because it provided a venue in which they could succeed *or fail*, and their parents' money would have no influence. They couldn't "buy" a sports record; they had to earn it. Losing and coming back for more led to better focus and greater discipline.

The Bible tells us Peter failed. Thomas failed. John Mark failed. From failure, they gained humility and perspective and, as a result, became heroes of the faith. Have you failed? Don't let that stop you. Ask God to teach you the lesson He has for you in the failure—and then get back into the game!

Hello God...it's me. Thank You for the honesty and encouragement of Your Word in recording stories of losers who became winners.

Unity in the Body

For as in one body we have many members, and the members do not all have the same function, so we, though many, are one body in Christ, and individually members one of another. Having gifts that differ according to the grace given to us, let us use them: if prophecy, in proportion to our faith; if service, in our serving; the one who teaches, in his teaching; the one who exhorts, in his exhortation; the one who contributes, in generosity; the one who leads, with zeal; the one who does acts of mercy, with cheerfulness.
ROMANS 12:4–8 ESV

A tornado ripped through an Oklahoma town in the fall of 2010 and left nothing standing. Debris covered the ground, power lines were down, and buildings lay flattened. One of the most unrecognizable buildings was the community chapel. The residents were devastated by the damage done to their beloved house of worship. Its beautiful stained-glass windows were shattered, and the pews, where they had sat and cried and prayed fervently, were now reduced to splinters.

Too often we think of the church as a building, and we confine God to that structure. But the church is more than drywall, carpet, and electrical wires. The church is the body of Christ, and we are all members of it. We are the church, and come what may—wars, famine, even tornadoes—God will reside in us.

Hello God...it's me. Thank You that You do not chose to live in a building, but in me.

The Fairy-Tale Life

How precious to me are your thoughts, O God! How vast is the sum of them!
If I would count them, they are more than the sand. I awake, and I am still with you.
PSALM 139:17–18 ESV

As children, we were delighted to read fairy tales and dreamed that once upon a time we, too, would fall in love with Prince Charming and live happily ever after. But as we grew older, we realized that real life seldom has a fairy-tale ending.

We only need to scan the headlines to realize all the disappointments, from failed celebrity relationships to scandals that cause millionaires to lose their castles. But those who let the Lord write their story find that He composes one that is redemptive and eternal.

Each person is unique and valuable to God. If you honor Him for what you've been given, whether it's much or very little, you may still experience troubles in this world. But if you've trusted Christ as Savior, your tale is guaranteed to end well—if not in this life, then in the next, where everything is perfect forever.

Hello God...it's me. Will You help me to live with authenticity in this life until the perfect arrives?

The Right Touch

I heard a loud voice from the throne saying, "Look! God's dwelling place is now among the people, and he will dwell with them. They will be his people, and God himself will be with them and be their God. 'He will wipe every tear from their eyes. There will be no more death' or mourning or crying or pain, for the old order of things has passed away."

REVELATION 21:3–4 NIV

Sorrow. Hardship. Affliction. Few of us escape these painful circumstances in our lifetime. When others don't notice the tears bottled up behind our eyelids, trickling down our cheeks, or flowing freely over our chin, God notices. And He cares.

With just the right touch God tenderly wipes away our tears. He might use a friend's hug, a phone call, or a Bible verse He brings to mind to demonstrate His love and comfort us. Or He may simply provide an awareness of His presence as we walk through the pain.

What resurrection work does God need to do in your life today? Reassurance? Comfort? Hope? Let God breathe new life into your soul as you depend on Him for joy. Let the smile on your tearstained face come because of who God is—even if the circumstances seem hopeless.

Do you need a tissue today? God's supply is stocked. Ask Him to wipe away your tears and to create the joy that comes from your new life.

Hello God...it's me. Thank You for Your touch that dispels my hopelessness.

God Will Not Deceive Us

*The Lord abides forever; He has established His throne for judgment, and He will judge
the world in righteousness; He will execute judgment for the peoples with equity. The Lord also
will be a stronghold for the oppressed, a stronghold in times of trouble; and those who know
Your name will put their trust in You, for You, O Lord, have not forsaken those who seek You.*
PSALM 9:7–10 NASB

Have you ever been betrayed? Many of us have experienced the disappointment of discovering that someone we trusted was not truthful with us. Others have suffered the crushing heartache of realizing that a close friend or loved one intentionally deceived or harmed them in some manner.

Since we live in a fallen world, lies and deception are a lamentable reality.

Yet what a blessing to know that our Creator—the One who designed us and formed us in our mother's womb—will never deceive us. His promises to care for us, to love us unconditionally, to provide for us, never to abandon us, and to prepare an eternal home for us are true. These promises cannot and will not be broken.

So when we put our trust in God and daily surrender ourselves to His leadership of our lives, we can rest completely in the fact that His Word cannot be broken. His promises in Scripture are ironclad.

Hello God...it's me. Thank You that I can rest so completely in Your promises.

Loss and Gain

I once thought these things were valuable, but now I consider them worthless because of what Christ has done. Yes, everything else is worthless when compared with the infinite value of knowing Christ Jesus my Lord. For his sake I have discarded everything else, counting it all as garbage, so that I could gain Christ and become one with him.

Philippians 3:7–9 NLT

Everything we have will one day be left behind. As the saying goes, you will never see a hearse pulling a U-Haul. This may be a rather morbid and depressing thought, but the reality is that no matter how hard we work and how successful we are during our years on earth, we can't take our stuff with us when we die. The only thing that will go with us into eternity is the soul we have entrusted to our God.

It is important to remember this perspective when we consider our belongings and ambitions. Everything we possess is only on loan from God, entrusted to us on a temporary basis. He wants us to be good managers of His resources, using what He has given us to increase His kingdom.

Are we willing to give what we cannot keep (our material goods, wealth, even our very lives) in order to gain what we cannot lose (our souls and eternal life in heaven)?

Hello God...it's me. Will You help me to loosen my grip on anything material and reach for more of the things that matter?

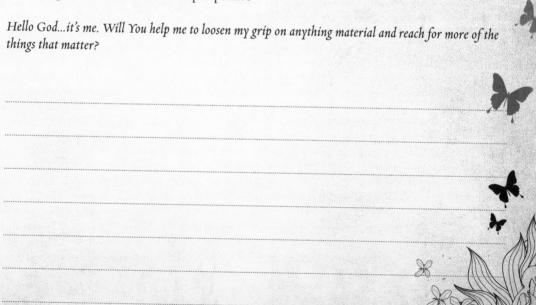

Heart Attitude

For the word of God is living and active and sharper than any two-edged sword, and piercing as far as the division of soul and spirit, of both joints and marrow, and able to judge the thoughts and intentions of the heart.

HEBREWS 4:12 NASB

When you pray, what is the attitude of your heart toward God? Are you assuming the posture of prayer and giving God lip service while your heart is secretly resisting His call to obedience and submission?

In the tiny Old Testament book of Obadiah, God's followers are warned about having a bad attitude. When we harbor anger, bitterness, or resentment, it affects not only those around us but also our attitude toward God. We should be showing gratitude, but are we?

The only way to overcome bad attitudes of the heart is to allow God to shine and reveal all the darkness that is there. But we also need to be willing to repent. Daily prayer and Bible study are essential for this to happen. We need to bow before God in our heart and show true thankfulness for His enduring grace.

Hello God...it's me. Will You show me if I am resisting Your call by the attitude of my heart?

The Specialist

When the spirit saw Jesus, it immediately threw the boy into a convulsion....
Jesus asked the boy's father, "How long has he been like this?" "From childhood," he answered.
"It has often thrown him into fire or water to kill him. But if you can do anything, take pity
on us and help us." "'If you can'?" said Jesus. "Everything is possible for one who believes."
Immediately the boy's father exclaimed, "I do believe; help me overcome my unbelief!"
MARK 9:20–24 NIV

After hours of work and effort, you finally accomplished a seemingly impossible task. With a sigh of relief, you energetically moved on to your next task. However, when your plan hits a pothole and you end up on the side of the road waiting for a tow truck, the opposite happens. Instead of relief and energy, you feel frustration and disappointment.

Are you dreaming for something today that seems out of reach? Do your needs seem impossible for you to meet on your own? Are you facing a challenge that seems unsolvable?

Take courage in the fact that God specializes in impossible situations.

When your circumstances seem impossible, don't look down in despair—look up to God and His goodness, graciousness, and mercy as you eagerly wait for His answers and provision. Redemption in Christ is just the beginning of what God has in store for you. Believe God for the impossibilities in life. He is able to handle anything that comes your way.

Hello God...it's me. Thank You that redemption in Christ is just the beginning of Your plan for me.

Don't Worry, Be Happy

Discover for yourself that the LORD is kind. Come to him for protection,
and you will be glad. Honor the LORD! You are his special people. No one who honors the LORD
will ever be in need.... If you trust the LORD, you will never miss out on anything good.
PSALM 34:8–10 ESV

It has been a long week, but today is Friday. The sun is brightly shining, with a blue sky, light wind, perfect temperature. Could it get any better?

"Could you come into my office?" your boss asks at lunchtime. "You've done great work this month. Take this afternoon off. Here are two tickets to that big show downtown. Fifth row. My treat."

On the way home, you make every green light, even that one at the complicated six-way intersection.

A good day? Believe it! Don't feel guilty. Be happy. Thank God for today (and for next Monday). And remember that He loves you—on the good days as much as on the bad days.

Hello God...it's me. Thank You for Your steadfast, guilt-free goodness.

Just As We Are

For there is no difference between us and them in this. Since we've compiled this long and sorry record as sinners (both us and them) and proved that we are utterly incapable of living the glorious lives God wills for us, God did it for us. Out of sheer generosity he put us in right standing with himself. A pure gift. He got us out of the mess we're in and restored us to where he always wanted us to be. And he did it by means of Jesus Christ.

ROMANS 3:23–24 MSG

Evangelist Billy Graham says he was saved in a revival meeting where "Just as I Am" was playing. A young woman named Charlotte Elliott had written the song almost a century earlier. She was in distress at the time, wondering if her faith was merely a collection of emotions. Her distress reached a breaking point, and she sat down with pen and paper to remind herself of the certainties of God.

She quickly wrote out the formula of her faith, acknowledging: *Just as I am without one plea / But that Thy blood was shed for me.*

God's amazing love accepts us no matter what mess we're in. His grace and mercy are poured out on us at the instant we open our hearts to receive Him. He is the origin of mercy. He is the definition of grace.

Hello God...it's me. Thank You for the certainty of Your love, just as I am.

I Did It

Boast no more so very proudly, do not let arrogance come out of your mouth;
for the Lord is a God of knowledge, and with Him actions are weighed.
1 SAMUEL 2:3 NASB

The lame man could walk. The leper was healed. The shriveled hand was restored. All were miracles accomplished by the power of God. But what if each individual had taken the credit instead?

The lame man bragged, "I used to be crippled, but I did a lot of physical training and over time I strengthened my legs so they could move on their own."

"I used to be a leper," another said, "but I cleaned myself constantly and eventually the spots went away."

The man who had a shriveled hand said, "I used to have a deformed hand, but I stretched it and put lotion on it every day for years and it healed."

Sounds ludicrous, doesn't it? Yet so often we take credit for blessings that come to us from God. Pride tells others that we accomplished the miracles in our lives—whether a healing, a renewed relationship, or some other success—on our own, when the credit belongs to God.

Hello God...it's me. Will You show me where I'm taking credit for something that belongs to You, and help me redirect the glory to You?

Home Away from Home

Therefore we are always confident and know that as long as we are at home in the body we are away from the Lord. For we live by faith, not by sight. We are confident, I say, and would prefer to be away from the body and at home with the Lord.

2 CORINTHIANS 5:1–8 NIV

A popular Christian author wrote a modern-day allegory about the Christian's desire to be close to God. This results in the believer diving in to a pool of God's grace and joyfully submerging in God's love, emerging from the water cleansed and renewed. He feels completely at home there, never wanting to leave.

We—the creation—long to be with our Creator. We yearn to be with Him in heaven, but for now, we're relegated to this earth.

However, we have the capacity to experience God's presence. He's blessed us with His Word. He's provided family and friends who encourage and love us. We have ministers, Sunday school teachers, and small group leaders who help us grow. We can listen and sing along to countless melodies that praise His name. He hasn't left us to fend for ourselves!

God's presence is in our hearts here, even as we long to be at home with Him.

Hello God...it's me. Thank You for making Your home in my heart, and for Your ability to reveal Your presence there.

Out of This World

But those who die in the Lord will live; their bodies will rise again! Those who sleep in the earth will rise up and sing for joy! For your life-giving light will fall like dew on your people in the place of the dead!
ISAIAH 26:19 NLT

Imagine a long vacation at a five-star hotel. A valet parks your car. A doorman greets you and welcomes you in. You enter, enjoying out-of-this-world amenities for a time.

Imagine death. Your body is parked in a cemetery—the underground garage. Your spirit approaches the doorway of heaven. It's opened, not by a doorman but by Jesus, the Proprietor and Architect of this dwelling—the same One who paid the price for you to come and stay. You enter, enjoying out-of-this-world benefits for eternity.

People sometimes say of a bad day, "Yeah, but it beats the alternative." No, it doesn't. For a believer, the alternative is heaven—an out-of-this-world experience that trumps any five-star hotel. Death is the doorway by which we can leave the limitations and pains of this existence and enter into the heavenly realm.

Death is loss, but heaven is the believer's gain.

Hello God...it's me. Thank You for heaven, our happy ending, made beautiful by You.

Divine Nature

Nevertheless I tell you the truth. It is to your advantage that I go away; for if I do not go away, the Helper will not come to you; but if I depart, I will send Him to you.
JOHN 16:7 NKJV

"Don't copy the behavior and customs of this world, but let God transform you into a new person" (Romans 12:2 NLT). Try as we may, that change—that transformation—is out of our reach. We vow to defeat the impulse to judge, the flare of anger, the habit that threatens our health. We stand at the door of need...a need for a helper. A helper who took on earthly wrappings, but whose divine nature did not die. Jesus's divine nature joined with our humanity to empower us to be transformed into new creations.

Be encouraged if transformation is out of your reach. Invite the Holy Spirit to lead you, to be your Helper. Let Jesus's divine nature live in you.

Hello God...it's me. I need Your help—will You continue Your work in me? I want more of Jesus.

October 31

Navigating the Moral Maze

There is a way that appears to be right, but in the end it leads to death.
PROVERBS 16:25 NIV

Some cornfield mazes have a platform where a knowledgeable person can shout out directions to anyone who is lost: "Take two rights and then four lefts." To those who are not too proud to accept them, such directions can take the stress out of traversing a maze and make it feel like more of an adventure.

Oh, that we would not be too proud to listen to God, who is trying, through His Word, to offer us direction as we wander the moral maze of this life! We could save ourselves a lot of panic and confusion if only we would consistently open our hearts to His wisdom and guidance.

Thankfully, we don't have to guess when to go right and when to go left in this maze. We have a knowledgeable Guide. And He is not shouting at us from above but rather walking through the maze with us at every twist and turn.

Hello God...it's me. Will You give me peace to be able to spend quiet time in Your presence when I am desperate for direction?

November 1

Prayer Power

The prayer of a righteous person has great power as it is working. Elijah was a man with a nature like ours, and he prayed fervently that it might not rain, and for three years and six months it did not rain on the earth. Then he prayed again, and heaven gave rain, and the earth bore its fruit.
JAMES 5:16–18 ESV

It's not exactly the superpower we would have asked for as kids. In fact, as children we may have thought prayer was just the appetizer to a meal or the precursor to bedtime. So how do we allow prayer to grow in our lives into what can only be described as a "superpower" from the Holy Spirit? It can't be how original our words are, for the Lord's Prayer, given to us by Jesus Himself, has great power even though we all pray the same words.

So how do our prayers have power? It begins first of all with the power of the Holy Spirit within us. Then, we get prayer power by putting our hearts into our prayers—by being genuine, by praying honestly about our desires, and by meaning what we say as we communicate with our Father.

The Holy Spirit will take your genuine words and infuse them with great power and wonderful results.

Hello God...it's me. Thank You for Your power working through my honesty with You.

No Limits

The heavens are telling of the glory of God; and their expanse is declaring the work of His hands. Day to day pours forth speech, and night to night reveals knowledge. There is no speech, nor are there words; their voice is not heard. Their line has gone out through all the earth, and their utterances to the end of the world.

PSALM 19:1–4 NASB

On a clear day, there's no limit to what we can see. On a clear night, countless shimmery stars light up the galaxy. Whether big or small, each star is part of the night's beauty. And as you gaze into the night sky, you gain a sense of being part of something bigger than yourself.

As we pour out our thoughts, fears, dreams, and hopes to God in prayer, we realize that we are part of something bigger than ourselves. What do you need to talk to Jesus about today? Your prayer is not a limited conversation. Just as no star is too big or small to take its place in our solar system, nothing we face is too big or small to take its place in our prayers.

We don't have to wait until the sky is clear to begin. Start the conversation now. There are no taboo subjects. There are no time limits. No matter what you need to talk to God about in prayer, He's listening.

Hello God...it's me. I want You to know that one of the things I love about You is that You are always listening, wanting to hear from me.

Your Heart's Desire

Trust in the LORD and do good. Then you will live safely in the land and prosper.
Take delight in the LORD, and he will give you your heart's desires. Commit everything
you do to the LORD. Trust him, and he will help you. He will make your innocence
radiate like the dawn, and the justice of your cause will shine like the noonday sun.
PSALM 37:3–6 NLT

Sit with an older believer and ask about the workings of God in his life. He will talk about answered prayers and amazing miracles. He may even make the statement, "Well, I thought I wanted this, but then God gave me that, and I found that what God gave me was better than anything I could ever have desired."

That's how God works. As we walk closely with Him, our desires become His desires. And when our own desires fall short, God is there, waiting with a gift beyond measure. God's "other plans" lead to things you never imagined. Suddenly you turn a corner—and find *His* plans satisfying your heart.

He will give you your desires by helping you to desire what He wishes to give. That's how much He loves you.

Hello God...it's me. Thank You for working in me so that I both want Your will and act on it.

All Grown Up

*I am sure of this, that he who began a good work in you
will bring it to completion at the day of Jesus Christ.*

PHILIPPIANS 1:6 ESV

Whether it's the first time a baby rolls over, crawls, take steps, or says "Mama" or "Dada," moms and dads want to be there for those milestone moments. But parents don't enjoy those moments of growth just because they're fun to watch; they enjoy them because growth is critical. The Bible says that God does something marvelous with the spiritual development of His children. Through the work of His Spirit, God gives His people spiritual birth. Then that same Spirit produces growth. Destructive thought processes and behaviors are sanctified, and the believer develops more and more into the likeness of Jesus.

But the best is yet to come! One day Jesus will return and gather His people from all corners of the earth. All wrongs will be made right, and God will complete His people, perfecting everything about them, making them like Jesus the Son.

Stop for a moment and reflect upon the growth you've experienced. Then take some time to anticipate what is yet to come.

Hello God...it's me. Thank You for the growth You continue to accomplish in me.

Going through the Motions

May these words of my mouth and this meditation of my heart
be pleasing in your sight, LORD, my Rock and my Redeemer.
PSALM 19:14 NIV

The Pharisees of Jesus's time were very good at giving God lip service. They kept the Hebrew laws, they quoted Scripture, and they stood on street corners and prayed. From all outward appearances, the Pharisees were holy. But Jesus knew their hearts. He saw the blackness that consumed them through their corruption and pride.

What does God see when He searches your heart? Do the words you speak and the prayers you pray accurately depict the meditations of your heart? Or are you just paying God lip service?

God wants our cheerful obedience. He wants us to show love, not just talk about it. He wants us to give generously, not out of compulsion but from a joyful spirit. He desires constant communication rather than a ten-second prayer before each meal. Our hearts should yearn for Him, dwelling in His power, flooded by His grace.

Don't just go through the motions—give God your sincere devotion today and always.

Hello God...it's me. I ask for help in making every word and thought acceptable to You.

A Cheap Inheritance

Jesus said to them, "I assure you: In the Messianic Age, when the Son of Man sits on His glorious throne, you who have followed Me will also sit on 12 thrones, judging the 12 tribes of Israel. And everyone who has left houses, brothers or sisters, father or mother, children, or fields because of My name will receive 100 times more and will inherit eternal life. But many who are first will be last, and the last first.
MATTHEW 19:28–30 HCSB

In the 1960s James Coburn starred in a movie titled *Dead Heat on a Merry-Go-Round*. Coburn played a con man. As part of one of his schemes, he wooed a woman, making her think he would marry her—when in reality, he was hoping to steal the money from her bank account. Ultimately, he was successful, cheating her out of fifty thousand dollars. Ironically, though, two days after the woman discovered she'd been swindled, she was notified that a relative had died and left her millions. Had the con man only been faithful, he could have shared in an utter fortune.

Like Coburn's con man, anyone who lives in falsehood—whether it's telling lies and cheating others or devoting oneself to pagan rituals, witchcraft, or other false religions—will one day discover that he or she has forfeited a glorious inheritance of eternal life in heaven. What a truly poor trade-off that is.

Hello God...it's me. Will You search my heart and reveal any motivations that are not pure and pleasing to You?

The Value of Being Available

God has chosen the foolish things of the world to put to shame the wise.
1 CORINTHIANS 1:27 NKJV

The Bible shows us over and over that God favors the unfavorable. He guided a nation to freedom through a stuttering shepherd. He placed the king's crown on the head of a gangly teenager. He delivered His people through an orphan girl turned unlikely queen. Through their stories, He is still celebrated today.

Jesus desired the undesirable. He broke bread with tax collectors and prostitutes. He touched the unclean and infirm. He conversed with foreigners and children. He used ordinary people. Through the lives of these misfits-turned-missionaries, He is known today.

Jesus doesn't require His followers to be *able*, just *available*. When Jesus enters the lives of those who are foolish, weak, lowly, or despised and changes them, people notice. When He accomplishes His will in spite of someone's natural weakness, He can't help but receive the glory. All throughout history God has used weak or broken vessels to accomplish great things for His glory. And He still does today.

Hello God...it's me. I love that my brokenness does not disqualify me in Your eyes. Thank You for Your long history of using brokenness for Your glory.

Grace First

You were saved by faith in God, who treats us much better than we deserve.
This is God's gift to you, and not anything you have done on your own.
It isn't something you have earned, so there is nothing you can brag about.
EPHESIANS 2:8–9 CEV

Most of us know that God's grace is free—but do we really believe it? Or do we still carry with us a nagging sense that we need to *do* something to be worthy of God's love and attention, such as have a daily quiet time, serve at church, or overcome a particular sin?

If we are honest with ourselves, performing these deeds makes us feel like we're earning God's favor or even that we deserve God's love. But the simple truth is that no matter what we do or don't do, we cannot earn God's grace. Grace is a gift.

As we celebrate the gift of God's grace to us, may we also be bearers of that grace to others. And may what we *do* for Jesus simply be the grateful response of our grace-filled hearts.

Hello God...it's me. Thank You for Your beautiful gift of grace—help me to show it off to others.

God Is

Thanks be to God, which giveth us the victory through our Lord Jesus Christ.
1 CORINTHIANS 15:57 KJV

God *is*. Meditate on this for a moment. His existence is without question. As we accept the reality of a God who is eternally present, our doubts are washed away.

If we examine our fear and break into its core, we will see that every fear is rooted in doubting God's existence—thus, doubting that anyone is out there who can help us. When we know that God *is*, however, we can be assured that His promises are true.

Knowing this, we can live fearlessly.

Because God *is*, He will be who He is eternally. He will keep His promises—to stay close, to walk with us through the trials, to turn evil to good, and to raise us again at the last day.

Be still and know that God is. And think about what that means to you today.

Hello God...it's me. Thank You for giving me the ability to live the life You desire: of peaceful trust.

Jesus, Our Great Reward!

We impart a secret and hidden wisdom of God, which God decreed before the ages for our glory.
None of the rulers of this age understood this, for if they had, they would not have crucified the Lord of glory.
But, as it is written, "What no eye has seen, nor ear heard, nor the heart of man imagined,
what God has prepared for those who love him"—these things God has revealed to us through the Spirit.
1 CORINTHIANS 2:7–10 ESV

Winnie the Pooh, written by A. A. Milne in 1926, is a classic children's story with many lasting lessons. In it we discover a delightful troupe of characters with their own unique personalities: Christopher Robin's kindness, Rabbit's nervousness, Tigger's playfulness, Pooh's curiosity, and Eeyore's sadness. In his perpetual gloom, a gray cloud follows Eeyore, raining down wherever he goes as he sighs, "Woe is me."

Many Christians have an Eeyore-like outlook on life. What's with the long faces on so many of God's children? Jesus said, "I came that [you] may have life and have it abundantly" (John 10:10 ESV)! If that is Jesus's intent, then as His followers, we need to enter the joy of the Lord more faithfully and earnestly.

Jesus Himself is our great reward! What else could we possibly want? Let's wipe off our frowns and choose to live in the joy of the Lord today.

Hello God...it's me. I love that You desire my joy.

Important Words

Therefore whoever hears these sayings of Mine, and does them,
I will liken him to a wise man who built his house on the rock.
MATTHEW 7:24 NKJV

One of the most important lessons that students learn in a writing class is to choose words carefully. They're taught to use plain, familiar, active words. They're taught to keep paragraphs short and to remove unnecessary details or descriptions. Every word must help communicate the point, and the point must be worthwhile. People today are too busy to read something meaningless. If a point isn't made by the end of the first paragraph, many people will stop reading.

When listening to a testimony, people want to hear the events that brought a person to Christ. When listening to music, the audience wants every note to lead fluidly to the next one. When listening to a speaker, a class wants to learn a memorable point. Once a person's attention is caught, it must be held. No word can be empty or meaningless.

Each word must be important, and that is especially true when we represent the Word made flesh. Instead of trying to impress people with our many words, let's follow Christ's example of communicating clearly and effectively, so that others may hear and follow Him.

Hello God...it's me. Help me to make every word count today.

Lord Above All

Come, my children, listen to me; I will teach you the fear of the LORD. Whoever of you loves life and desires to see many good days, keep your tongue from evil and your lips from telling lies. Turn from evil and do good; seek peace and pursue it. The eyes of the LORD are on the righteous, and his ears are attentive to their cry; but the face of the LORD is against those who do evil, to blot out their name from the earth.

PSALM 34:11–16 NIV

When we obey God, we sometimes feel strong enough to take on any opposition. However, how do we feel when we humbly obey, only to see evil continue to get the upper hand? What happens when, even with all of our obedience, things don't quite turn out as planned? Did we mess up? Did we misread God? We might even be tempted to wonder if obedience was worth it.

We must never forget that we are in a spiritual battle. Our obedience naturally stirs up the world of evil, with our enemy seeking to discourage us and make us doubt our God. Instead of doubting, remember that in obedience is strength. When we obey God, when we put our faith and trust in Him, He imbues us with such power that evil has no hope of ruling over us. Our strength may falter and fail at times, but the strength of the Lord is everlasting. He is Lord above all, including evil.

Hello God...it's me. Thank You that Your strength lasts forever.

Setting the Table

Look at the birds of the sky: They don't sow or reap or gather into barns, yet your heavenly Father feeds them. Aren't you worth more than they?... Learn how the wildflowers of the field grow: they don't labor or spin thread. Yet I tell you that not even Solomon in all his splendor was adorned like one of these!

MATTHEW 6:26, 28 HCSB

As a child, learning to set the table can be a daunting task. The piles of glasses, plates, and utensils in the middle of the table can be confusing. Where does everything go?

Regardless of how you learned to set the table—from a family member, a sample place setting, or a diagrammed place mat—the plate is key to the proper arrangement. Once the plate is in its rightful place, the center, everything begins to make sense.

In prayer, God's character is the plate we start with. When we focus on who God is first and foremost, our confidence in Him grows. As His attributes form the foundation of our prayer, our needs are put in perspective. His priorities become our priorities. All prayer begins with the character of God.

Set the plate of God's character first today in your prayers. And answered prayer? Put it right in the center of the plate for all to see!

Hello God...it's me. I want You to know that I desire Your character to be my character.

A Treasured Possession

For you are a people holy to the LORD your God. The LORD your God has chosen you to be a people for his treasured possession, out of all the peoples who are on the face of the earth. It was not because you were more in number than any other people that the LORD set his love on you and chose you, for you were the fewest of all peoples, but it is because the LORD loves you and is keeping the oath that he swore to your fathers,

DEUTERONOMY 7:6–8 ESV

The Bible describes the Israelites as a stiff-necked people. Often prideful and stubborn, they chose to go their own way time after time. They were a small nation, yet God made them mighty. They were foolish, yet God trusted them with His very Word. They were unfaithful, yet God continually drew them back, rescuing them when they called out for help.

A human father might tire of the antics of such a rebellious child, but the Lord refused to break His covenant with His children. The Israelites couldn't earn His love after their failures, because they had not earned it in the beginning. They were a holy people only because God made them holy. He treasured them, and it was because of His grace that He remained faithful toward them despite their wayward spirits. He chose them, bought them, and because of His great love, He refused to abandon them.

He feels the same way about us today.

Hello God...it's me. I want You to know that Your faithfulness is incredible. Please help me to love others with the steadfast love You have for me.

The Affair

Do not let sin control the way you live; do not give in to sinful desires. Do not let any part of your body become an instrument of evil to serve sin. Instead, give yourselves completely to God, for you were dead, but now you have new life. So use your whole body as an instrument to do what is right for the glory of God. Sin is no longer your master....

ROMANS 6:12–14 NLT

In a popular romance novel, the night before her wedding, a bride is caught with her former boyfriend. She had left him, and the pain he'd caused her, for the prospective groom, who loved and protected her. Her life had improved marvelously, yet despite her fiancé's love, she'd returned to her former sweetheart. His lies possessed her mind, telling her that he was the one she loved, that he was better for her than the groom. She ran back to her ex-boyfriend even though he had made her feel betrayed and worthless.

The readers turn the pages faster and faster, eager to discover whether the girl will come to her senses and return to the one who truly loves her.

In like manner, we too often return to the very sins Jesus saved us from. Yet even when we betray Him, He takes us back in His arms, loves and forgives us, and enables us to be who He created us to be. Our relationship with Jesus is a love story that has a happy ending.

Hello God...it's me. For forgiveness, but also for continued guidance in becoming who You've created me to be, I worship You.

Gracious Guide

*In all the travels of the Israelites, whenever the cloud lifted from above the tabernacle,
they would set out; but if the cloud did not lift, they did not set out—until the day it lifted.*
EXODUS 40:36 NIV

After a collapse at the gold and copper mines in New South Wales, Australia, in November 1999, there was only one way to rescue the fifty-seven miners trapped below: the rescuers used rope as a guide through the debris and moved them all to safety. It wasn't possible to see the path ahead; the only option was to believe in the carefully placed rope and move one step at a time.

The Israelites finally learned that lesson. The only way to stay out of trouble was to follow the message in the cloud of the Lord. If it had lifted, it was time to move.

Otherwise, stay put, be patient, and wait on God. He showed His faithfulness to them by visible signs during the day and through the night, and it was up to them to be obedient.

This same God, who had the power to form a cloud over the tabernacle and fill it with fire at night, is still our strong Deliverer. He speaks, He beckons, He commands, and sometimes He communicates through silence, but always He is our Guide. In all these ways He leads us along His path and displays His glory in our lives.

Hello God...it's me. I want You to know I will wait on You for guidance.

The Blessed Life

Delight thyself also in the LORD: and he shall give thee the desires of thine heart.
PSALM 37:4 KJV

The movie *Chariots of Fire* tells the story of Eric Liddell, a Scottish Christian born to missionary parents in China who competes for God's glory on the track in the 1924 Olympics.

After Eric misses a prayer meeting, his sister—who disapproves of his athletic pursuits—questions just how much his running really honors God. "I believe that God made me for a purpose," Eric responds. "But He also made me fast, and when I run, I feel His pleasure."

The activities we enjoy are blessings from God. Liddell eventually returned to China and, upon his death, all of Scotland mourned. His was indeed a blessed life.

Find those pursuits where you feel God's pleasure—and you, too, will be blessed.

Hello God...it's me. Thank You for being pleased when we use the gifts and talents You've given.

November 18

Whatever

So whether you eat or drink, or whatever you do, do it all for the glory of God.
1 CORINTHIANS 10:31 NLT

The young man pushed and shoved his way through the crowd with little concern for who or what was in his way, rushing to who knows where. He knocked some shopping bags out of a lady's hands with barely a glance.

It's hard not to judge a moment like that, especially when his T-shirt has one word emblazoned on it in all capital letters: WHATEVER.

Jesus is constantly redeeming our attitudes and behaviors. A T-shirt that no doubt was meant to express a clear statement of indifference might suddenly mean something entirely different when the wearer is devoted to God. As we come to know and follow Jesus as Lord and Savior, the *whatever* of apathy becomes the *whatever* of submission. Our actions begin to reflect the character of Christ, and the Holy Spirit indwells and empowers our lives, our actions, our decisions.

With God's purposes in mind, that same T-shirt means, "Whatever I'm doing, I'm doing for His glory!"

Hello God...it's me. Whatever I do today, I'm doing for Your glory.

A Gift

Because of his great love for us, God, who is rich in mercy, made us alive with Christ even when we were dead in transgressions—it is by grace you have been saved. And God raised us up with Christ and seated us with him in the heavenly realms in Christ Jesus, in order that in the coming ages he might show the incomparable riches of his grace, expressed in his kindness to us in Christ Jesus.
EPHESIANS 2:4–7 NIV

A friend holds a package out to you. The paper covering it is stained and crumbled, but your friend assures you what's inside is beautiful and life-changing. What would you do? Do you trust your friend and open the gift despite its package, or do you turn away in disgust and exclaim, "I don't care what you say; I'm not opening that ugly gift"?

It amazes us as believers that God would give us—the undeserving—new life through the torment of His Son on the cross. The fact that He would take something as ugly as crucifixion and make it beautiful causes us to wonder.

And even more wondrous, God does the same with us. He takes our ugly, sin-stained lives and regenerates them with the purity of His Holy Spirit. He offers us a life-changing package that could be wrapped only one way: the blood of Christ. Only by opening this gift will we receive new life from Christ.

Hello God...it's me. Thank You for taking the torment of the cross to give me the unending gift of life.

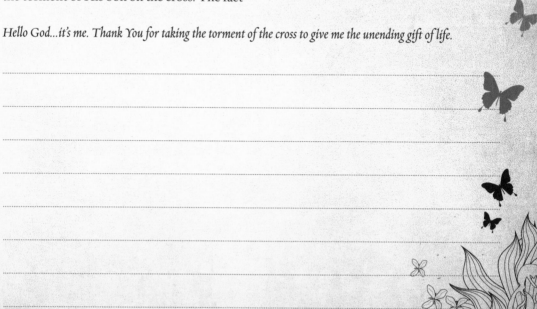

Heaven's Answers

But you, when you pray, go into your inner room, close your door and pray to your Father who is in secret, and your Father who sees what is done in secret will reward you.
MATTHEW 6:6 NASB

Have you ever thought God wouldn't want to hear about a deep longing of your heart? Have you spent your quiet time talking with God about what He wants you to pray, rather than what was really on your mind?

Prayer is one area where we need not hesitate or fear. We can run to God and tell Him honestly about the desires of our heart—the need for a job, concerns for a spouse, the desire to conceive a child, handling health issues, facing financial struggles.

God longs to hear whatever is troubling us, whatever is occupying our thoughts. And as we come to Him with our problems, requests, and desires, He asks only that we lay them at His feet and trust His answers to come in His time, His way.

He knows us far better than we know ourselves. He knows the beginning from the end. So when you pray, be open to His answers, for He will respond according to your true needs.

How can we know this for certain? Because He knows and loves us best.

Hello God...it's me. Thank You for wanting to hear the deep longing of my heart.

Broken

At noon, darkness fell across the whole land until three o'clock. At about three o'clock, Jesus called out with a loud voice, "Eli, Eli, lema sabachthani?" which means "My God, my God, why have you abandoned me?"
MATTHEW 27:45–46 NLT

Emotional pain so severe it feels as though daggers are actually ripping through muscle. Anguish that seems to have no end... These can't possibly be things to embrace. In the suffering of a broken heart, it feels impossible that any good could possibly come from such bad. But God offers a salve to our wounded world: His sovereignty.

Kicking and screaming, we reject His calming words in search of explanations and immediate relief. Unfazed, the Son leaves His arms around us until, through the slowing tears, we can focus on the hands. The nail-scarred hands that changed the world.

A broken heart is often the first avenue through which the world is changed. Will you dare to find the purpose for yours? Through the broken heart of our heavenly Father and the sacrifice of His Son, the world is free from sins' bondage. Transformation is possible! Restoration can be ours!

Hello God...it's me. Thank You for Your gentle, compassionate heart that heals me.

No Sacrifice Too Great

In this the love of God was manifested toward us, that God has sent His only begotten Son into the world, that we might live through Him. In this is love, not that we loved God, but that He loved us and sent His Son to be the propitiation for our sins. Beloved, if God so loved us, we also ought to love one another.

1 JOHN 4:9–11 NKJV

He didn't have to do it. When sin entered the world, God could have turned away and left humanity to fend for itself. Instead, out of His great love for us, He sent His one and only Son to give up the glories of heaven to take on a human body. Christ lived among us, felt the physical pangs of hunger and thirst, and experienced the pure exhaustion after a long day in the heat. He experienced sorrow at people's unbelief; He wept at what death does to us.

Then He gave the ultimate sacrifice on the cross, for only His death could bridge the gap of sin between us and God. Only His death could cover our sin. Instead of *us* dying, Jesus Christ—the sinless Son of God—died *for* us.

When we contemplate what He did for us, is any sacrifice too much for us to make for Him?

Hello God...it's me. You created the human body, then stepped into one. How can I possibly thank You for giving up heaven and dying for me?

The Firm Peace of God

Rejoice in the Lord always; again I will say, rejoice! Let your gentle spirit be known to all men.
The Lord is near. Be anxious for nothing, but in everything by prayer and supplication
with thanksgiving let your requests be made known to God. And the peace of God,
which surpasses all comprehension, will guard your hearts and your minds in Christ Jesus.
PHILIPPIANS 4:4–7 NASB

Suffering can make the world feel like an unstable place. In the midst of suffering, what we thought was a solid foundation beneath us turns to sand. During those dark times, our faith may be tested. In those dark times, we discover if the peace of God is truly in our hearts, for that peace will show itself even in the midst of dire suffering.

We have a choice about how we will undergo these trials. When we are filled with God's peace, we can view our suffering with a calm and understanding spirit. We still suffer, but the peace of God that "surpasses all understanding" (Philippians 4:7 NKJV) will help to restore our sense of stability. When we turn to God in times of great suffering, His peace will be our comfort.

In our suffering, we find God's peace. Without Him we would be lost; with Him we are forever found.

Hello God...it's me. Thank You for the many times the peace of Your presence came when I needed it most.

No Option

The LORD God gives me the right words to encourage the weary. Each morning he awakens me eager to learn his teaching; he made me willing to listen and not rebel or run away.
ISAIAH 50:4–5 CEV

If you want to follow Christ, making Jesus Lord of your life isn't optional. He doesn't wait on the sidelines of our lives, tossing in a little grace here and there while we run back and forth considering the decision of total devotion to Him. As disciples of Jesus Christ, we are already on His team. We are committed, and that commitment means accepting His lordship over our lives as well.

Lordship means that Jesus is the center of our lives—not an extra addition thrown in, mixed with all our other priorities and focuses and desires. As the King of kings and Lord of lords, Christ is over all and in all and through all. He is the very reason for our existence.

Lordship means that our lives revolve around Him in every decision, every word, and every step.

Lordship means that we walk with Him every step of the way.

Lordship means we are His and He is ours—totally and completely.

Hello God...it's me. Today, I want my every decision, my every word, and my every step to revolve around You.

What Would He Do?

Love your enemies, do what is good, and lend, expecting nothing in return.
Then your reward will be great, and you will be sons of the Most High.
For He is gracious to the ungrateful and evil. Be merciful, just as your Father also is merciful.
LUKE 6:35–36 HCSB

In the 1990s, the question "What would Jesus do?" spread across America as youth groups studied Charles Sheldon's 1896 novel *In His Steps* and wore bracelets with the letters WWJD. This question called believers to ask themselves whether or not they were living as Christ would have them live. It encouraged them to model their lives after Christ's and to become walking testimonies of the Savior.

The Lord has called us to be more like Him, to show His love to the unlovable, and to reach out to the unreachable. Jesus loved Judas, who betrayed Him, and Pilate, who sent Him to the cross. And He taught His followers to follow His example by loving their enemies and praying for those who persecuted them.

If we truly are to do what Jesus would do, then we will respond to others in love, not hate. We will love others as Jesus Himself loves them.

Hello God...it's me. Will You help me to respond like You did when betrayed, even loving the people who gossip about me?

Our Kind Priest

*We do not have a high priest who is unable to empathize with our weaknesses,
but we have one who has been tempted in every way, just as we are—yet he did not sin.*
HEBREWS 4:15 NIV

The idea of a merciful and compassionate high priest was powerfully appealing to the Jewish Christians of the first century. No such priestly attributes are found in the Old Testament, and in New Testament times, the Sadducee priests were notoriously unfeeling and cruel. In addition, these people were being persecuted socially and physically by both Jews and Romans. So imagine how they felt at hearing,

"Listen—Jesus understands. He was tempted just like we are. He walked in our shoes, and He knows exactly how it feels to go through the battles that we face. But here's the good news: *He knows exactly how to help.* He feels our pain, but He is God."

It's still true today. Jesus is in a unique High Priest position where He remains exalted, holy, and faithful to God and yet is merciful in an everyday, understanding way toward His people who are feeling the pull of sin. He intercedes, reconciles, strengthens, encourages, loves—every day...all the time. How great is the Lord!

Hello God...it's me. You are so powerful and mighty, yet so compassionate and merciful. You are beyond amazing.

Eager to Fill

*You will show me the way of life, granting me the joy of your presence
and the pleasures of living with you forever.*
PSALM 16:11 NLT

Jesus wept and laughed. He fed the multitudes and taught thousands. He grew angry at the moneychangers and welcomed the children with open arms. He expressed many emotions during His ministry on earth, but Jesus was the most gentle and tender toward those who came to Him simply to worship Him, soaking in His presence and power.

Mary of Bethany, who sat and listened at His feet, earned a place of honor. Jesus defended the woman who came to Him and drenched His feet with her tears, saying she wanted only to be near Him and to worship Him.

Each of these believers came to Jesus to worship Him—to pour out their longings, their fears, and their devotion to Him. In return, Jesus eagerly filled them with His love, His healing, and His peace.

Spending time worshiping Jesus unites His heart with yours. When you draw near to Him, He responds by eagerly filling you with His presence and love.

Hello God...it's me. Thank You for the depth of Your emotions towards me and for caring about my deep emotions.

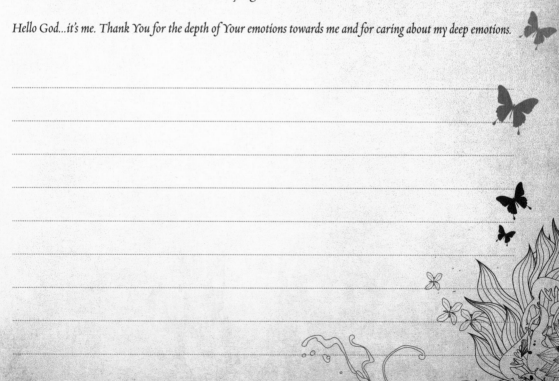

Our Abba Father

For as many as are led by the Spirit of God, they are the sons of God. For ye have not received the spirit of bondage again to fear; but ye have received the Spirit of adoption, whereby we cry, Abba, Father.

ROMANS 8:14–15 KJV

We are part of a family. Not just the physical family we were born into, but also our spiritual family. When we invited Christ into our lives, God adopted us as His own children and welcomed us into His family. When we look to God to take care of us as a father would, we look to the God who has a Son of His own. When we read the Bible and see the faithfulness Jesus showed to God's plan and the trust He placed in His heavenly Father, we can begin to understand how magnificent this intimate, familial relationship with God can be.

The word *Abba,* the Hebrew word for "father," is a term of affection much like "daddy" spoken by a child. It describes more than just the intimacy between Jesus and God. It describes closeness, familiarity, and a trusting love that is bigger and deeper than we can imagine. And *Abba* is what we, His children, are invited to call our heavenly Father.

Hello God...it's me. Thank You for the invitation to call You Daddy. Thank You for Your desire to have me close.

Secure in Power

In your relationships with one another, have the same mindset as Christ Jesus: Who, being in very nature God, did not consider equality with God something to be used to his own advantage; rather, he made himself nothing by taking the very nature of a servant, being made in human likeness. And being found in appearance as a man, he humbled himself by becoming obedient to death—even death on a cross! Therefore God exalted him to the highest place and gave him the name that is above every name.

PHILIPPIANS 2:5–9 NIV

There's an odd thing about power: the more powerful you are, the less you need to tell people about it. We all know by experience that the more people need to talk about themselves, the less secure they are.

Imagine for a moment, then, the immense majesty of a God so secure in His power that He is willing to be born to poor parents in a drafty barn; to mingle with dirty, flawed human beings; and, ultimately, to be mocked, scorned, and publicly executed.

We often forget just how much dignity Jesus could have claimed. As the Ruler of the universe, the King of kings would have been justified in commanding humanity to afford Him *proper* respect. Yet the Lord of creation humbled Himself. Why then do we cling to dignity when our all-powerful God never asked for fanfare?

Hello God...it's me. Thank You for Your example of a serving Savior. Help me to follow You by serving others.

Ache Joyously for God's Glory

*I consider that the sufferings of this present time are not worthy to be compared
with the glory that is to be revealed to us. For the anxious longing of the creation
waits eagerly for the revealing of the sons of God. For the creation was subjected to futility,
not willingly, but because of Him who subjected it, in hope that the creation itself also will be
set free from its slavery to corruption into the freedom of the glory of the children of God.*
ROMANS 8:18–21 NASB

After a first winter snow, when the earth is blanketed with a fresh, white quilt, life seems serene. Muffled sounds travel farther, and people whisper so as not to disturb the quiet. Such a winter scene can mesmerize us, encouraging us to stop, to be still, and to think deeply.

Then it happens. In the freshly laid snow, the first set of car tracks, a stranger's careless footsteps, or even worse, the city's snowplow rips down the street with no regard, even contempt, for our winter scene. We sigh from regret at the loss of the pristine.

God sighs too when He sees the glory of His creation corrupted by our sin and evil. Can He fix things? Certainly, but He has chosen not to do so completely until the end of time. Until the Day arrives, we look upon our sin-stained world and ache for God's glory to be fully displayed.

Hello God...it's me. Thank You for the anticipation of Your glory fully displayed.

December 1

Perfection Needs No Alterations

Jesus Christ is the same yesterday, today, and forever.
HEBREWS 13:8 NLT

One of the themes we revisit every Christmas season is an individual's capability of changing bad character to good. Ebenezer Scrooge goes from being a rude, miserly skinflint to a generous, loving old man. Even the Grinch finds his heart growing in kindness, to the point that he returns all the stolen gifts to the citizens of Whoville. The reasons these stories resonate with us is that we all recognize the depravity of mankind, and we yearn for a universal peace that too often eludes us.

Christ, however, has no need for change. He was and continues to be perfect. Hebrews 13:8 promises us, "Jesus Christ is the same yesterday and today and forever." The Jesus who made the blind see, the lame walk, the leper clean, and the unrighteous pure is the same Jesus who today comforts our souls, hears our prayers, and meets our needs. He is timeless, flawless, and immutable. Hallelujah!

Hello God...it's me. Thank You for Your perfection, for Your mighty power working in us that never changes.

December 2

Conquering Snowdrifts

*Therefore take up the whole armor of God, that you may be able to withstand in the evil day,
and having done all, to stand.... Above all, taking the shield of faith with which
you will be able to quench all the fiery darts of the wicked one. And take the helmet of salvation,
and the sword of the Spirit, which is the word of God.*
EPHESIANS 6:13–17 NKJV

If we tried to battle four-foot snowdrifts in our driveway without the right equipment, we wouldn't be very effective. Wearing shorts and flip-flops in the bitter cold, we'd soon start sniffling, shivering, and shaking. And without the right tools for the job—shovels and maybe even a powerful snow blower—we'd never make any headway. The snowdrift would defeat us no matter how hard we tried. The key to success is being prepared.

We may chuckle at the idea of fighting snowdrifts in flip-flops, but how many times have we tried to tackle life's spiritual battles without the right armor? We forget to put on the shield of faith to protect our hearts, or the helmet of salvation to protect our minds, or the sword of the Spirit—God's Word—to show us the truth.

Whether you're heading out to shovel snow or simply going out your door to face the day ahead, be prepared. Then, no matter what happens, you'll be able to stand your ground.

Hello God...it's me. Thank You for outfitting us for success with salvation, faith, and Your Word.

Relax into Grace

We do not have a high priest who cannot sympathize with our weaknesses, but One who has been tempted in all things as we are, yet without sin. Therefore let us draw near with confidence to the throne of grace, so that we may receive mercy and find grace to help in time of need.

HEBREWS 4:15–16 NASB

"Relax, relax, relax," chant the explorers as they lean into the freezing arctic wind on the way to their destination. Their mantra reminds them to resist the urge to tense up because doing so only causes the body to lapse into shivers. Staying calm will help them stay warm. Tensing up in fear makes it difficult for grace to enter in.

If we believe that we need to rely solely on our abilities, we will experience fear, for we know that most of our problems go beyond our ability to understand or solve. Like oil and water, fear and grace do not mix. Fear involves taking back control over circumstances that God promised to handle. Grace allows humbly accepting that there is nothing in us able to provide the solution.

Once we understand His grace, God can pour more of it into the places left empty by fear, and then through His power we can have the confidence to move forward. So relax. And let His grace fill you.

Hello God...it's me. Will You help me to relax and let Your grace fill me?

Know the Unknown

So Paul, standing in the midst of the Areopagus, said: "Men of Athens...what therefore you worship as unknown, this I proclaim to you. The God who made the world and everything in it, being Lord of heaven and earth...gives to all mankind life and breath and everything.
ACTS 17:22–25 ESV

The Greeks addressed their unexplainable questions of origin through intricately woven stories of gods and goddesses. Thousands of years and technological light-years later, scientists break down the smallest pieces of life and travel to planets beyond our own in the continued pursuit of discovering answers to the unknown.

Every mystery cries out for an explanation. Humans find it hard to allow a question to remain unanswered. God summarized the answer to all of life's unknown questions when Jesus entered the world as a baby; though at first glance, a virgin birthing a child raises more questions than it answers.

Today, allow yourself to move past the mysteries of the manger and enter into deeper intimacy with Jesus. Sit quietly. Talk to Him. Search for evidences of Him in even the smallest details. Experience His presence and discover the answers to your most desperate questions.

Hello God...it's me. I want You to know that, more than anything, I desire to experience Your presence.

Managing Stuff

We humans are merely grass, and we last no longer than wild flowers.
At the LORD's command, flowers and grass disappear, and so do we.
Flowers and grass fade away, but what our God has said will never change.
ISAIAH 40:6–8 CEV

When Jesus stated that it's easier for a camel to go through the eye of a needle than for a rich man to enter into the kingdom of God, He wasn't implying that rich people never go to heaven; He was highlighting the distraction of "stuff" instead.

Is there any doubt about the downside of owning too much? In large quantities, stuff roars up and threatens to take over our thoughts. Even possessions that start off as blessings end up requiring attention. What is it you find yourself focused on? If the tasks of today include "stuff management," consider taking a break. Let go of the longing for the latest and greatest.

Give up the comparisons and remember where true contentment resides.

Hello God...it's me. Help me to love Your mercy and grace over anything I have or desire to have.

Come with Me

The apostles returned to Jesus from their ministry tour and told him all they had done and taught. Then Jesus said, "Let's go off by ourselves to a quiet place and rest awhile." He said this because there were so many people coming and going that Jesus and his apostles didn't even have time to eat. So they left by boat for a quiet place, where they could be alone.

MARK 6:30–32 NLT

Jesus was a busy man. Healing the sick, casting out demons, teaching, traveling, and communing with His Father kept Him busy from dawn until the evening hours. But Jesus frequently pulled away from the crowds to find quiet and rest. He was fully God yet fully man—and as a human being, He needed time to physically rest and recharge.

Sometimes He invited His friends to come along with Him into the quiet places. He used these times of solitude with His disciples to explain, to mentor, and to train. Away from the crowds, Jesus taught them the meanings of His parables and shared secrets that they couldn't yet understand. His followers used these times to ask questions, to seek answers, and to share their deepest thoughts with their Teacher.

Jesus still longs for quiet time with us today, so He can teach us and train us. It is in these times of quiet and rest that He answers our questions and the deepest stirrings of our hearts.

Hello God...it's me. Will You help me to make quiet time with You a priority so I may know Your will?

Finding Joy

Therefore, since we are surrounded by so great a cloud of witnesses, let us also lay aside every weight, and sin which clings so closely, and let us run with endurance the race that is set before us, looking to Jesus, the founder and perfecter of our faith, who for the joy that was set before him endured the cross, despising the shame, and is seated at the right hand of the throne of God.

HEBREWS 12:1–2 ESV

Sometimes pain is necessary in order to bring about health. Healing may require surgery to remove an ailment or to reset a broken bone. When we're in the operating room, our wounds are tender and we often cannot see anything good during our time of pain—but it is in those very wounds that joy can settle.

God wants the very best for us. He works in all of His people's lives to create beauty instead of ashes (Isaiah 61:3) and to restore us to spiritual health so that we might glorify Him. He takes our pain and gives us joy.

Every little step of trust and faith that we take—even when we are wounded in life's battles, even when we're in pain—is a step that pushes back the darkness and confusion Satan uses to overwhelm us. Each step of faith says to God, "I hurt, but I trust You."

Then joy has a soft place to settle.

Hello God...it's me. Help me in my pain to know Your peace, joy, and healing.

Reality Check

We have a great high priest, who has gone into heaven, and he is Jesus the Son of God. That is why we must hold on to what we have said about him. Jesus understands every weakness of ours, because he was tempted in every way that we are. But he did not sin! So whenever we are in need, we should come bravely before the throne of our merciful God. There we will be treated with undeserved kindness, and we will find help.

HEBREWS 4:14–16 CEV

How would you describe your life right now—does the word *peace* come to mind? Many believers struggle with experiencing God's peace in the midst of our real, here-and-now difficulties. We think that the only way we'll find peace is by pretending everything is just fine. But God knows the reality you are facing, as well as what is ahead tomorrow and for the rest of your life.

Finding God's peace doesn't mean we have to deny our struggles or pretend that our life is calm and serene. Our Lord never asks us to lie to Him, to others, or to ourselves about reality. On the contrary, God wants us to confront our difficulties, knowing that when we approach the cross, we approach an omnipotent God who is intimately aware of the difficulties we are facing.

When God offers us His abiding peace, we can trust that He will give it to us, even in the midst of our reality.

Hello God...it's me. I want You to know how grateful I am that You listen to my problems and give me the peace to get through them.

Leave the Future to God

Thus says the LORD, your Redeemer, and He who formed you from the womb: "I am the LORD, who makes all things, who stretches out the heavens all alone, who spreads abroad the earth by Myself; who frustrates the signs of the babblers, and drives diviners mad; who turns wise men backward, and makes their knowledge foolishness; who confirms the word of His servant, and performs the counsel of His messengers....
ISAIAH 44:24–26 NKJV

Tarot card readers. Astrologists. Psychics. Fortune-tellers. All claim to foretell the future. And all are frauds!

The Lord warns against these forms of evil. Deuteronomy 18:10–14 admonishes us to avoid such practices and those who practice them. He wants us to trust Him for what lies ahead and rely on no one else.

But in case we applaud ourselves for avoiding such evil, 1 Samuel 15:23–26 reminds us that rebellion is as sinful as witchcraft and stubbornness as bad as worshiping idols. We may not be running to palm readers or consulting mediums to see what the future holds, but is our rebellious and stubborn nature keeping us from seeking God's purposes for our lives? What He wants may not be what we had planned. Our job is to love and obey Him anyway.

Hello God...it's me. Thank You that Your Words says You will tell us great and mighty things when we come to You. Thank You for Your desire to lead us.

The Perfect Lover

Dear friends, let us love one another, because love is from God, and everyone who loves has been born of God and knows God. The one who does not love does not know God, because God is love. God's love was revealed among us in this way: God sent His One and Only Son into the world so that we might live through Him.

1 JOHN 4:7–9 HCSB

To love people is risky. The greater the love, the greater is the risk. We long to be loved completely by someone who will never disappoint us or hurt us. But we soon discover that mere humans—no matter how well-intentioned—simply aren't capable of loving perfectly. After we experience the heartache of receiving a "Dear John" or "Dear Jane" letter we might feel that it's not worth the pain to give our heart away in love to another, only to have it broken again.

We can never completely insulate our hearts from the pain in loving others. Nor should we. As humans, we are all imperfect, so we are not able to love perfectly. We can, however, let our heartache lead us to the One whose perfect love casts out fear. When our hearts know His love we no longer try to find from humans the love that we can only receive from God, our perfect Lover.

Hello God...it's me. Will You help me to run to You when I hurt?

Good Always

Give your entire attention to what God is doing right now, and don't get worked up about what may or may not happen tomorrow. God will help you deal with whatever hard things come up when the time comes.
MATTHEW 6:25–34 MSG

How would you define the word *good*? Based on your definition, is there someone or something you would consider good *all* of the time? Fifty percent of the time? Perhaps you have a friend who is a good friend most of the time, but sometimes he or she frustrates you or makes you mad. Or perhaps you read a book you thought was good once, but now you can't stand it.

God alone is good 100 percent of the time.

But at times, our view of God's goodness can change, especially when we are going through difficult circumstances. Sometimes our definition of *good* is like shifting sands—changing based on feelings. But the Bible assures us that God is good all of the time, regardless of our circumstances or feelings. And because He is good, He cares about our needs.

Believe that God is good and that He delights to make His goodness known.

Hello God...it's me. Thank You for delighting to make Your goodness known by providing for us.

Heroic Humility

He humbled Himself by becoming obedient to the point of death—even to death on a cross. For this reason God highly exalted Him and gave Him the name that is above every name, so that at the name of Jesus every knee will bow—of those who are in heaven and on earth and under the earth.

PHILIPPIANS 2:8–10 HCSB

Most children have a hero, a man or woman they look up to as someone they want to be like. Adults often have heroes too. More than just admiration for their accomplishments and skills, we are inspired by such heroes to try harder, to live braver, to go farther than we would have without their examples. By imitating their lives we hope to accomplish more, to be more than we could on our own. Yet all earthly heroes have their blemishes, some more glaring than others.

Then upon the human stage enters Jesus.

Being both fully man and fully God at the same time, He alone is our true hero, elevating the human heart to true heights of greatness. By imitating His life of humility and service, we become more human— the way God intended humanity to be.

Our hero, Jesus Christ, humbled Himself and became obedient to death on a cross on our behalf. Through His sacrifice we gain our glorification so that for eternity we may live fully like Jesus.

Hello God...it's me. I want You to know You will always be my hero. I want to be more like You every day.

Make Your Choice

If it seem evil unto you to serve the LORD, choose you this day whom ye will serve;
whether the gods which your fathers served that were on the other side of the flood, or the gods
of the Amorites, in whose land ye dwell: but as for me and my house, we will serve the LORD.
JOSHUA 24:15 KJV

We love to sit around with cups of steaming coffee and talk about ideas. How would we solve the budget problems in our country, or what's the best way to grill a steak? We express our opinions and walk away changed or unchanged, ready to act or not. It doesn't really matter—we were just discussing ideas.

Many people treat God as if He were just an idea we could discuss and then walk away unchanged. That is precisely why God did not leave us with just a set of ideas; He gave us a person, Himself. He gave us some*one* to follow rather than an idea to discuss.

Because God gave us a person, that leaves us with a choice. We have to *do* something about this Person. We have to decide whether to believe what God said about Himself or not. We have to choose. And that choice makes all the difference.

Hello God...it's me. Thank You for choosing to give Yourself. I chose to give myself to You.

December 14

Too Busy?

For thus saith the LORD God, the Holy One of Israel; in returning
and rest shall ye be saved; in quietness and in confidence shall be your strength.
ISAIAH 30:15 KJV

How often has someone responded to your question, "How are you?" with the answer: "I am so busy," followed by a verbal list of tasks completed that day? Somehow, being busy has become a marker of success in our culture. We have come to believe that *busy* is a synonym for *productive*, *useful*, and *important*.

What happens, however, when our very busyness not only affects our physical rest but our spiritual rest as well? Are we so focused on our tasks that we miss the soul-strengthening moments within a day—sitting quietly before God in silence, enjoying creation, being thankful?

What if we adopted a new way of living, reflected in a new answer to "How are you?" What if we learned to say (and live out) these words: "I am giving myself permission to slow down and find moments of silence and solitude in each day"?

Might we have healthier hearts? Might we be closer to our Father?

Hello God...it's me. Help me to slow down and remember that spending time with You is my success.

For His Glory

Don't hoard treasure down here where it gets eaten by moths and corroded by rust or—worse!—stolen by burglars. Stockpile treasure in heaven, where it's safe from moth and rust and burglars. It's obvious, isn't it? The place where your treasure is, is the place you will most want to be, and end up being.

MATTHEW 6:19–21 MSG

The latest computer, the most upgraded cell phone, the newest reading device, the latest car, the largest screen TV...often, this obsession with possessing something new gets in the way of what is most important in life—pleasing the Lord and seeking to glorify Him. We can end up more focused on buying the latest technology than we do in becoming more like Christ.

It's not that we can't or shouldn't enjoy the latest computer or cell phone or other gadget, but we must always keep a biblical perspective on our possessions. Are we buying these things and considering them "our own," or are we carefully using them so that they are pleasing to the Lord and helpful in promoting His glory? As Christians, we are to seek the things that please God.

Don't settle for bells and whistles. Instead, invest in the treasure that lasts: the eternal rewards of our infinitely generous Creator.

Hello God...it's me. I ask Your help in using all my possessions to glorify You.

December 16

Keep Going

Endurance builds character, which gives us a hope that will never disappoint us.
ROMANS 5:4–5 CEV

Your full key ring clinks and clatters as you struggle with your bags and try to find the right key to open the door. When the first key doesn't work, you try another. And another, and another, and another, and another. Just when you are ready to give up, you finally hear a clicking sound as the key turns in the lock. Perseverance has given you victory and hope.

When circumstances last longer than we expect, are harder than we thought they would be, or just plain don't go as planned, persevering is often the last thing we want to do. But God calls us to endure so that we can discover the hope that is unlocked by perseverance.

What challenges are you facing today? Perseverance may be the key you need not only to survive, but to thrive. With this key you can open the door victoriously because God has strengthened your character, built your trust in Him, and given you hope.

Put perseverance in the lock today, and watch what God does.

Hello God...it's me. Help me to persevere so I can learn the lessons You want me to learn.

December 17

The Event Coordinator

After this manner therefore pray ye: Our Father which art in heaven, hallowed be thy name. thy kingdom come, thy will be done in earth, as it is in heaven. Give us this day our daily bread. And forgive us our debts, as we forgive our debtors. And lead us not into temptation, but deliver us from evil: for thine is the kingdom, and the power, and the glory, for ever. Amen.
MATTHEW 6:9–13 KJV

When we have a jam-packed schedule, it's easy to fall into the trap of approaching the day like a busy event coordinator. Excited about our plans, our prayer—if we make time to offer one—becomes a passionate monologue telling God everything we're going to do that day. We approach God looking for His stamp of approval on our plans instead of asking for His direction.

But, oh, the blessings that come when we let God be the Event Coordinator and we humbly take our place as His assistant. When we give control of our daily schedule to God, things may not turn out exactly as we would have planned, but isn't God the ultimate planner? He is omniscient, omnipotent, and omnipresent—attributes that make Him the greatest Event Coordinator possible.

Ask Him to not only fulfill His plan for you, but to lead that plan. Do more than just include Him in your plans—let Him be in charge.

Hello God…it's me. Help me to make You the ultimate Event Coordinator of my day.

Unmasking Impossibility

Ah, Lord God! It is you who have made the heavens and the earth by your great power and by your outstretched arm! Nothing is too hard for you.
JEREMIAH 32:17 ESV

"It's impossible," we say with a resigned sigh. We can't see a way out. All the choices lead to unpleasant results—if there are any choices at all. We may be tempted to give up in despair in the face of what appears to be an impossible situation. What a change of perspective, then, when we see that impossible situation as an opportunity from God that has merely been brilliantly disguised!

God wants us to look at our difficult situations as if we were attending a masquerade party—what we think is impossible and scary is merely an illusion. Like the moment of unmasking at a party, it's time to reveal the true identity of what has appeared to be an impossible situation—opportunity.

Take off opportunity's disguise today. As you unmask your impossible situation and reveal it as an opportunity from God, the greatness of God is just waiting to show itself in your life.

Hello God...it's me. Help me to see behind the mask of my impossible situations to Your greatness waiting.

Where Is God?

*Do not fear, for I am with you; do not anxiously look about you, for I am your God.
I will strengthen you, surely I will help you, surely I will uphold you with My righteous right hand.*
ISAIAH 41:10 NASB

When we walk through a storm, where is God? When the floodwaters sweep under the door of our hearts and crash into our lives, where is God? When our hearts hurt until we think they will burst from the pain, where is God?

The deep and abiding truth is that God will never leave us or forsake us...no matter what. That does not mean we will not feel the wrench of pain. It does mean that God will walk with us through it. He waits for us to invite Him to carry the load.

God knows all about our struggles and trials. His Word states that they are the very link to identifying with Jesus. Through struggles we taste the suffering Jesus endured. It is then that His life can be seen in us.

Hello God...it's me. I thank You for walking beside me today again. I invite You to carry my load.

Undeserved

Now apart from the law the righteousness of God has been made known, to which the Law
and the Prophets testify. This righteousness is given through faith in Jesus Christ to all who believe.
There is no difference between Jew and Gentile, for all have sinned and fall short of the glory of God,
and all are justified freely by his grace through the redemption that came by Christ Jesus.
ROMANS 3:21–24 NIV

Are you tempted to give in to the comparison obsession? Do you wonder why God chooses to lavish good gifts on people who don't even care about Him, while faithful believers sometimes go without even the most basic necessities? Maybe you've even wondered why God hasn't distributed gifts to you according to the good things you've done for Him?

If it were up to us, the largest share of blessings might go to pastors, missionaries, and others whom we see making huge sacrifices for the sake of God's glory. This way of dividing God's riches seems fair, after all.

But attempting to run God's world in this way overlooks the most important blessing in God's economy: grace. It's the lavish gift of forgiveness that He offers to anyone who simply longs for it. This we could never deserve.

Hello God...it's me. Thank You for Your enormous blessing of Grace.

Hide and Seek

There is nothing concealed that will not be disclosed, or hidden that will not be made known.
What I tell you in the dark, speak in the daylight; what is whispered in your ear, proclaim from the roofs.
MATTHEW 10:26–27 NIV

Something makes us want to search for hidden treasures. We seek for birthday presents tucked away in closets or basements. We explore the recesses of couch cushions hoping to find some change. We shake the gifts piled under the Christmas tree, straining to hear a crinkle or jingle that might give away the contents.

Jesus knew our penchant for seeking hidden things. He spoke in parables and riddles, using word games to capture the attention of His audience. He hinted at things to come and a time when all would be made known. His whispers caused the listeners to lean in closer. He related stories of places unseen, of secrets soon to be unveiled, of heavenly riches for those who believe.

Like children, we wait eagerly, imagining all Jesus has planned for us, watching for a glimpse of the glory He's prepared for us. In the meantime, we can tell His secrets to others.

Hello God...it's me. Will You show me the best way to share Your treasures with others?

Happily Humbled

He disciplines us for our good, that we may share his holiness. For the moment all discipline seems painful rather than pleasant, but later it yields the peaceful fruit of righteousness to those who have been trained by it.
HEBREWS 12:10–11 ESV

The prodigal son envisioned a life of entertainment and pleasure outside the confines of his country home. He longed to broaden his horizons beyond his boring life and the watchful eye of his father. So he demanded his inheritance and struck out on his own. But he squandered his wealth, lived a wild existence, and returned home broken and humbled.

Before, the boundaries of his father's land had felt confining. Now the son longed for the security of home. Once, his father's wealth had given him all the food he needed to survive. But the inheritance he left home with only fed his folly. Previously, his father's arms made him struggle for liberty; now they offered protection.

The son learned the difficult lesson that freedom comes within the margins of lovingly set boundaries.

Our loving heavenly Father also gives us limits. His boundaries are not to keep His children in, but to keep danger and evil out. His rules are not to limit us, but to sustain us. Within His walls we find refuge, acceptance, and provision. In His arms, we find our home.

Hello God...it's me. Thank You for my home in Your arms.

Experience Him

Therefore I...do not cease to give thanks for you, making mention of you in my prayers:
that the God of our Lord Jesus Christ, the Father of glory, may give to you the spirit of wisdom
and revelation in the knowledge of Him, the eyes of your understanding being enlightened.
EPHESIANS 1:15–18 NKJV

In today's world, logic is the standard we most often use. We tend to measure the validity of something by how logical it is. We think logically about our choices. We solve dilemmas by using logic. We readily toss aside choices because they just "make no sense."

Too often people do this with God. After all, a lot about God simply isn't logical; it doesn't seem to make sense. But God's ways don't always follow our human rules of logic. It isn't that we have to set aside all logic in order to believe in God; instead, we have to be willing to realize that as finite human beings, we can never completely understand an infinite God. He is beyond and outside of our reasoning abilities.

We should understand what we can logically, but we should also let ourselves *experience* God, for only then will we understand more than we ever can with our minds. We experience the reality of true love, of peace, of having a life with purpose and meaning.

With our hearts, we know Him. Our minds will follow.

Hello God...it's me. Thank You for giving me the ability to take logic off the throne and experience You.

What About You?

Simon Peter replied, "You are the Christ, the Son of the living God." And Jesus answered him, "Blessed are you, Simon Bar-Jonah! For flesh and blood has not revealed this to you, but my Father who is in heaven."
MATTHEW 16:16–17 ESV

One day as Jesus and His disciples walked along the road, He posed a question. "Who do people say the Son of Man is?" Did Jesus ask that question because He didn't know what people were saying? Had He been warned that some mistook Him for John the Baptist, Elijah, or Jeremiah? Had He heard the whispered debates of His followers?

It's likely that Jesus used the question as an opening to the real question He wanted His disciples to answer—"Who do you say I am?" Peter answered for himself, but did all the disciples agree? Could they have each answered according to who they thought He was? Savior. Teacher. Messiah. Rabbi. Brother.

Who do *you* say Jesus is? Can you answer for yourself, or must you rely on the answers of your parents, your spouse, or your church leaders?

One day every knee will bow and every tongue confess the name of Jesus Christ our Lord. What about you? Who do you say He is?

Hello God...it's me. Thank You for how You make Yourself known to me. Give me wisdom on how to describe You to others.

The Most Profound Mystery

The angel said to [the shepherds], "Do not be afraid. I bring you good news that will cause great joy for all the people. Today in the town of David a Savior has been born to you; he is the Messiah, the Lord.
LUKE 2:10–11 NIV

A newborn evokes deep awe and great delight from adults. We exclaim, "Just look at the little fingers and toes. Listen to those cute baby sounds. What an adorable button nose."

Imagine the wonder Mary and Joseph must have experienced as they saw their firstborn baby wrapped in swaddling clothes and lying in a manger. As they exclaimed in delight over His little fingers and toes, endearing baby noises, and His tiny nose, they no doubt recalled Gabriel's words to them—this baby was conceived by the Holy Spirit.

Did they grasp the fullness of that miracle? Their newborn son, who seemed so finite and powerless, was the One who created the stars on that night, the donkey that carried Mary to Bethlehem, and the angels from the heavens who heralded to shepherds their baby's birth. Mary and Joseph must have looked in awe upon the most profound mystery—their tiny, helpless infant was the Son of God, the Maker of heaven and earth!

Hello God...it's me. Thank You for the ultimate gift I could never deserve: You.

Echoes of Joy

Offer to God thanksgiving, and pay your vows to the Most High.
Call upon Me in the day of trouble; I will deliver you, and you shall glorify Me.
PSALM 50:14–15 NKJV

"Thank you." These two small words are among the first in a child's vocabulary. They roll easily off our tongues to convey common courtesy—to the grocery clerk, the waitress, or the stranger who holds the door.

Yet sometimes those two little syllables seem very inadequate. How can the same two words convey the tidal wave of emotion we want to express to the organ donor, the birth mother, or the friend who listens without judgment?

How can we express our gratitude for all God has given us? How can we tell Him how grateful we are for all He's forgiven us? Our words of deep gratitude would fill a book, if we were to write them down. Our sacrifices of thanksgiving would reach to heaven, if we were to pile them up. Yet all God requires is our life, lived for His glory, returning to Him all the goodness He has freely and graciously bestowed upon us.

Hello God...it's me. Thank You for reading my heart when words aren't enough.

Love Story

*For no one ever hated his own flesh, but nourishes and cherishes it, just as the Lord does the church.
For we are members of His body, of His flesh and of His bones. "For this reason a man
shall leave his father and mother and be joined to his wife, and the two shall become one flesh."
This is a great mystery, but I speak concerning Christ and the church.*
EPHESIANS 5:29–32 NKJV

The classic love story has a formula: man meets woman and falls in love. Though the woman's heart may be difficult to win, though her suitor may have to overcome many obstacles to gain her love, we always hope that, in the end, their story culminates in a memorable "happily ever after."

How does the man know he's in love? It's not just that his heart races whenever she walks into the room, or that he gets tongue-tied when he tries to speak to her. He also knows he's in love because he would do anything for this woman. He would gladly give his life for hers, knowing that even though he'd be gone, she'd have another chance at life and happiness.

So, too, with Christ and the church. The church is His beloved, His bride. He didn't just *say* He'd do anything for her; He actually sacrificed His life, giving *everything*—all because of love. What a love story that is! And it can be yours. Christ's deep love for you held Him to the cross, where He died so that you might live.

Hello God...it's me. Thank You for writing me into Your love story.

Light in a Dark Place

Then Jesus again spoke to them, saying, "I am the Light of the world; he who follows Me will not walk in the darkness, but will have the Light of life."

JOHN 8:12 NASB

It is no secret that some days are dark. At times, our darkness might be so deep that we cannot see the next step on the path—so we sit on the side of life's road, afraid to take a step because we might fall or trip or walk over the edge of a cliff.

Darkness can be frightening. But our Lord, the Light of the world, understands. In our darkest hours, He shines the brightest of His glory on our gloomy paths. When we look to the Father, He will give us light and show us the way.

When you are lonely, *He is there.* When you are anxious, *He is there.* When you see only darkness, *He is there with the light of life.*

Hello God...it's me. Thank You for Your light that takes away my darkness.

Becoming More

Our citizenship is in heaven, and from it we await a Savior, the Lord Jesus Christ, who will transform our lowly body to be like his glorious body, by the power that enables him even to subject all things to himself.

PHILIPPIANS 3:20–21 ESV

The Grand Canyon is renowned for its majesty and grandeur. Two hundred and seventy-seven miles long, eighteen miles wide, and up to a mile deep...few places can make a human feel so small. Yet, if someone has never been to the Grand Canyon, how can we describe it? Mere words aren't enough to capture its breathtaking beauty and magnitude.

Our eternal state is similarly impossible to describe adequately. Some depictions of our eternity in heaven even make it seem boring. But God promises us something far greater: a place of eternal fulfillment. In heaven we will be more, not less, than we are here on earth. What that means, we do not yet know. But one day, we will.

We can trust that God will make our eternity better than we can even imagine.

Hello God...it's me. Thank You for the beautiful gifts here, and the promise of more in heaven.

The Finish Line

Consider it a sheer gift, friends, when tests and challenges come at you from all sides. You know that under pressure, your faith-life is forced into the open and shows its true colors. So don't try to get out of anything prematurely. Let it do its work so you become mature and well-developed, not deficient in any way. If you don't know what you're doing, pray to the Father. He loves to help. You'll get his help, and won't be condescended to when you ask for it. Ask boldly, believingly, without a second thought.

JAMES 1:2–6 MSG

On October 20, 1968, the Mexico City Olympic Stadium was both the starting line and the finish line of the Olympic marathon. During the race, John Stephen Akhwari of Tanzania stumbled and seriously hurt his leg. Medics bandaged the man's bloody calf, and then Akhwari rose and began to hobble forward. Though in agonizing pain, Akhwari continued, mile after mile. As he finally entered the stadium, he completed the final lap, hobbling all the way. The crowd rose and cheered, but Akhwari simply finished the lap and left the stadium. Later, a sportswriter asked, "Why didn't you just quit?" Akhwari responded, "My country did not send me seven thousand miles to *start* the race. It sent me to *finish* the race."

Our God finishes what He starts. James tells us "perseverance must *finish* its work" (italics added) so that we can be mature in our righteousness. Let us also complete the good work we start.

Hello God...it's me. Thank You for giving me the ability to focus and finish what I start.

Mighty Tenderness

Therefore God exalted him to the highest place and gave him the name that is above every name,
that at the name of Jesus every knee should bow, in heaven and on earth and under the earth,
and every tongue acknowledge that Jesus Christ is Lord, to the glory of God the Father.

PHILIPPIANS 2:9–11 NIV

God with skin on. God in the flesh—with beating heart, healthy mind, and blood coursing through His veins. God come to earth in the skin of our humanity in order to bring the message that He is eager to relate to us, know us, understand us, intercede for us.

This is Jesus.

Jesus—who walked along the dusty roads of Judea, reached out to heal the lepers, cast out demons, calmed the sea, held children on His lap. Jesus—who lived, laughed, wept, died, and rose again.

This is Jesus.

So in love with you that He not only cares enough to know you completely but loves you intimately, unconditionally, without wavering.

This is Jesus.

Hello God...it's me. Thank You for Your love that knows and plans every detail about me: past, present, and future.

Ellie Claire® Gift & Paper Expressions
Franklin, TN 37067
EllieClaire.com
Ellie Claire is a registered trademark of Worthy Media, Inc.

Hello God...it's me 365-Day Devotional Journal
© 2015 by Ellie Claire
Published by Ellie Claire, an imprint of Worthy Publishing Group, a division of Worthy Media, Inc.

ISBN 978-1-63326-053-5

Stock or custom editions of Ellie Claire titles may be purchased in bulk for educational, business, ministry, fundraising, or sales promotional use. For information, please e-mail info@EllieClaire.com

Cover photo by Thinkstock Photos

Cover and interior design by Studio Gearbox | studiogearbox.com

Printed in China

4 5 6 7 8 9 10 11 12 – 22 21 20 19 18 17 16